Ready-to-Use Information & Materials for Assessing Specific Learning Disabilities

VOLUME I

COMPLETE LEARNING DISABILITIES RESOURCE LIBRARY

JOAN M. HARWELL

Chapter opening illustrations by Colleen Duffey Shoup

JOSSEY-BASS
A Wiley Imprint
www.josseybass.com

Published by Jossey-Bass
A Wiley Imprint
989 Market Street, San Francisco, CA 94103-1741   www.josseybass.com

Jossey-Bass books and products are available through most bookstores. To contact Jossey-Bass directly call
our Customer Care Department within the U.S. at (800) 956-7739, outside the U.S. at (317) 572-3986 or fax
(317) 572-4002.

Jossey-Bass also publishes its books in a variety of electronic formats. Some content that appears in print may
not be available in electronic books.

Library of Congress Cataloging-in-Publication Data

Harwell, Joan M.
     Complete learning disabilities resource library : ready-to-use
information & materials for assessing specific learning disabilities,
Volume 1 / Joan M. Harwell.
        p.   cm.
     Includes bibliographical references.
     ISBN 0-87628-279-6 (v. 1)
     ISBN 0-7879-7232-0 (paperback)
     1. Learning disabled children—Education—United Staes.
   2. Learning disabled children—Services for—United States.
   3. Learning disabilities—United States.   I. Title.
LC4705.H367   1995   95-24094
371.91—dc20

FIRST EDITION
    10 9 8 7 6 5 4 3 2 1

ABOUT THE AUTHOR

Joan M. Harwell has over 30 years of experience as a regular classroom teacher and special education teacher for learning disabled students in the schools of San Bernardino, California. She has run several remedial programs for slow learners and spent 14 years as a learning handicapped Resource Specialist. Currently, she supervises student teachers for the University of Redlands. She is the author of *How to Diagnose and Correct Learning Disabilities in the Classroom* (Parker, 1982), *Complete Learning Disabilities Handbook* (Center for Applied Research in Education, 1989), and *Ready-to-Use Learning Disabilities Activities Kit* (Center for Applied Research in Education, 1993). She is listed in Marquis' *Who's Who in American Education.*

Ms. Harwell earned a B.A. degree from San Jose State College and an M.A. from the University of Redlands.

ABOUT THIS RESOURCE LIBRARY

My purpose in writing the *Complete Learning Disabilities Resource Library*, volumes I and II, is to share with you some of the things I have learned in my thirty years of working with learning disabled (LD) students, both in mainstreamed classes and in special classes, at the elementary and secondary levels.

When I began teaching special education classes for educably mentally retarded students in 1964, the educational fields of learning disabilities was brand new. When I heard the term for the first time, I was immediately able to attach it to three students in my junior high special education class, who were able to pick up skills more quickly than other students in the class. Although we did not use the term "mainstreaming" in those days, I was able to find teachers willing to have these three students in their regular classes for half the day, where they received extra help and encouragement so they could maintain passing grades. It was with great satisfaction that we—the teachers and the parents—saw those three students go on to complete a vocational nurses' program. As I watched their success, it aroused in me a fierce and abiding interest in the field of learning disabilities.

By 1971, I found myself working with learning disabled students in pull-out programs at the elementary level. In those days, we sincerely believed that if we provided LD youngsters with the right curriculum and concerned teaching, students would overcome or compensate for their disabilities. We would "fix" them. Sad to say, experience over the last 25 years has not borne this out. Students with learning disabilities grow into adults with learning disabilities. Once they leave school, these students find niches where they try to blend in with other adults with varying degrees of success. We now realize how important the parent's role is in determining whether these students will be successful.

Unfortunately, economic and social pressures within today's society have created a situation where parents are not exerting the influence they were able to exert in the 1960s. Parents say they simply do not have time to spend with their children. You will note Volume I continuously mentions the importance of involving parents of LD students in being the children's helpers and advocates. When students are originally identified as LD, do not be afraid or timid to tell parents how critical it is that they maintain weekly contacts with teachers, give encouragement to their children, and offer one-to-one help with their children's assignments at home.

Some parents report that they have never met with the Student Study or I.E.P. teams. Even though the law mandates parent involvement, obviously on occasion some schools are not involving them in any other way than having them sign papers. This is a very questionable practice. It is imperative that you enlist parents' (1) input in planning for their youngster's educational program and future, and (2) help with homework and the teaching of social skills.

The *Complete Learning Disabilities Resource Library* will show you how to involve parents in their LD children's education—and much more!

• Volume I, *Ready-to-Use Information & Materials for Assessing Specific Learning Disabilities*, provides you with a helpful background on the field of learning disabilities.

It is intended to assist both the regular class teacher dealing with mainstreamed students and the special education teacher. If you are a beginning teacher, Volume I provides a wealth of information to help you as you begin your work in the field. The book is also of interest to school principals and to medical practitioners as a desk reference. While Volume I mentions some of the research that has occurred in the field, it does not do so in technical terms; the book is written at a level that is understandable to parents.

- Volume II, *Ready-to-Use Tools & Materials for Remediating Specific Learning Disabilities*, provides you with ready-to-use materials and activities you can use with students in the areas of reading, language arts, and mathematics. The majority of learning disabled students (even those leaving our high schools) have achievement scores that fall in the 1.0 to 5.0 range; for this reason, the difficulty of the materials in Volume II are confined to that range. (Keep in mind that the materials included in Volume II are not intended to replace those supplied by your district; rather, they are supplements. Colleagues have found them particularly helpful as homework.)

I look forward to watching the developments in our field, and am confident we will find more effective ways to help LD students. There are still far too many students who slip through school without acquiring those skills necessary to enable them to feel good about themselves. It is my hope that the information you find in the *Complete Learning Disabilities Resource Library* will make a positive difference in what you are able to do to help students.

Joan M. Harwell

ABOUT VOLUME I

Volume I of the *Complete Learning Disabilities Resource Library* offers you the following:

- Chapter 1 presents an overview of the LD field. It addresses such subjects as the history, causes, incidence, definition, symptomology, and behaviors associated with the condition. The chapter briefly discusses the prognosis for LD individuals.

- Chapter 2 gives background information about the medical aspects of learning disabilities so that you are familiar with medical terms associated with LD and, when asked questions by parents, you know the answers.

- Chapter 3 briefly describes some of the laws educators work under and how they affect students', parents', and teachers' rights.

- Chapter 4 provides a very brief overview of the early childhood program for at-risk students, including those with learning disabilities. The chapter dispels the myth that we have to wait until grade 3 or 4 before helping these students.

- Chapters 5, 6, and 7 talk about identifying students who need extra help and planning educational programs to meet their needs.

- Chapter 8 describes the current shift in how we provide services to identified and at-risk students. It describes the collaborative-consultive Resource Specialist model and the Inclusion model.

- Chapters 9 and 10 give teachers numerous tips on classroom and academic management.

- Chapters 11, 12, and 13 offer tips on how to teach the core subjects of reading, language arts, and mathematics. (These three subject areas are discussed in further detail in Volume II of the *Resource Library*.)

- Chapter 14 is a plea that we include in-depth social and life skills in the curriculum at all grade levels.

- Chapters 15 and 16 address the changing needs of LD students after they leave elementary school.

- Chapter 17 seeks to pique your interest in using technology to help you teach across all areas of the curriculum. New advances offer teachers materials that meet students' multiple achievement levels, interests, and needs. When properly selected and used, they should be a boon to your efforts in ways students find exciting.

- Chapter 18 suggests some of the directions we may be taking in the coming years.

Volume I concludes with appendices that provide you with a list of organizations and sources of help; a parent's and teacher's guide to attention deficit disorder; and a parent's and teacher's guide to learning disabilities. A bibliography is also included.

ACKNOWLEDGMENTS

I would like to thank the following persons (all were my colleagues in the San Bernardino City Unified School District) for their help in compiling this book:

Dr. Neal Roberts, Superintendent of San Bernardino City Unified School District

Colene Pate, Pat Wright, and Linda Paule, Program Specialists

Sharon Kilpatrick and Sandi Laurenco of the Early Childhood Program

Sheila Berger, regarding technology

Diane Wheeler, Director of Psychological Services

Pat Kimerer, Psychologist

Marge Lumbley, Parent Liaison

Clifford Harwell and Ann Land, middle school teachers

Janet Nickel, high school resource specialist

Bobbie Pregmon, Principal, Thompson School

Suzi Negron, Counselor

Connie Carlson, Tutorial Assistant

Chris Le Roy, Transition Office

Marion Klein, Director of Special Education

CONTENTS

About This Resource Library — v

About Volume I — vii

CHAPTER 1 LEARNING DISABILITIES—AN OVERVIEW 1

Historical Perspective — 4

Causes of Learning Disabilities — 6

Incidence of Learning Disabilities — 7

Definition of Learning Disabilities — 7

Facts About Learning Disabilities — 7

List of Learning Disability Symptomology — 8

Visual Perceptual Deficits 8 Visual Perceptual-Motor Deficits 9 Auditory Perceptual Deficits 9 Memory Deficits 10 Conceptual Deficits 10 Spatial Relationship and Body Awareness Deficits 11

Behavioral Components Associated with Learning Disabilities — 11

Attention Deficit Disorder 11 Failure Syndrome 12 Serious Emotional Overlay 12

Prognosis — 13

How Parent Expectancy and Teacher Expectancy Affect Learning — 14

CHAPTER 2 MEDICAL ASPECTS OF LEARNING DISABILITIES 15

The Central Nervous System and Learning — 17

Helping Children Learn How to Learn — 18

Parts of the Brain and Their Functions — 19

Understanding the Learning Process — 21

Encoding Data 22 Storing Data 22 Retrieving Data 23

The Physician's Role in Learning Disabilities — 23

Conditions Associated with Learning Difficulties — 24

Developmental Reading Disorder/Dyslexia 24 Tourette Syndrome 25 Teratogenic Insult as a Cause of Learning Disabilities 25 Extreme

Environmental Stress 26   Deficits in the Immune System 26   Chronic Ear Infections 26   Infectious Diseases/Accidents 26   Epilepsy/Seizure Disorder 27   Developmental Arithmetic Disorder/Dyscalculia 27   Infantile Autism 27 Developmental Language Disorder 27   Attention Deficit Disorder 28 Conduct Disorder 31   Oppositional Disorder 31   Separation Anxiety Disorder 31   Child Abuse and Neglect 32   Substance Abuse 33   Serious Emotional Disorder (SED) 33

CHAPTER 3   UNDERSTANDING THE LAW   37

The Intent of Public Law 94-142   39
Parents' Rights Under P.L. 94-142 40   Students' Rights 40 Student/Parental Rights Regarding Suspension or Expulsion 41 Behavioral Contingency Plans 41   Court Decisions and Teachers 41

The Intent of Section 504 of the Rehabilitation Act of 1973   42

Public Law 98-199, Section 626 (1983)   44

Public Law 99-457 (1986)   44

The Regular Education Initiative (REI)   44

CHAPTER 4   EARLY CHILDHOOD EDUCATION FOR AT-RISK STUDENTS   47

Referrals for Assessment   49
Normal Child Development/Developmental Milestones 49

Eligibility for Special Education Services at Ages Birth to 3   53
What Services Are Provided for Ages Birth to 3? 54

Eligibility for Special Education Services at Ages 3 to 5   54
What Services Are Provided for Ages 3 to 5? 54

Assessment of Individuals with Exceptional Needs, Ages Birth to 5   55

What Does a Play Assessment Look Like?   56

The Components of an Effective Early Childhood Education Program   57

Maturation and "Readiness" for Kindergarten   57

Tips for Parents of Children Identified for Preschool Services   58

CHAPTER 5   THE ROLE OF THE STUDENT STUDY TEAM   59

Making a Preliminary Study   61

Talking with Parents and Getting Their Support   61

Initiating a Request for Help   66

The Student Study Team Process   66

Instructional Interventions for SST Meetings   74

Specific Interventions by Subject   74

*Reading 74   Spelling 75   Mathematics 75   Social Studies/Science 75
Illegible Handwriting 76   Attentional Deficits 76*

List of Academic and Behavioral Interventions by Specific Problem   76

*Visual Perceptual Deficits 76   Auditory Perceptual Deficits 78   Spatial
Awareness Deficits 79   Conceptual Deficits 81   Memory Deficits 83
Attentional Deficits 85   Excessive Absence 87   Poor Work Habits 88   Poor
Social Relationships 89*

Storage of SST Information   94

Follow-Up SST Meetings   94

CHAPTER 6   THE ROLE OF THE MULTI-DISCIPLINARY TEAM IN ASSESSING THE NEEDS OF STUDENTS   97

The Purpose of Assessment   99

Eligibility for Special Education Services   101

The Intellectual Assessment   101

*Assessing IQ 101   Assessing Visual Perception 102   Assessing Auditory
Perception 103   Assessing Memory 104   Assessing Language 105
Assessing Adaptive Behavior 106   Assessing Emotional/Behavioral
Problems 106*

The Academic Assessment   107

*Classroom Observations 107   Doing a Time-on-Task Assessment 110
Formal Testing for Academic Assessment 110   Informal Reading
Inventories 112*

The Health Assessment   114

The Social Assessment   114

Sample Multi-Disciplinary Assessment Report   114

CHAPTER 7   THE ROLE OF THE MULTI-DISCIPLINARY TEAM IN DEVELOPING THE I.E.P.   121

Understanding the Jargon   123

The Discrepancy Model   124

Exclusionary Situations   125

Assessment Scores and Their Implications for Learning   128

The Individual Education Plan   128
"Delivery of Services" Models 128   The "Least Restrictive Environment"
Decision 129   The "Number of Hours" Issue 129   Writing Objectives 129
Modifications and Accommodations 131   Dissenting Opinions 132
Differential Standards—Promotion, Placement, and Retention 132

The Annual I.E.P. Review and the Triennial Review   133

Exiting a Student from Special Education Services   133

CHAPTER 8   MAKING THE CHANGES REQUIRED BY THE REGULAR
              EDUCATION INITIATIVE   139

Implementing the Collaborative-Consultative Model   141
The Roles of the Rsp and the Regular Classroom Teacher 142

Implementing the Inclusion Model   142
The Role of Special Education Personnel in the Inclusion Classroom 144

The Status of the Regular Education Initiative Today   145

CHAPTER 9   CLASSROOM MANAGEMENT   151

Environmental Decisions   153
Creating a Utilitarian and Attractive Classroom 153

Behavioral Management Decisions   154
Use a Classroom Aide Effectively 154   Plan the First-Week Activities 154
Establish Rules 155   Create a Positive Feeling 157   Shift from "Teacher" to
Learning Facilitator 157

Preventing Misbehavior   158
Find Better Ways to Talk to Students 158   Provide Alternatives for More
Able Students 159   Provide Alternatives for Less Able Students 159
Keep Environment Consistent and Structured 160   Use Contracts to
Prevent Misbehavior/Assure Work Production 160   Use Lotteries to Prevent
Misbehavior/Assure Work Production 161   Use Token Economies to
Prevent Misbehavior/Assure Work Production 161

Academic Enhancers   161
Build Class Spirit/Increase Feelings of Belonging 161   Offer Rewards 162
"Earn a Grade" 163   Involve the Principal 164

Handling Misbehavior   165
"Ball in Your Court" Technique 165   Timeout 166   Level Systems 166

Involving Parents in Positive Ways   166

Involve Parents in the Classroom 166   Money Therapy 167

Record Keeping   168

Profiles 168   Portfolios 168   Report Cards 168   Teacher-Parent-Pupil Conference 169   Update I.E.P.s 169   Hold Special Reviews to Rewrite I.E.P.s 169

21 Tips for Classroom Management   170

Chapter 10   Academic Management Considerations   173

Curriculum for the Learning Disabled   175

How Can a Teacher Increase Student Learning?   175

The Importance of Task Analysis and Setting Goals 175   Direct Instruction and Effective Lesson Design 178   Peer Teaching 179 Cooperative Learning 179 Metacognition 180   Advance Organizers and Story Mapping 180

Strategies for Learning   183

Higher Level Questioning 183   The Importance of Feedback 184

6 Tips for Academic Management   184

Chapter 11   Teaching Reading   187

Methods and Techniques for Teaching Reading   189

Whole Language Approach 189   The Basic Skills/Phonics Approaches 189 Combining Whole Language and Phonics 189   Language Experience Approach 190   Neurological Impress Method 190   Programmed Reading Instruction Method 190   Daily Word Lists 190   Cloze Method 190

Techniques for Improving Comprehension   191

Marginalia 191   Self-Questioning 191   Predicting/Inferential Thinking 191

Teaching Safety Words   193

Teaching Reading During Science and Social Studies   193

Multi-Scan 193

Help! Johnny Still Can't Read and I Must Help Him: A Teacher's Guide for Helping the Child Who Finds Reading Extremely Difficult   194

15 Tips for Teaching Beginning Readers   198

Chapter 12   Teaching Language Arts   201

The Value of Keeping an Ongoing Language Arts Notebook   203

Vocabulary Development   203
  Vocabulary Development and Its Relationship to Paraphrasing 204
  Words That Describe Feelings 204   Words That Drive Kids Crazy 204

Teaching Spelling   206
  Which Words? 206   Effective Ways to Teach Spelling 206

Teaching Writing   208
  Penmanship 208   Written Expression Deficits of LD Students 209

12 Tips for Teaching Language Arts   210

CHAPTER 13   TEACHING MATHEMATICS   213

Manipulatives vs. Representational Instruction   215

Making Math Activities Relate to Real-Life Situations   216

Using Math to Develop Critical-Thinking Skills   217

20 Tips for Teaching Math   217

CHAPTER 14   TEACHING LIFE AND SOCIAL SKILLS   231

Do Schools Need to Offer Life and Social Skills Courses?   233

How a Lack of Social Skills Affects Success in Life   233

Techniques for Teaching Life and Social Skills   234

Making Time to Teach Life and Social Skills   234

Curriculum for Teaching Life and Social Skills   234
  Going to School 234   Social Skills 235   Making Friends 235
  Understanding the Feelings of Others 235   Understanding Myself 235
  Etiquette 236   Protecting Myself 236   Handling Emergencies 236
  Working with Authority Figures/Obeying the Law 237   Understanding My
  Handicap 237   Dealing with Stress 237   Family Living 237
  Organizational Skills 238   Prevocational Skills 238   Work-Related
  Skills 238   Dating 238   Money Management 239   Consumer Skills 239
  Community Services 239

CHAPTER 15   THE ROLE OF THE SECONDARY SCHOOL   243

The Changing Needs of the Junior High School LD Student   245

**Efforts to Engage the Student in the Educational Process
at the Junior High Level**   246
  Departmentalization/School Within a School 246   Resource Rooms 246
  Self-Contained Special Day Classes 246

Curriculum for the Junior High School   246

Strategies to Increase Metacognition and Learning 247   Reading in Junior High School 247   Mathematics for Living 248   Teaching LD Students to Be Their Own Advocate 248

The Changing Needs of the High School LD Student   250

Efforts to Engage Students in the Educational Process at the High School Level   250

Peer Counseling 250   Family Involvement and Transition I.E.P.s 250 Vocational Programs 250   Independent Study Programs and Continuation High Schools 250

Curriculum for the Senior High School   251

CHAPTER 16   BEYOND HIGH SCHOOL   253

Services Available to LD Students Going to College   255

Vocational Rehabilitation Services for the Learning Disabled   256

Learning Disabled Adults   257

CHAPTER 17   THE ROLE OF TECHNOLOGY IN LEARNING DISABILITIES   259

Computer-Assisted Learning   261

What Does Research Say About Computer-Assisted Learning?   262

Hardware   263

Software   263

CHAPTER 18   A CALL TO ACTION   265

How Can We Prevent Learning Disabilities?   267
Discourage Teenage Pregnancy 267   Initiate Early Infant Program 268

Early Screening and Identification   268

Attendance   268

Getting Parents Involved with Education   268

Strengthening Vocational Programs   269

Adult Education   269

Professional Issues   270

APPENDIX 1   LIST OF ORGANIZATIONS AND SOURCES OF HELP   273

APPENDIX 2   TEACHER'S GUIDE TO BEHAVIORAL PROBLEM SOLVING   277

APPENDIX 3   WHAT YOU NEED TO KNOW ABOUT ADD:
A GUIDE FOR PARENTS AND TEACHERS   281

APPENDIX 4   WHAT YOU NEED TO KNOW ABOUT LD:
A GUIDE FOR PARENTS AND TEACHERS   287

BIBLIOGRAPHY   293

LEARNING DISABILITIES— AN OVERVIEW

Cameron was repeating first grade when the Student Study Team referred him for formal assessment. It was January and his teacher was concerned because he was still a nonreader. His mother was concerned because she thought he might be dyslexic; his father and his uncle were. On that first day, I asked Cameron which he liked better—reading or math. His answer stunned me! He said, "I can't do anything." Cameron was deep in failure syndrome and was reluctant to attempt anything he had had trouble with before. At the ripe old age of seven, he had given up on learning to read. He had significant delays in visual perception, memory deficits, and attentional deficits.

Sarah is 27 years old. She reads well and writes beautifully but math is extremely difficult for her. She is a junior in college, majoring in journalism. After taking "bonehead math" three times, she was finally declared dyscalculic and will be allowed to finish college with no further math.

Cameron and Sarah are identified as being "learning disabled." Known as the "invisible handicap," these disabilities can cause their victims as much distress as physical handicaps. Some conclude they are dumb and cannot cope with school, becoming dropouts. Most are underachievers, who often go to great lengths to avoid situations where others might discover their problems. Figure 1-1 shows a note that was intercepted by a high school teacher in which one such victim verbalizes his frustration with his disability.

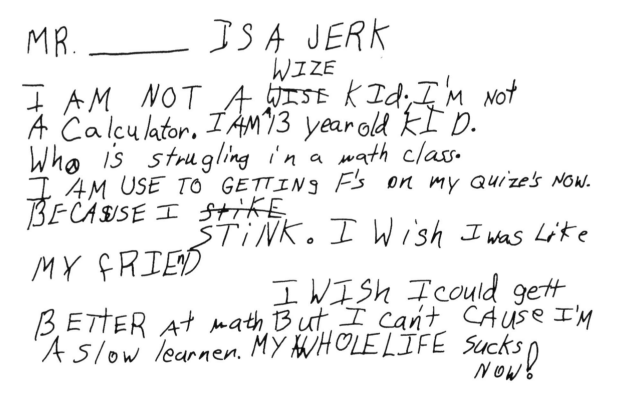

Figure 1-1

Without appropriate assistance, these individuals may develop an emotional overlay that will further hamper their efforts.

3

With early identification, sound remedial teaching, training in social skills, vocational guidance and training, and personal as well as family counseling, the majority of learning disabled persons could become responsible and productive citizens.

HISTORICAL PERSPECTIVE

Learning disabilities is a relatively young field. Prior to this century, individuals with these problems probably found employment in agriculture, service industries, or were taken care of by their family. With the rapid technological advances that occurred in the 1940s and the decline in the family, demands were made on the educational system to do something for these children. It was felt that because of their difficulties, they would need to be in special classes with specially trained teachers, using a curriculum that was at their level. Learning disabled students were often clumped with mildly educably retarded students.

Two schools of educational theorists emerged:

1. The *Perceptual-Motor Theorists* noted that many children with learning problems had perceptual and motor difficulties. This group contained such well-known names as Goldstein, Strauss, Werner, Bender, Kephart, Cruickshank, and Frostig. Out of their experience came the following educational suggestions:

   - We needed to reduce distracting stimuli in the classroom so pupils could attend to their work and accomplish more. This would be facilitated by carpeting floors, using carrels ("blinders"), and reducing light levels.
   - By using various techniques, a youngster's awareness of the material to be learned could be heightened. Color-coding, large print, highlighting, sandpaper letters, and configuration are some examples.

2. The *Language Theorists* noted that many learning handicapped children had deficits in the area of language. Some of the famous names in this group are Orton, Fernald, Mykleburst, and Kirk. Out of their thought came the following suggestions:

   - Phonics training
   - Teach to the child's primary learning channel. It had been discovered that most people have a preferred way to acquire information (visually, auditorily, or tactiley), so it was presumed that if information was presented in that mode, it would be assimilated quicker. While this certainly makes sense, it turned out that children learned more when information came through multiple channels or modalities.

We can see remnants of these two schools' positions still being used in the field today.

By the 1960s, disturbing new research showed that segregating children into special classes had detrimental effects.

1. First, it often carried with it a stigma.
2. Children in special classes learned less than similar children who were not in segregated classes.

3. The behavior of children in special classes was more problematic because the handicapped children imitated each other rather than the behavior of nonhandicapped peers.

4. After years of special treatment, these children were not able to integrate themselves into the work-world because they could not relate to their nonhandicapped fellow workers. Without special treatment from understanding employers, they could not cope.

In 1962, Dr. Samuel Kirk introduced the term "learning disabilities." He defined the term as "a retardation, disorder, or delayed development in one or more of the processes of speech, language, reading, spelling, writing, or arithmetic resulting from a possible cerebral dysfunction and/or emotional disturbance and not from mental retardation, sensory deprivation, or cultural or instructional factors."

In 1963, the Association for Children with Learning Disabilities (ACLD) was founded.

Parents of children with learning disabilities demanded that their children be moved back into regular educational settings with resource room help from a teacher who specialized in learning disabilities.

During this period, new terms came into general use. There was an effort to describe these disabilities in more specific terms such as:

"dyslexia"—referred to a deficit or delay in acquisition of reading.

"dyscalculia"—referred to deficits in the acquisition of mathematical skills and concepts

"dysgraphia"—referred to deficits in the writing area

In 1975, the Congress of the United States passed Public Law 94-142 (The Education of All Handicapped Children Law) that guaranteed a "free and appropriate education" in the "least restrictive environment" for each child, ages 3-21 who was identified for services. Known as the "mainstreaming" law, it said that children would be educated in the regular classroom unless the nature and severity of the disability indicated they could not learn there. With this law came the idea of the multi-disciplinary assessment, and the development of the Individualized Educational Plan (I.E.P.).

Public Law 94-142 had one enormous shortcoming. It did not provide school districts with adequate monies to provide the services it mandated. At the time of its passage, it was presumed that roughly 2 percent of school children would require such services for learning disabilities. No one predicted at the time of its passage that by 1987 almost 5 percent of children would qualify.

In the mid-1980s a number of new approaches became available for the treatment of learning disabilities. Practitioners of these approaches attributed startling positive results to them. The treatment approaches included dietary changes (restricting sugar, eliminating artificial flavorings and colorings, taking megavitamins and trace elements). At this time, vision training and auditory-perceptual training were touted to help LD children learn to read. Chiropractic interventions and patterning were supposed to bring great improvement. Unfortunately, research has not supported the claims of the practitioners providing these services so they are no longer recommended to parents by special educators.

In the late 1980s, instruction shifted to skills development. Teachers of the learning disabled found themselves working on developing basic skills in reading, writing, and arithmetic. The methods used closely resembled those of remedial teachers.

By this time it had been noted that most learning disabled students were not active learners. Active learners have strategies they use to learn new materials (metacognition) while LD students do not. Out of this *Inactive Learner Theory* has come new teaching techniques. Special education teachers were encouraged to use direct teaching rather than functioning in a tutorial mode. They were inserviced in how to teach children strategies for learning and how to use advance organizers to help students extract the most important parts of the lesson. Regular class teachers were trained in cooperative learning techniques. These strategies have students teaching and giving emotional support to other students. Last, the computer and new software show great promise because inactive learners often respond to computer-assisted learning with enthusiasm.

In the late 1980s, advances in the medical field (EEG, CAT and Pet Scans, NMR and MRI) allowed clinicians to begin to study the brains of living and functioning people. Post-mortem studies revealed new information that suggested brains of dyslexics are different from those of persons without reading difficulties in several ways. There was a renewed interest in studying the etiology of learning problems.

As the 1990s opened, the nation was in the grip of a severe recession. The problem of how to serve so many needy students without increasing taxes led to efforts to find ways to use special educators more effectively. The Collaborative-Consultative Resource Specialist and Inclusion model will bring special educators into the regular classroom, where they can help regular teachers with both identified special education students and "at-risk" students.

CAUSES OF LEARNING DISABILITIES

We are now aware of a number of factors that are associated with learning disabilities.

1. First, we know there is a strong familial connection. It is not uncommon to find several members of the same family have the problem, which suggests a genetic basis. Recently, scientists announced they believe they have isolated a gene for dyslexia.

2. We also know that certain prenatal conditions can harm the fetus. Among these conditions are infectious disease during the first three months of pregnancy, use of chemical substances (alcohol, drugs, smoking), any condition that interferes with the fetus receiving adequate oxygen or nutrition, intrauterine infections, or maternal stress. Statistics show the incidence of problems is higher in the babies of women who are over 40 years of age or under 16. Babies of low birth weight are considered at risk.

3. Prematurity, birth trauma, oxygen deprivation at birth, and failure to thrive have all been associated with later learning problems.

4. Recent studies show that infants who are born into nonstimulating environments (lack of attention, toys, talk) are at risk. Likewise, so are youngsters who experience head trauma, intracranial infections, long sustained fevers, anorexic episodes, near drowning, and ingestion of neurotoxins.

Lead poisoning, and contamination by aluminum, arsenic, and mercury have been shown to cause learning impairment. Children with learning disabilities often have deficits of the immune system such as asthma and allergies. Children who experience chronic ear infections in the first five years are likely candidates for LD.

INCIDENCE OF LEARNING DISABILITIES

How many people have learning disabilities? We really don't know. In the literature you will find estimates ranging from 2 percent to 20 percent. It depends on who you count. While the identified population is around 5 percent, there are many more individuals who probably have some degree of the problem but never showed the significant discrepancy, so were never identified. There are also children who, for one reason or another, slipped through the school system. The true nature of their problems was not recognized. They may have appeared to be just lazy or unmotivated.

DEFINITION OF LEARNING DISABILITIES

The definition used by 20 states and with only minor modification by nine others is:

> "Disorder in one or more psychological processes involved in understanding or in using language, spoken or written, which may manifest itself in an imperfect ability to listen, think, read, write, spell, or do mathematical calculations. The term includes such conditions as perceptual handicaps, brain injury, minimal brain dysfunction, dyslexia, and developmental aphasia. The term does not include children who have learning problems which are primarily the result of visual, hearing, or motor handicaps, or mental retardation or emotional disturbance, or of environmental, cultural or economic disadvantage." (U.S. Office of Education, *Federal Register*, 1977)

Once believed to be a condition one outgrew or learned to compensate for, we now know that true learning disabilities exist across the life span. Some newer definitions state this.

FACTS ABOUT LEARNING DISABILITIES

1. More boys than girls are identified as being learning disabled; the ratio is about 3:1 (Cone et al., 1985).
2. Students with learning disabilities are usually identified when they reach third or fourth grade. While they were lagging behind their classmates earlier, they finally reach the "significant discrepancy" stage required for eligibility for services. Unfortunately, they also have developed feelings of being academic failures and feel they have no control over their learning (Bender, 1992).
3. More students are identified as having disabilities in the area of reading and language arts than in math. The deficits occur in the area of *semantics* (word meaning), *syntax* (putting words together to form sentences), and *pragmatics* (the subtleties of language usage that make the speaker's meaning clear) (Smith, 1991).
4. IQs of LD students are typically in the 90-95 range (Bender, 1992).

5. Many LD students have deficits in short-term memory and in attention.

6. LD students are inactive learners. They do not learn incidentally. They require many repetitions to master a skill.

7. Studies suggest that students with reading disabilities will read better in the long run if they have phonics training (Ross, 1976).

8. All dyslexics are learning disabled but not all learning disabled are dyslexic. The typical dyslexic shows severe difficulty reading but no difficulty with math.

9. Studies that measure time-on-task indicate nonhandicapped students are on-task 60 to 85 percent of the time while LD students are on-task only 30 to 60 percent of the time (Bryan and Wheeler, 1972; McKinney and Feagans, 1983).

10. Drug intervention is often effective in reducing behaviors that interfere with learning (Benson, 1987).

11. Students with LD are not generally as socially acceptable as other students when rated by their peers/teachers (Bender et al., 1984).

12. LD students rarely attain skills levels beyond sixth grade (Deshler, Schumaker, and Lenz, 1984).

13. As many as 50 percent of students with LD will drop out of school prior to high school graduation (Levin, Zigmond, and Birch, 1985).

14. Students with learning disabilities are more likely to be in trouble with the law (Keilitz and Dunivant, 1986).

15. Parents of students with LD expect less of their children both in academics and behavior than other parents expect (Bryan and Bryan, 1983).

LIST OF LEARNING DISABILITY SYMPTOMOLOGY

Visual Perceptual Deficits

These deficits occur when the brain misinterprets what is seen. Among the symptoms associated with this deficit are:

- reversal of letters (such as b/d, p/q)
- inversions (such as u/n, m/w)
- yawns while reading
- complains the eyes itch, hurt, tear, or the print becomes blurry
- loses place frequently, rereads or skips lines
- sequencing errors (was/saw, on/no, there/three)
- erases excessively
- turns paper or head at odd angles to read or write
- cannot copy accurately
- does not recognize an object or word if part of it is not shown (has trouble with poor quality dittoes)
- not alert to visual detail (likenesses/differences, changes in environment)

- reading improves when print is larger, or there are fewer items on the page or a marker is used
- does not see the main theme of a picture but notices some minute detail instead
- mirror writes—in this phenomenon the student writes things exactly reversed and if the writing is held up to a mirror, then it appears as it should look
- reversals of numbers (2, 3, 4, 5, 7, 9)

Visual Perceptual-Motor Deficits

These include deficits that occur because the brain misinterpreted what it saw, as well as deficits resulting from poor motor control, such as:

- deficits in depth perception; the individual bumps into things and steps on things instead of passing by them
- cannot color within lines
- letters are not on a line; they are above, under or are intersected by the line
- cannot cut on a line
- does not use paste efficiently—it oozes out or the picture has lumps under it
- forms letters in odd ways
- poor fine motor control reflected by poor quality of the handwriting
- breaks pencil lead or crayons due to too much pressure; holds pencil too tightly
- there is a deficit in the spacing of letters; letters collide, no space between words or in math, the student has difficulty with operations that require keeping columns of numbers straight

Auditory Perceptual Deficits

These deficits occur because the brain is slow to interpret what it hears, or it misperceives what it hears. Common among these deficits, we find:

- auditory processing delays; not able to process conversation at normal speed but can understand if information is repeated very slowly
- auditory discrimination deficits; unable to hear differences in sounds—most likely sounds are b/p confusion, d/t confusion, and v/f confusion; also cannot distinguish between short "e" and short "i" sounds; may have trouble with the "sh"/"ch" sounds
- cannot tell where a sound is coming from
- does not recognize common sounds for what they are
- cannot filter out extraneous noises; cannot distinguish the teacher's voice from competing voices, therefore gets the wrong information and steadfastly maintains "the teacher said it"
- mispronounces some words such as "chimney," "spaghetti," "particularly"

Memory Deficits

Memory deficits are quite common among children with learning disabilities. They usually are most notable in the short-term memory. The child is not able to hold onto something he or she sees or hears long enough to do anything with it, such as repeat it or write it. Therefore, the child is unable to benefit from instruction because literally "out of sight" or "out of hearing" is "out of mind." Of course, there is some selective memory operating here; very traumatic experiences such as burning oneself or being promised a highly meaningful award are usually remembered. Among the symptoms of memory deficit are:

- cannot remember what was just seen/shown
- cannot remember what was just heard
- when copying, can retain only one letter at a time in memory and has to refer back to the book after writing each letter
- poor sight vocabulary; only a few words recognized at the automatic level
- limited receptive and expressive vocabulary; does not recall the names of common objects and says "that thing"; semantic and syntax errors are common
- slow to memorize poetry; even after multiple exposure there are many errors
- may appear to know something one day or one hour and has forgotten it by the next
- makes the same error over and over; does not benefit from experience
- extremely slow to acquire the habits of spacing, punctuating, capitalizing, indenting, etc.
- has great difficulty getting his or her ideas on paper (will tell you what he or she is going to write but will forget it after writing only a few words)
- general knowledge scores on standardized tests are low; does not pick up and retain information that is only heard occasionally

Conceptual Deficits

These are deficits in an individual's ability to think or make associations between similar kinds of information. Many kinds of symptoms are shown. Some examples are:

- cannot "read" social situations; does not understand body language; for example, when you are really angry, he or she may laugh because you look funny
- cannot generalize learning from one situation to another without someone guiding him or her to do so; for example, may get a word right on a spelling test and then misspell it a few minutes later
- cannot do inferential thinking; has trouble deciding why something happened and trouble making predictions
- cannot see how things are alike and different when subtle discriminations are required; has trouble with classification activities
- does not understand time relationships: yesterday, today, tomorrow, after/before; 15 minutes vs. 2 hours; concepts such as "hurry"

- reads but is not able to attach meaning to the words
- does not associate an act with its consequences: "If I talk I will get detention" and when the detention is assigned screams loudly that the teacher is just picking on him or her
- little imagination; not able to create poetry or original stories
- no sense of humor; does not recognize a joke or pun
- tends to be expressionless
- slow responses
- bizarre answers; correct answers obtained in bizarre ways; classroom comments are "off track"
- cannot think in orderly, sequential, logical ways
- does not understand concepts such as beauty or bravery
- has trouble formulating sentences (written expression looks like "word salad," i.e., all the words are there but they are in the wrong order)
- slow to grasp any new idea, such as place value, rounding of numbers, more/less
- excessively gullible

Spatial Relationship and Body Awareness Deficits

These are deficits in an individual's ability to organize spatially. The following types of problems belong in this category:

- becomes lost even in familiar surroundings such as the school or the neighborhood
- is awkward/clumsy and prone to have accidents
- cannot skip, hop, hit, or catch a ball
- very confused over directionality, so may not read left to right; is confused by concepts such as over, under, around, first, last, front, back, up, down
- very disorganized; loses things; messy desk
- drops pencil over and over; falls out of chair

BEHAVIORAL COMPONENTS ASSOCIATED WITH LEARNING DISABILITIES

Attention Deficit Disorder

This is not a learning disability. Confusion about this exists because in the earlier days, it was mentioned frequently when speaking of "minimal brain dysfunction." In our minds, however, it continues to be associated with learning disabilities because research shows that it is a condition found in about 20 percent of children and adolescents with learning disabilities. Therefore, it will be helpful to list some of the symptomology of Attention Deficit Disorder (ADD) here:

- impulsivity; does not consider the consequence before acting
- cannot sit still; cannot stand still; blurts out

- low frustration tolerance/short fuse
- does not finish assignments in the allotted time; little work produced
- visually and auditorily distractible
- fidgety: drums fingers, taps toes, fools with objects
- demanding; cannot share or await turn
- disorganized, loses things
- short attention span: flits from activity to activity
- spaces off/daydreams
- negativistic; oppositional; argumentative
- mouth noises; incessant talking
- reads something correctly but comprehension is poor
- overreacts to stimuli, yells out
- cannot mind his or her own business; intrusive; interrupts
- does not follow rules; often claims not to have heard them
- moody/mood swings
- may be cruel; mean to others; makes fun of others
- poor social relationships with peers and siblings; other children sitting nearby complain about being "bothered"
- wets or soils self after the age of five
- appears tired; cannot sit up or cannot hold head up
- performance varies from day to day (good/bad days)
- sleep disturbances

There are two forms of this disorder: Attention-Deficit Hyperactivity Disorder (ADHD) and Undifferentiated Attention-Deficit Disorder (UADD). Children with the second type often just sit and do nothing. Since they are not usually disruptive, they rarely get referred to a physician. Both forms hamper a child's ability to take full advantage of schooling.

Failure Syndrome

- describes self as "dumb"
- does not take reprimands well
- tends to avoid group activity
- claims illness without any evidence of illness
- class clown; acts out
- immature behavior: babyish, dependent, seems younger
- not able to do the work assigned

Serious Emotional Overlay

The following conditions are not a part of a child's learning disability. Unfortunately they sometimes occur. When these conditions are present, they should not be ignored.

It is best to request that the I.E.P. team reconvene for a special review if these conditions are present:

- explosive, unpredictable, bizarre, and dangerous behavior
- preoccupation with death and destruction
- prevailing mood of sadness; lack of interest in anything
- cannot distinguish reality from fantasy; bizarre stories
- withdrawal; fearfulness; anxious; tense

PROGNOSIS

Whenever a child is diagnosed as having learning disabilities, invariably the question arises, what is the prognosis for the child? That is hard to predict because it depends on many factors, such as:

1. the nature and severity of the disability
2. whether attention deficit disorder is also present
3. the intellectual potential of the child
4. the quantity and quality of the intervention
5. when intervention begins to occur (earlier is better)
6. the quantity and quality of the parental relationship (Does the parent talk with the child, read to the child, expose the child to lots of wholesome experiences, work on social skills, use parenting skills that involve effective discipline, supervise home-work and give help as needed?)
7. the temperament of the child (how much frustration the child can tolerate)
8. the maturity and social skills of the child
9. the quality of communication between teacher and parent
10. the stability of the home
11. luck

If the nature and severity of the disability is mild and all of the other factors are positive, the outcome will probably be good.

If the nature and severity of the disability is moderate but all other factors are positive, the outcome will probably be satisfactory.

A few years ago research showed the teacher-pupil relationship was the most important gauge of school success. Today, because of the decline in the amount of time parents spend with their children, it is the quantity and quality of the parent-child relationship that is most critical. For this reason, schools are trying to involve parents in their children's education by offering parenting classes. Some employers are joining the schools by allowing parents time off from work to help in the classroom.

When parents are dysfunctional or barely functionally literate themselves or are too busy or too stressed to help, the prognosis for the child's success becomes more bleak.

Being learning disabled does not, by itself, doom a person to failure. Many famous persons have had the problem. Thomas Edison's teacher described him as being "addled" and he left school at an early age. He went on to invent the electric light and thousands of other useful products. It is suspected that Leonardo da Vinci and Albert Einstein, two of the greatest thinkers in the history of the world, may have been learning disabled. Winston Churchill and Woodrow Wilson had learning difficulties but became great national leaders. Hans Christian Andersen and George Bernard Shaw became great writers in spite of earlier difficulties. In our time, we have several celebrities who are learning disabled—Cher, Tom Cruise and Henry Winkler—yet they are certainly successful. All of these people found their way by concentrating on their abilities rather than their disabilities. As teachers, we need to find ways to help students look at themselves from the same perspective.

How Parent Expectancy and Teacher Expectancy Affect Learning

Research clearly shows that parents of most LD children expect less of their children academically than do parents of nonhandicapped children (Chapman and Boersma, 1979). Likewise, teachers also tend to expect less of them. It may well be that this lack of expectancy may be one reason LD students have such a high dropout rate. In my own experience, I have found that LD students are able to achieve fairly difficult objectives when given *daily* practice and when they are motivated to want to achieve it. I sometimes compare them to rubber bands. We want to stretch them to their potential but not cause them to break under undue stress.

Occasionally you will encounter parents who expect far more than the child can achieve. Under their undue pressure, the child may play sick, develop real psychosomatic illness, become depressed, develop acting-out escape behavior (drug use or run away), become school phobic, or try to manipulate the situation so school and parents are in conflict (make up stories of injustices done to them by school personnel).

We need to counsel some parents to raise their expectations and others to lower them.

Learning disabilities is a relatively new field. It is one offering tremendous challenges. The debate continues over what is the best way to deliver services to identified students and what is the best curriculum for these children. We're seeking better ways to assess student progress and to encourage student progress. Over the next few years, the medical field probably will come forth with both new information on etiology, but also new drugs to help. Computer technology and the information Superhighway may revolutionize how we teach. What an exciting and dynamic field to be a part of!

MEDICAL ASPECTS OF LEARNING DISABILITIES

When you become a part of this field, you will soon find yourself dealing with various medical aspects of the condition. Perhaps a colleague will ask you to observe a child with ADHD or a parent will ask whether she should restrict her child from consuming sugar or you will encounter a child in your program who also has epilepsy. It is possible that in the future you will read articles that will tell of new medications that improve central nervous system functioning. You will need some background knowledge of how that system works.

THE CENTRAL NERVOUS SYSTEM AND LEARNING

The Central Nervous System is composed of the brain and spinal cord. Nerves all over the body pick up sensory stimuli and send messages via the spinal cord to the brain. The brain interprets what is seen, heard, felt, smelled, and tasted, and integrates that information with previously stored information.

The system is run by electrical and chemical factors. To understand how this works, here is a rather simplified explanation.

The smallest unit of the system is a single cell called a neuron. Billions of neurons lie in close proximity but do not actually touch each other as shown in Figure 2-1. When a sensory stimulus is received by a neuron, we say the neuron "fires." This refers to the fact that an electrical charge is generated. This charge then jumps a gap called the synaptic gap to the next neuron, causing it to "fire"; in turn, it stimulates the next neuron and so on until the message either reaches its destination or loses impetus. The system produces chemicals that either help the message cross the synaptic gap or inhibit its passage. Those that help are call "neurotransmitters" and those that inhibit are called "neuroinhibitors." In each category, there is not a single kind of substance but many, so we are finding new names (such as dopamine and acetylcholine) coming into the literature as scientists discover them. Each has a different effect on how we feel or how we learn. At the present time these relationships are not well understood; but as scientists learn more, it is probable they will be able to develop new drug therapies to assist persons who have behavior and learning problems.

Neurons

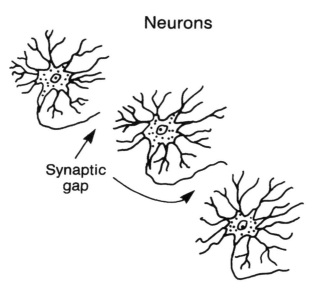

Synaptic gap

Figure 2-1

17

As learning begins to occur, the gap between the neurons decreases and finally closes. A learning connection has been created. We know that these connections form more quickly when we use verbal rehearsal, visual stimuli, activities that involve doing a skill (kinesthetic and tactile senses are brought into play).

HELPING CHILDREN LEARN HOW TO LEARN

Beginning in grade one, and every year thereafter, our primary goal is to teach children "how" to learn. First you say to the children:

"Today I'm going to give you a gift made of pure gold. (pause) If you can learn to remember to use it, you will find going to school and working on a job easier." (pause)

Draw several neurons on the board, leaving a gap between each. (It is better to do this while the children watch. It enhances their interest in what you are about to say.)

"In your brain, you have cells called neurons. These neurons help you learn. (pause) Let's say you are trying to learn to spell a new word" (for older kids, you can say "learn your time tables"), "each time you really look at the word and verbally rehearse it out loud, this little gap gets smaller. (pause) Oh, by the way, verbally rehearsing means saying the thing out loud. I'm going to tell you to talk to yourself. (pause) Let's say I want to learn to spell the word *learn.* Now watch! I'm going to show you how to do this."

Write each letter down and say the name of each letter out loud as you write it: " 'l–e–a–r–n spells learn.' Now I want you to write this word on your blackboard/paper and say each letter as you go." (Do the letters in unison.)

"Good, _____, _____ (name a couple of students who you saw doing it correctly). Is everyone saying it with us? Let's do it again together." (Watch to see which kids are not and have an aide, or one of the kids who understands, teach those children later.)

"Let me show you what is going on in your head. See these little spaces between the neurons? Let me show you what happens to those spaces as you say it out loud. (Using the chalk, move the ends of the neurons closer together.) Let's say it again. L–e–a–r–n spells learn. (Move the ends of the neurons closer.) Can anyone spell this word without looking?" (Have a child demonstrate.)

"This is what has happened in _____'s head." *(In your drawing, make the ends of all the neurons touch each other.)* "_____ has made a learning connection. He (She) has learned this word." (pause)

"Some people can make those neurons move together by doing something five times; other people have to do something twenty times. But you **can** make them move together if you keep doing it because each time you do it, they are getting closer and eventually they will connect. Then you will have learned the word."

You will need to go through this explanation for at least three or four days in a row. On the third day you can have your brightest child explain it to the class; on the fourth day, have another bright child explain it. After that, bring up the method each time it is appropriate to the task (such as 4 + 3 equals 7). Show students they don't need to count the objects each time; rather, they just stop and memorize the fact using the technique above. You may want to have the class do group practice with spelling words or math facts.

As part of your daily opening exercises, you may want to impress students with the fact that *they are powerful*. They can make themselves learn. They can use this technique at home and at school. They can explain to their parents how learning occurs. You may want to use the *Pride Pledge* (author not known):

> Today, I'll do my best, to be my best.
>
> I will listen!
>
> I will follow directions!
>
> I will be honest!
>
> I will respect the rights of others!
>
> **I can learn and I will learn!**

PARTS OF THE BRAIN AND THEIR FUNCTIONS

The brain stem, cerebellum, and cerebrum are the three parts of the brain. The brain stem is in charge of automatic functions such as breathing, heart beat, digestion, etc. The cerebellum controls bodily movements such as balance, posture, and other deliberate kinds of bodily movements. The higher level functions such as thinking and learning take place in the cerebrum. Moving from the front of the brain to the rear, there are four lobes. The frontal lobe is involved in abstract thinking as well as emotional control. The temporal lobe, which lies just behind the frontal lobes near the ears, is involved with hearing and remembering. The parietal lobe is concerned with the tactile senses and the occipital lobe deals with vision and visual perception. (See Figure 2-2.)

The cerebrum is divided into two hemispheres. If you are right-handed, oddly it is the left hemisphere where that function originated. Conversely, if you are left-handed, it originated in the right hemisphere. By far, the majority of humans are right-handed and have, therefore, a dominant left hemisphere which is actually larger in size than the other hemisphere. Each hemisphere seems to be somewhat specialized in the types of functions it performs, as shown in Figure 2-3.

When brain injury occurs, however, there is a remarkable effort by other areas of the brain to take over functions that were lost.

The brain is shaped by experience. The first five years of a child's life have been called "the formative years." Babies are born with billions of brain cells. Within a few months linkages begin to connect the cells into a learning network. Where there were once synaptic gaps, there are now learning connections called synapses. During this first period of growth, the sensorimotor period, babies move their bodies, look around, and listen. They integrate visual, kinesthetic, tactile, and auditory messages to learn about their immediate world. They learn about size, relative position, and contour.

Brain Anatomy and Hemispheric Functioning

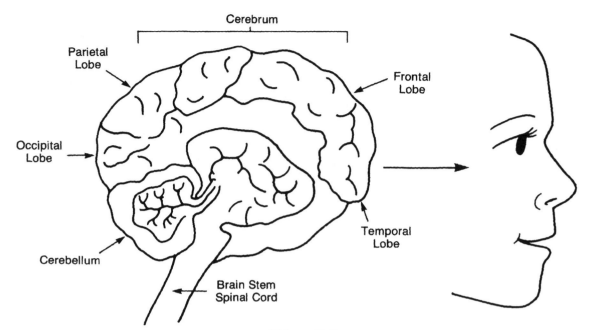

Figure 2-2

Left
- Receptive/Expressive Language
- Logic
- Analytic
- Reading
- Arithmetic
- Complex Motor Functions
- Conceptual Similarities
- Writing
- Sequential Processing (Parts)

Right
- Spatial Orientation
- Intuitive Problem Solving
- Music
- Arts
- Picture/Pattern Sense
- Facial Recognition
- Tactile Perception
- Visual Imagery
- Nonverbal Thinking
- Humorous Thought
- Simultaneous Processing (Whole)

Hemispheric Functioning
Summarized from Various Sources

Figure 2-3

According to a study conducted by the Carnegie Foundation, by three months of age, the baby's brain has formed trillions of synapses. Then the brain begins to trim away synapses that are not being used. It appears that once lost, later experiences are less likely to produce results. In other words, "use it or lose it." "Children raised in poor environments can display cognitive deficits by 18 months that may be irreversible" (*Wall Street Journal*, April 12, 1994).

Studies suggest that early stimulation-singing to the baby, talking to the baby, exposure to appropriate toys for the age, and touching/cuddling are critical to the child's later intellectual well-being.

It is helpful to understand how a child's cognitive development progresses. The chart shown in Figure 2-4 was adapted from *Piaget's Theory of Cognitive Development*, second edition, by Barry J. Wadsworth, copyright © 1979 by Longman Publishing.

Figure 2-4

Sensorimotor (ages 0–2)	Begins at birth; babies go through many random movements and pay attention to sensation. Gradually the child is able to make purposeful movements, such as rolling and reaching. Language begins with cooing, responding to, and imitating sounds. Toward the end of this stage, the child understands that out of sight does not mean that something ceases to exist.
Preoperational (ages 2–7)	Understands what is said; gradually increases number of words he/she can say; gains the ability to think in symbolic terms. Can think in one direction. At the beginning of the stage, the child is very egocentric (I want). This gives way to being able to share and understand the feelings of others.
Concrete Operational (ages 7–11)	Begins to be able to solve problems. Ability to conserve develops (when counting does not have to start with one; can see things are the same size even though their shape is different); reversibility develops (counts forward and backward, can do and undo). Able to classify and arrange things (such as numbers in order of size).
Formal Operations (ages 11–15)	Able to solve problems abstractly. Able to hold onto and integrate multiple ideas. Begins to understand social issues. Sense of separate identity begins.

UNDERSTANDING THE LEARNING PROCESS

The process by which learning occurs is complex. It involves:

1. *encoding* data from the sensory system
2. *storing* data for future use
3. *retrieving* stored data

Encoding Data

A person is bombarded day and night with data coming from our senses. Every sight, sound, and feeling begins a journey. Most of us possess normal sensory input (we are not blind or deaf, etc.), the chemicals in our bodies are balanced in such a way that we are able to stay alert but are also able to weed out stimuli that are not really important. When a message reaches its destination, we are able to accurately interpret its meaning. Many children with learning problems are not able to do these things. They have deficits in arousal. They are either not alert to incoming stimuli or they are overwhelmed by the multitude of messages arriving simultaneously and cannot distinguish which ones to attend to. To illustrate, some children do not hear what you say while others hear every noise, no matter how insignificant, and cannot distinguish the teacher's voice above other sounds (auditory figure-ground distortion). Other people receive the message but cannot interpret it; for example, they are not able to distinguish between seeing similar words such as *being, begin* and *bring* or cannot tell a "b" from a "d." These kinds of problems are called perceptual learning disabilities. Perceptual deficits are found in a majority of people with LD.

Storing Data

Most people are able to receive data, interpret it accurately, integrate it with already known data, and decide on ways to keep up with it (metacognition). Some things are stored where they can be immediately recalled; others are stored where they can be retrieved with a little thought.

The average person can hold on to a visual message or auditory message long enough to record it on paper. But for many children with learning disabilities, the message is lost as soon as it disappears from sight or as soon as the teacher says it.

We have memory for what we see, what we hear, what we feel, and what we do. Most people have a preferred modality. About 67 percent of people prefer the visual channel; 15 percent the auditory; and 10 percent the tactile. For the other 8 percent, it appears they find learning difficult no matter how it is presented. Research has found that the most efficient lessons involve all three modalities.

Short-term memory will hold a message only for a few seconds. To convert it to long-term memory, some sort of "verbal/visual rehearsal" must occur. You do this as you keep repeating a phone number from the time you look it up until you dial it. If you use that number frequently, you store it in your "working memory."

Obviously, there is a "selective" feature to memory. For most of us, we can remember anything we want to remember. This is not true for some persons with memory deficits. They forget important information. Life is a nightmare of "forgetting" and "losing."

Can memory be improved? The answer is a resounding "yes." By getting a person to rehearse (repeat it verbally, write it over and over) what he or she needs to remember, short-term memory information can be converted to long-term. Rewards and other techniques help focus a child's attention on what is to be learned and encourage him or her to want to learn it. In the case of children and adults with attention deficit disorder, we know the normally prescribed medicines help improve both perception and memory for the user.

There are techniques that will assist in aiding memory. When a new piece of information can be linked to something already known, it is more likely to be remembered.

Retrieving Data

Once data is stored in long-term memory, it will stay there provided it is reinforced occasionally. The necessary *reinforcement* schedule varies from person to person. At first, the concept must be reinforced daily. Most people need about 20 to 30 exposures to grasp a piece of information. For the average person, five daily exposures to a new word, repeated for four days, is sufficient to "fix" a spelling word in his or her memory. Maybe this is why teachers still often require students to write the words five times each. The word is then maintained in memory by the rate at which students normally encounter it in reading. This technique does not often work for LD kids because they are inactive learners. They will copy the word over and over without ever knowing what the word is, without any verbal rehearsal and often with copying errors.

Even if you get them to focus their attention and they learn the word for the spelling test, the next time they see the word or need to spell the word, they may not recognize it as being the same word. I have had children get 100% on a spelling test (and they were not cheating) and an hour later ask me how to spell one of the words from the test. Finally, for most people, once a word is learned or a math concept mastered, it is maintained by daily experiences. This is not true with LD kids who have memory deficits. At first, the concept must be taught daily. When it is mastered, it has to be deliberately reinforced on whatever schedule is required by that student. It may be every other day or once a week. For these kids you will find the typical monthly or six-week review may not be sufficient to maintain their accuracy. If these children are in regular classes, some provision for this necessary reexposure must be made or they learn very little, which is reflected by poor achievement test scores.

The *rate* at which a person retrieves also varies from person to person. A child may have learned the spelling words but not be able to write them with the rest of the class because of a slow retrieval rate. Instead of slowing the whole class down so that he can think about each word, test this child at a later time or have a helper test him. Given additional time, the student often does quite well. Likewise, if you ask a question and she cannot answer it, put it on the board and tell her you are going to come back to that question in a few minutes and she is to get ready to answer it.

THE PHYSICIAN'S ROLE IN LEARNING DISABILITIES

Some physicians recognize that youngsters are born "at risk" for learning problems and make referrals to their local school systems for early intervention. Others recognize a child's early development does not meet the normal milestones expected and make a referral to the local school district.

These doctors, through thorough history gathering, interviews, listening, and examination do find signs that would indicate learning disabilities and suggest parents seek formal assessment from the school.

When youngsters are having medical or behavioral problems, the physician's or psychiatrist's recommendations need to be solicited and followed exactly. Medication can often either alleviate or eliminate troublesome behaviors. When a child needs to take medication at school, the parent must give written permission and the doctor must send specific directions. In the case of medications for ADHD, it is sometimes not possible for the parent to remember to give the morning dose or the parent is not home to give it. It certainly behooves the school to try to get permission to give it.

If you are working with a child and you do not know much about his or her condition or the medication prescribed, physicians and pharmacists are a great source of information. It is important to be alert for untoward side effects whenever medication is being taken. If the child reports daily headaches, stomachaches, mood changes, nervousness, sleeplessness, etc., the parent will want to report it to the doctor.

CONDITIONS ASSOCIATED WITH LEARNING DIFFICULTIES

Developmental Reading Disorder/Dyslexia

One child out of seven will have trouble learning to read. Some are victims of "dysteachia" (poor teaching); others are victims of "dyslearnia" (poor attendance, poor attention, lack of effort); some are truly dyslexic. Dyslexics have incredible difficulties with language, both spoken and written. Despite having normal intelligence, they have trouble storing, organizing, and retrieving language information.

Because of the symptomology observed, researchers first sought for the cause in the areas of the brain associated with visual perception. *Newsweek* (October 24, 1994) reported that research by Rosen, Galaburda and Menard of the Harvard Medical School suggests that these individuals have irregularities in brain formation. The language processing centers (left side of brain) had fewer neurons of the type that make it possible to process certain sounds. Researchers for California, Colorado, and Nebraska who have been analyzing the DNA of members of families having serious reading problems now believe that dyslexia occurs due to a genetic deviation on chromosome #6. If further research confirms this, in the future dyslexia could possibly be diagnosed by a simple blood test, allowing us to give these children specialized reading help before they experience school failure.

Dyslexics whose IQs typically fall in the normal range tend to show the following problems.:

- Left–right confusion; may "mirror write"
- Poor retention of information
- Impaired sound discrimination (have trouble with i/e, p/b, d/t)
- Hesitant speech; stammer; have difficulty finding words
- Confusion (may shake their heads as if the shaking rearranges information or helps them retrieve it)
- Difficulty getting thoughts on paper; poor fine motor skills
- Poor spelling (often the words they write bear no resemblance to the word dictated)
- Visual processing errors (was/saw, on/no)
- Distractibility, inattention (33 percent have Attention Deficit Hyperactivity Disorder [ADHD])
- Complain that print "swims" on the page or that some parts of a word look darker (for example; other is seen as o**ther**)
- Word guessing; give up easily
- Often awkward and clumsy; may have spatial deficits

In the case of the truly dyslexic student, early identification and service definitely is better. Special reading approaches are required. These youngsters will not learn to read through the standard approaches used in regular classrooms.

Dyslexia is a life-long problem. Dyslexia occurs more often in boys than in girls (4:1). For more information, contact the Orton Dyslexia Society.

Tourette Syndrome

Once believed to be a very rare condition, Tourette is now believed to occur about once in 300 children. It may be a factor in as many as one out of four special day class students. It seems to occur more frequently in boys than in girls, and is often associated with ADHD. It is typically characterized by motor tics—rolling eyes, rapid eyeblinking, facial grimacing, tongue protrusion, sniffing, mouth opening, and involuntary jerking of the upper body; and vocal tics—ranging from clicking, grunting, and whistling to barking and profanity. Sometimes these children chew on their clothing or lick their lips (lips look chapped). They tend to have sleep disturbances. They may show obsessive-compulsive tendencies or be oppositional/negativistic. Sometimes they imitate the movements of someone being observed. Making racial slurs is sometimes a part of the condition as are panic attacks, school phobia, fear of testing, being mean to others, as well as aggressive behaviors. Their learning deficits usually fall in the areas of memory, fine motor control, and writing. The onset of the condition occurs between ages 2–13. It is a genetic, not a psychological, disorder. For more information, contact the Tourette's Syndrome Association (Comings, 1990).

Teratogenic Insult as a Cause of Learning Disabilities

We know that certain substances can cause learning difficulties. We refer to these substances as teratogenic influences. Here is a brief review of some common ones.

Fetal Alcohol Syndrome (FAS)/Fetal Alcohol Effects (FAE).   The detrimental effects of alcohol on the fetus have been documented for many years and publicized in recent years; yet statistics indicate that 2 out of 3 women of childbearing age consume alcohol on a fairly regular basis. We know that even a modest amount—1.5 ounces—may cause damage. FAS, the more serious condition, occurs in about one out of 750 births. FAE occurs is one out of 300 births.

Children with these conditions show deficits in cognition, arousal, and attention as well as diminished IQ.

FAS children often have facial (midline) dysmorphia, cardiac problems, speech problems, sleep disturbances, attention deficit hyperactivity disorder, mental and growth retardation, and behavioral problems. FAS children find their way into full-day special education programs while FAE children (same symptoms but without the facial malformation and IQs in the low-average range) are found in resource room or least-restrictive situations.

Smoking.   Women who smoke during pregnancy often have babies who have a low birth weight. These babies are also more likely to develop asthma and allergies, and to be LD.

Maternal Drug Usage.   We are beginning to see the results of maternal drug use on children. They may have learning problems in the areas of attention, concept acquisition, and memory. The research on the problems of these children is on-going. Unfortunately, once damaged, the problems are not outgrown.

Lead Poisoning.   We are now aware that children with even a mild blood lead level may experience reading and spelling difficulties (Moon et al., 1985).

Prematurity/Low Birth Weight.   Babies who weigh less than five pounds are more likely to have learning problems and visual and hearing problems.

Extreme Environmental Stress

One in five youngsters lives below the poverty line. Some are homeless. Some live in shelters; others live in the family car. They enter a school and the teacher is alarmed at how little they know. Children from this background do have a higher incidence of LD, but some are just victims of inadequate school exposure or cultural deprivation.

When a divorce occurs, children often feel fearful and anxious. They may not be able to concentrate. For a five- to seven-year-old, a divorce can undermine the child's whole life. They may not get the foundation for future learning, which leads to low self-esteem.

When a parent suddenly loses a job, this can create enormous stress on all members of the family. It may necessitate a move, a change of school and loss of friends (McLoyd, 1989).

Many children are living in environments where domestic violence is a regular occurrence.

Deficits in the Immune System

Allergies and asthma are found in many LD kids. Research continues to determine whether there is a causal link.

Chronic Ear Infections

When children have chronic ear infections from birth to four years of age, they frequently will have learning disabilities later—especially in the area of written expression. When ear infections are present, the child's hearing is diminished. I am told they hear about the same way you do under water. It is in these early years that language is acquired and the extra amounts of fluids in the ear seem to prevent them from acquiring a true picture of how words are pronounced and how they are combined to form sentences. Doctors may put tubes in the ears to prevent this kind of impairment.

Infectious Diseases/Accidents

Some children seem to begin life normally, but have a disease or a head injury and then do not progress well. A high sustained fever can cause damage to the central nervous system, vision, or hearing.

Epilepsy/Seizure Disorder

Seizure Disorder or epilepsy is a neurological disorder. Seizures can range from being very mild (virtually unnoticeable) to severe (resulting in loss of consciousness and violent spasms). Most seizure activity can be controlled with medication. For more information, contact the Epilepsy Foundation of America.

Developmental Arithmetic Disorder/Dyscalculia

The essential characteristics of this disorder is the student's limited ability to grasp mathematical concepts. The disorder may exist in combination with reading or spelling disorders or alone.

When the student is able to read and write satisfactorily, he or she is rarely referred for evaluation for special education.

Infantile Autism

Infantile autism is a condition that occurs before age 2.6. There is a failure to develop interpersonal relationships as well as a lack of interest in/responsiveness to people. The child does not like to cuddle, does not establish eye contact, and does not develop cooperative play. They are alone in their own world. Language development is absent or extremely limited and immature.

Ritualistic behaviors are often present. These include rocking, rhythmic body movement, hand clapping or other hand motions, giggling without a stimulus, and staring at objects that move (such as running water or a fan). These children often like music. They invariably end up in special education settings.

Developmental Language Disorder

This disorder affects about 5 percent of children. It ranges from articulation deficits to failure to acquire adequate language. Speech therapists work with children who have mild language delays, but children with moderate to severe delays are most often assigned to classes for the communicatively handicapped.

Children with articulation problems normally have difficulty with /s/, /r/, /sh/, /th/, /f/, /z/, /l/, and /ch/ sounds. They may have immature speech, such as "Her wants to go."

The child with language delays speaks and understands at a significantly lower level than is appropriate for his or her age. It is not uncommon to find a kindergartner with a two-year language development delay. Remediation entails lots of talking, reading to them, asking questions to check their understanding, and providing them with the words they need to express themselves. These children often make dramatic gains once they get daily one-to-one assistance.

Older children with this problem normally do not get referred for help until fourth or fifth grade when the teacher realizes just how inferior their writing is. Their writing resembles that of a child who is two or more years younger. It is often characterized by poor fine motor control. Their written expression has been referred to as "word salad"— the ideas are there but the words used to express them are jumbled up so that their sentences do not make sense. These students often have few organizational skills.

Of course, with good instruction given on a daily basis, these children do make some improvement. They need to write, write, write!

Attention Deficit Disorder

Attentional deficits are deficiencies in an individual's ability to concentrate, to accurately complete a task, and to cope with frustration. While this condition *is not* currently considered to be a learning disability, which qualifies a child for service from special education personnel, it is a component that affects the person's learning and, in some cases, hampers his or her life-long functioning. *It is* a recognizable condition under Section 504 of a civil rights protection law passed in 1973 called the Rehabilitation Act. *It is* also a condition frequently found in dyslexic children.

You are not in the educational field long before it becomes apparent that activity level varies from child to child. It can be charted as in Figure 2-5.

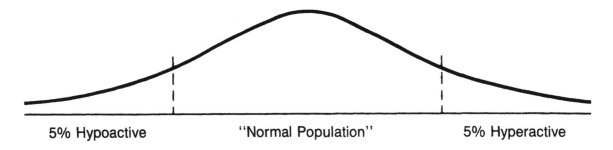

5% Hypoactive   "Normal Population"   5% Hyperactive

Figure 2-5

Most children's activity falls within the limits considered to be normal, but for the 10 percent of children in the tails of the curve, activity level is a problem. They are not able to complete their schoolwork satisfactorily (which often results in poor grades and retentions). Students may get in trouble for rules violations (leads to detention/suspension). In turn, their self-esteem is in jeopardy. Lowered self-esteem may increase the risk of delinquency, pregnancy, mental illness, and suicide during the adolescent years. Once believed to be a condition of childhood that was outgrown, we now know that about half of the people with the condition will carry it into their adult years, making them more prone to accidents and aggressive acts that get them in trouble with the law, divorce, and various forms of domestic violence including child abuse. They are less able to stay on a job due to the impulsivity and low frustration tolerance associated with ADHD.

The symptomology of ADD is described in Chapter 1. When a child displays eight or more of the symptoms described, it is appropriate to suggest to the parent that they take the child to their physician. Since there is no medical test to diagnose the condition (diagnosis is based on the symptoms), a referral letter from the school can be extremely helpful to the doctor. Most doctors will not do anything without a report from the school. Figure 2-6 offers a sample of such a letter. If you plan to mail the letter or talk to the physician, you will need to get the parent's written permission to release information about the child.

Figure 2-6

(To the Physician of the Parent's Choice)

Jane Doe, d.o.b. 2-8-88, is a student in the second grade at Panacea School. She was referred to our Student Study Team because she is not making satisfactory progress.

Her teacher, Mrs. Sally Stern, reports that Jane regularly displays the following symptoms, which are associated with Attention Deficit Disorder:

1. She rarely completes an assignment in the allotted time frame; and requires almost constant 1:1 help to get anything done. (Parent reports that homework is an ordeal.)
2. Jane is frequently off-task, talking or looking around.
3. She stays in her seat, but fidgets and squirms.
4. She is intrusive. When you are trying to talk with another student, she jumps in and either starts tattling on the student or taking the child's side in opposition to you.
5. Her mother reports she loses her lunch box, her coats, her papers; would "forget her head if . . ."
6. Her papers contain multiple careless mistakes.
7. If you tell her she has an error, she gets mad and wads up her paper.
8. Her mother reports the home is a battlefield because of Jane's aggression toward her siblings.

Rest assured that if a trial on medication is pursued, we will be happy to monitor its effectiveness.

Sincerely,

NOTE: A word of caution must be interjected here. Not all children with these symptoms are ADHD. There are other conditions that can produce similar behaviors. For instance, use of street drugs is a possibility among older kids. Very young children—those in their first year of school—may appear to have an attentional problem but really do not. They may come from homes where any kind of behavior is permitted. Children are not born knowing to sit quietly. Some are not talked with, so when they reach school, they are so used to amusing themselves that they are oblivious to the teacher's requests and do not even hear them unless the teacher is yelling or touches them on the shoulder.

These children must be taught by:

1. Clear explanations of what behaviors are expected
2. Modeling of the expected behavior
3. Consistent use of rewards for compliance and aversives for noncompliance

    *With very young children, referral to a pediatrician would not be appropriate until behavior modification has been attempted for a period of six months.

Treatment for ADD/ADHD includes:

- pharmacological therapy
- parent counseling and training in child management
- teacher awareness and training in child management

Drug therapy is usually begun on a trial basis, using a minimal dose. The medications most often prescribed are Ritalin and Cylert. These medications are central nervous system stimulants. Their effectiveness needs to be monitored by someone who has been familiar with the child's behavior *before* medication and can follow it afterward to see if there is any change. Some change should be noted immediately because it takes only about 25 minutes for the drug to begin to affect behavior. (It takes about three weeks to properly evaluate the total effect of the medications.) Many children experience loss of appetite, and an inability to fall asleep the first few nights; but generally by the end of the first week these side effects disappear. If they continue to go on, they could be significant. Occasionally, a child will experience more unusual symptoms—dizziness, excessive nervousness, rashes, changes in the heart beat, hallucinations, nausea, stomachaches, or become tearful and overly sensitive to criticism. If these symptoms occur, the parent will want to inform the doctor immediately.

The minimum dosage of Ritalin is 5 mg. It is effective for about 3 to 4 hours (this varies from child to child and requires monitoring). Generally, the dosage is repeated around noon. If the minimum dose helps but doesn't completely solve the problem, talk with the physician because it usually takes several visits before he or she can determine the optimal dosage since this varies from child to child.

Cylert is a time-released medication. The usual dose is 37.5 mg. and its effective period is about 10 to 12 hours.

While drug therapy offers the easiest, quickest and often the best results for these children, there are some parents who will not even consider it. Usually they reject it out of fear that drugs will either harm their child in some way or will make their child more likely to use street drugs. The best approach to parents with these concerns is to encourage them to talk to their physician about drug therapy. It is helpful if they go prepared with a written list of questions. You could help them make such a list. You may also want to refer the parents to a support group for parents of children with attentional deficits. (For your own information, you should know, however, there is no evidence to support that children on medication for attention deficits are more likely to use street drugs than other children.)

Since attention deficits occur so often in LD children, you will want to become completely familiar with it. *How to Reach and Teach ADD/ADHD Children* by Sandra F. Rief offers a thorough working knowledge of the condition as well as techniques and strategies for working with these children. Also see Chapter 5 for interventions listed under "Attention Deficits" and "A Parent's Guide to Attention Deficit Disorder" at the end of this book. You may reprint the parent's guide and use it as a handout at the time you discuss the subject with parents.

Conduct Disorder

People with conduct disorders are totally self-serving. They lack concern for the wishes, feelings, or well-being of others. If they do something for another, it is because there is something in it for them. Because of these characteristics, they rarely have friends.

They repeatedly disobey rules, display inappropriate behavior, and violate the rights of others. They frequently say they are not treated fairly, yet in their own dealings, they do not exercise fair-play ethics. When caught at a transgression, they may deny it in the face of all evidence (even when you saw them do it) or they may project blame to others ("he made me do it" or "I didn't do it, he did.") There is no sense of remorse or guilt.

Students with conduct disorder often engage in repeated lying, cheating, and stealing. They may set fires. As they get older they may become involved in extortion, physical violence toward others, truancy, drug abuse, drinking, running away, and early sexual experimentation. It is not uncommon for a conduct-disordered child to be seen as being ADHD.

Conduct disorder is common in home situations that would be described as dysfunctional; for example, situations where there is shifting of parental figures (foster homes, group homes, multiple short-term marriages by the custodial parent); in homes where there is domestic violence, alcohol or drug abuse; in homes where there is criminal activity going on; and in homes where discipline is inconsistent or nonexistent.

Oppositional Disorder

The primary characteristic of this disorder is that the child seeks to deliberately provoke you by being disobedient, negativistic, and defiant with authority figures. It is as though the only purpose for a rule—in the child's opinion—is to break it. When asked to do something—even something where compliance would be easy such as "Capitalize the first word of the sentence and any proper names"—he (much more common among boys than girls) may make the first word a lower-case letter and randomly capitalize other words in the sentence.

The onset of this condition is generally between ages 3 and 18. (REMEMBER: It is normal for all children to go through the "no" stage at age two.) These children are seen as being stubborn and argumentative, and may have temper tantrums. Unlike those with conduct disorder, they usually have age-appropriate behavior and respect the rights of others (are not liars, cheats or thieves, and are not physically aggressive).

Separation Anxiety Disorder

While many children experience some anxiety about new situations, this child experiences panic when separated from familiar people or situations. These children show the following behaviors:

- clinging to parents, crying, temper tantrums, may hit or kick the person trying to separate them from the parent
- can't be left in a room alone
- stomachaches, headaches, vomiting if separated or anticipate separation
- difficulty or fear of falling asleep/nightmares
- fear of animals, monsters, burglars, car accidents
- extreme fear that something will happen to their attachment figure

This condition may have its onset between the ages of 2.6 and 12 and may come as a result of some traumatic event such as a death in the family or the death of a pet. When it occurs, it usually occurs in close-knit caring families.

Allowing the child to have the favored person present in a new situation until the child feels more comfortable may make the eventual separation less traumatic.

Child Abuse and Neglect

An article in the April 25, 1994 issue of *Newsweek* magazine reported that there were over a million confirmed cases of child abuse or neglect in the United States in 1993. Most states have laws that require school personnel to report even suspected cases, with fines and jail terms for failure to report. You will want to find out what your responsibility is in this regard.

Some of the clues that a child may be *abused* are:

- physical injury—The easy cases are when you notice a child has bruises or wounds and ask what happened and the child tells you the parent did it. Less easy are those situations where the child has repeated episodes of "falling"; and the hardest of all are the children who are kept home until the bruises heal (the "flu" cases).
- the child flinches if you make a sudden movement, or withdraws when touched
- evidence of abuse creeps into the child's conversation or writing; the "I know a kid who . . . what should he/she do" scenario
- early/inappropriate preoccupation with sex, sexual topics, or self stimulation of the genitals
- history of urinary tract infections or complaint of pain in area of genitals/rectum; "It hurts when I walk/sit"
- does not want to go home; stays at school as long as possible
- moodiness
- aggressive behavior
- speaks of running away/runs away
- withdraws, will not talk

Some of the clues to *neglect* are:

- dirty, unkempt appearance
- always saying he or she is hungry; steals or begs food from other children

- excessive absence/tardiness
- arrives at school much too early
- medical conditions (toothache, earache) go untreated
- constantly tired
- always home alone
- clothing does not match weather conditions
- clings to adults; inordinate need for affection

Substance Abuse

There are five classes of substance abuse—alcohol, barbiturates, opiates, amphetamines, and cannabis (marijuana). Substance abuse often involves use of several substances. When substance abuse begins early in life, it often results in failure to complete school and a life-long pattern of underemployment.

Alcohol abuse seems to have a familial factor. It usually involves daily use of alcohol with occasional binges where the person drinks until he or she blacks out.

People who abuse barbiturates, opiates, and amphetamines are customarily intoxicated all day long. Their drug usage results in fights, loss of friends, absences, and eventually arrest.

There has been a lot of research on the effects of cannabis use. One study will tout its harmful effects while another will show it to be helpful to people who otherwise would be extremely anxious. The one point of agreement is that it diminishes the user's will to get things accomplished. All agree that when used constantly and in moderate amounts, it may cause the user to lose interest in more worthwhile activities.

Serious Emotional Disorder (SED)

When a person's behavior departs from the norm to the point her or she is seen as being weird or bizarre, we must be concerned about mental illness. Having a mental illness does not in itself necessitate classification of the person as SED. Every effort should be made to avoid this special educational classification because when a school district so labels a child, it follows the person throughout life—making it impossible for him or her to enter the military and some civil service jobs, even if the person should be able to function adequately later. Such a classification may open the district to lawsuit later, so this is an extremely serious matter.

Social maladjustment does not make a person SED. The following characteristics may:

1. "An inability to learn which cannot be explained by intellectual, sensory, or health factors.
2. An inability to build satisfactory interpersonal relationships with peers and teachers.
3. Inappropriate types of behavior or feelings under normal circumstances exhibited in several situations.

4. A general pervasive mood of unhappiness or depression.

5. A tendency to develop physical symptoms or fears associated with personal or school problems." (Ed Code 53030-i, California)

These conditions must have existed "over a long period" (6+ months); "to a marked degree" (the disturbing behavior must be intense, severe, consistent, habitual, and seen in multiple settings) "which adversely affects educational performance" (in the judgment of the I.E.P. team). These definitions *exclude* Conduct Disorder, Attention Deficit Disorder, simple phobias, identity distress or crisis reactions, and social immaturity. They *do include* Schizophrenia, Depression, Pervasive Developmental Disorder, and Affective Disorders (Ed Code 53030-i, California).

Schizophrenia   Schizophrenia has its onset in adolescence or early adulthood. The person shows marked deterioration in functioning. The person may have delusions that have no basis in fact; for example, being spied on, being talked about, being controlled by an outside source. The person may complain about hearing noises, or feeling a tingling or burning sensation. They have a tendency to withdraw from the outside world, to deteriorate in self-care, or to show disturbances in psycho-motor function (speak in a monotone, be expressionless, show affect that is inappropriate to the situation).

Depression   Again, the person "changes" from his or her former self. Common traits of this disorder are:

- loss of interest/pleasure in activities previously enjoyed
- no appetite/overeating
- insomnia/sleeping most of the time/fatigue
- feelings of worthlessness
- inability to concentrate
- repeated thoughts of death; wishing to die or commit suicide
- overwhelming sadness

Childhood-Onset Pervasive Disorder   This condition manifests itself between the ages of 2-1/2 and 12. The symptoms may include bizarre ideas, preoccupation with morbid thoughts, fantasies, sudden unexplainable anxiety that may reach panic stage; oddities of motor movement (for example, walking on tiptoe); lack of appropriate affect, speech abnormalities, self-mutilation (biting, hitting self, head banging); insistence on doing things in the same way every time and resistance to changes in schedule. These students will need special education services.

Affective Disorders   There are several kinds of disorders under this classification. People with them often have tremendous swings in affect: depressed/slothlike for a period of time and then turn manic/full of energy. They may have hallucinations or delu-sions.

Many more disorders may interfere with learning, but it is not feasible to examine all of them here. In this section we have looked at only the more common ones you may encounter.

UNDERSTANDING THE LAW

The Intent of Public Law 94-142

When P.L. 94-142 (The Education of All Handicapped Children Act) passed in 1975, it contained this wording:

> "... more than half of the handicapped children in the United States do not receive appropriate educational services which would enable them to have full equality of opportunity;
>
> ... It is in the national interest that the Federal Government assist State and local efforts to provide programs to meet the educational needs of the handicapped children in order to assure equal protection of the law.
>
> ... It is the purpose of this Act to assure that all handicapped children have available to them ... a free appropriate public education which emphasizes special education and related services designed to meet their unique needs, to assure that the rights of handicapped children and their parents or guardians are protected."

(In 1990 the name of this law was changed to the Individuals With Disabilities Education Act [IDEA]). As a result of the passage of this law, a number of significant changes occurred in special education:

First, the law soon became known as the "mainstreaming" law because it said "To the maximum extent appropriate, handicapped children" (including children in public or private institutions or other care facilities) are to be "educated with children who are not handicapped and that special classes, separate schooling, or other removal of handicapped children from the regular educational environments occurs only when the nature and the severity of the handicap is such that education in regular classes with the use of supplementary aids and services cannot be achieved satisfactorily." The term LRE is used to mean "least restrictive environment." When the law was passed, each child's program had to be reviewed to determine what services were needed and where they were to take place (LRE).

Interpretations of the law led to additional requirements that directed: "Each district, special education services region or county office shall actively and systematically seek out all individuals with exceptional needs, ages 0 through 21 years, including children not enrolled in public school programs." After P.L. 94-142 was enacted, the number of handicapped children enrolled in special education programs rose steadily.

The law specified procedures for assessment and placement of handicapped children. Each identified child's educational progress and program must be reviewed yearly with the parent or guardian. Every three years, a review of the child's eligibility and need for continued services is held. At these times, the results of these reviews are written up on a *legally binding document* called an Individualized Education Plan (I.E.P.) that specifies where services will be given, what services are needed, and what materials and methods will be used.

The law said that handicapped students should have related services such as transportation, developmental, corrective, and other supportive services (including speech and audiology services, psychological services, physical and occupational therapy, recreation, medical and counseling services). Public Law 94-142 also provides for the services of advocates. These people apprise parents of their rights and assist them in obtaining the related services guaranteed in the law. Districts are finding themselves hard-pressed when required to provide expensive equipment—such as home computers or motorized wheel chairs. In some cases they have even had to pay for private school tuition of $50,000+ a year for a single child.

At the time P.L. 94-142 was passed, our nation was enjoying an expanding economy. No one predicted that by the 1990s we would be struggling as a nation to pay our bills. The intent of the law was to help each child reach his or her maximum potential. Today, we simply do not have enough money in school budgets to do what the law says is guaranteed. Many people are upset about the fact that in order to provide the services mandated in this law, districts are having to go into the general education fund, thereby short-changing regular class students.

Parents' Rights Under P.L. 94-142

In addition to the provisions listed above, parents also have a right to:

- confidentiality
- review and inspect records, to know where they are stored, to know who else can inspect those records; to grant permission for anyone other than school district employees to have access to the information in those records; to have copies of all records
- be notified in advance (ten days) of meetings pertaining to their child, to bring anyone they choose to the meeting; to tape-record meetings
- request that their child be assessed and to have that assessment occur swiftly
- give permission for the child to be assessed; have the child tested in his or her native language and to have an interpreter at the meeting to explain the proceedings if language is a barrier
- have the child tested with devices that do not have racial/cultural/sexual bias
- have the child assessed by a multi-disciplinary team and be assured that no single test will be used as the sole criterion to determine the child's eligibility for special education services
- have input into the development of the educational plan; to refuse services or placement of the child in special education
- request an independent evaluation at public expense if they disagree with the evaluation obtained by the school district
- a fully paid private school placement if it is deemed necessary to meet the child's best interest
- request and have a fair hearing if disagreements occur in regard to assessment, identification, placement, or services

Students' Rights

The courts and laws have given students the following rights:

If a student gets into trouble at school, he or she has the right to due process. The student shall know the charges that are being brought against him or her.

The pupil has a right to be heard in his or her own defense and to review all documents in support of the charges brought. The pupil has a right at all times to be treated with courtesy and respect by all members of the school staff. If the student is suspended, faces expulsion or involuntary transfer, the student has a right to a prompt hearing.

Student/Paternal Rights Regarding Suspension or Expulsion

Students with special needs enrolled in special education classes are subject to the same policies and provisions regarding suspension as regular education students, except they may not be suspended for more than ten school days without a court injunction. If a special education student commits an offense that warrants expulsion, the full I.E.P. team should be recalled to determine if the student is correctly placed (setting where student receives special education services is appropriate to his or her needs). This requires that tests and assessments of a comprehensive and recent nature have been done. Next, it must be determined if the behaviors being displayed are part of the student's handicapping condition. The student *may not be expelled* if the team determines (1) the pupil's misconduct was caused by the handicapping condition or (2) if the student was not correctly placed at the time of the offense.

Parents must be given 48 hours' notice of any pre-expulsion meeting. They may request that the meeting be postponed for an additional three days. The meeting can be held without the parent being present. Parental consent is not required for a pre-expulsion assessment, but the parent must be notified of the pending assessment and must be notified of his or her due process rights concerning all aspects of the expulsion process.

Behavioral Contingency Plans

If you have a student who has regular or serious behavioral difficulties, it is a good idea to develop a Behavioral Contingency Plan and to write behavioral goals on the I.E.P. This plan will address which behaviors are part of the handicapping condition and which are not. If the student commits an offense that is not related to his or her handicapping condition, the regular district discipline standards are applied. If the student commits an offense that is related to his or her handicapping condition, you will have a plan developed for dealing with it. You will find it much easier to develop such a plan before a student commits a serious offense than to have to deal with a parent who is fearful or angry because his or her child is in trouble or in danger of suspension/expulsion.

Court Decisions and Teachers

You need to be aware that courts have rendered recent judgments against teachers that resulted in teachers having to pay damages to students. These damages have been awarded for such things as:

- failure to write sufficient goals to meet student's needs
- refusal by teacher to give student accommodations guaranteed by the I.E.P.
- consistant failure to see student for the number of minutes stated on the I.E.P.

If a parent of a special education student is not happy, he or she may file a complaint with the Office of Civil Rights, or request a due-process fair hearing. *Specific due-process issues* you need to carefully comply with are:

- written notification to parents before evaluation
- written notification to parents when initiating or refusing to initiate a change in educational placement
- allowing parents the opportunity to obtain an independent evaluation of the child, if they wish it

Insurance companies are becoming aware of these suits and you can obtain coverage for a reasonable fee.

THE INTENT OF SECTION 504 OF THE REHABILITATION ACT OF 1973

While some of the students do not qualify for special education assistance (when assessed by the I.E.P. team, the student did not show a significant discrepancy between potential and achievement), the I.E.P. team must determine whether that youngster falls under the provisions of Section 504. If it is determined that the individual does, the district must provide appropriate educational services to that student. There are seven conditions that might make the child eligible. They are:

1. drug or alcohol dependency
2. ADD/ADHD
3. health needs
4. communicable diseases
5. social maladjustment
6. learning disabled without the severe discrepancy
7. student removed from special education (having a record of a disability)

Eligibility under 504 is based on "impairment which substantially limits one or more major life activities such as caring for oneself, performing manual tasks, walking, seeing, hearing, speaking, breathing, learning and working." To illustrate, consider the case of a child who is under a physician's care for severe sleep disturbances. While he is not eligible for services under P.L. 94-142, his "major life activities" may very well be disturbed. He may be irritable and have a short fuse, but can he be suspended? Is his behavior related to not being able to get enough sleep? Some districts have their I.E.P. teams sit as 504 teams to deal with 504 issues such as developing service plans or behavioral contingency plans to ensure the individual's rights to a free and appropriate education are met.

(See Figure 3-1 for a comparison of IDEA and Section 504.)

Figure 3-1

	IDEA (P.L. 94-142)	Section 504
PURPOSE	Federal statute to ensure appropriate services for disabled children	Civil Rights law to protect the rights of individuals with handicaps in programs that receive federal financing
SCOPE	All school-aged children who fall into these categories: —Specific Learning Disability —Mental Retardation —Speech Impaired —Seriously Emotionally Disturbed —Other Health Impaired —Multi-Handicapped —Orthopedically Impaired —Deaf, Hearing Impaired —Visually Impaired —Traumatic Brain Injury —Autism —Deaf-Blind	All school-aged children qualified as handicapped who have/have had a physical/mental impairment that substantially limits a major life activity
FUNDING	Provides additional funds for eligible students	Does not provide additional funds
ENFORCEMENT	U.S. Department of Education (Office of Special Education)	U.S. Office of Civil Rights
ACCESS EVALUATION	Requires written notice to parent and informed parent consent (written)	Requires notice to parent—suggests it be written
	Full comprehensive evaluation by a multi-disciplinary team	No formal evaluation; decisions made by a group of knowledgeable professionals (may be same people who serve as I.E.P. team)
	Provides for independent evaluation at public expense if parent disagrees with school evaluation	Does not provide for independent evaluation
PLACEMENT	Reevaluation not required for a change of placement; change is an I.E.P. team review decision	Reevaluation is required for a significant change of placement
DOCUMENTATION	Both laws dictate that there should be thorough documentation	
DUE PROCESS	Both laws require impartial hearings for parents/guardians who disagree with the identification, evaluation, and placement of student	

PUBLIC LAW 98-199, SECTION 626 (1983)

Named the Secondary Education and Transitional Services for Handicapped Youth, this law provides grants for the development of transition programs to assist learning disabled students gain the skills necessary to adequately function in the area of employment.

PUBLIC LAW 99-457 (1986)

The Education of the Handicapped Amendments provide for services to children with developmental delays from birth to age 2. Research has shown that early intervention is very beneficial for learning disabled children.

THE REGULAR EDUCATION INITIATIVE (REI)

In 1986, Madeleine C. Will, the Assistant Secretary for the U.S. Office of Special Education and Rehabilitative Services, said:

"At the heart of the special education approach is the presumption that students with learning problems cannot be effectively taught in regular education programs even with a variety of support. Students need to be *pulled out* into special settings where they can receive remedial services. Although well-intentioned, this so-called *pull out* approach to the educational difficulties of students has failed in many instances to meet the educational needs of these students and has created, however unwittingly, barriers to their successful education."

Following this speech, an enormous debate was set off, resulting in an initiative designed to merge special education with regular education. Many special education youngsters previously served in resource room pull-out or special day classes are now to be served in the regular classroom.

Will's speech suggested having special and general education join their resources into a coordinated educational delivery system (sharing methods that have a strong research record of effectiveness). This movement advocates that "the general education system assume unequivocal primary responsibility for all students in our public schools—including identified handicapped students as well as those who have special needs of some type" (Davis, 1989).

We now find our schools pondering how to make this initiative a reality; thus, the emergence of the collaborative-consultative model for Resource Specialist service and the inclusion model for moderately or severely handicapped students.

The proponents of the initiative believe this movement will relieve schools of excessive administrative/teaching costs of the categorical system of providing services to a wide variety of exceptional students without being detrimental to those students. They feel the students will benefit by having normal social role models to emulate. Others will tell you that the pull-out system deprives special education students of their equal education rights since they do not have the "opportunity" to access the core curriculum as it is presented to nonhandicapped students.

The opponents of the initiative fear all students will learn less because there is only so much one teacher can do.

Nevertheless, this is the direction that special education throughout the United States is taking. As educators devoted to improving the lives of our students, we will accept this challenge and do our best to help our students.

EARLY CHILDHOOD EDUCATION FOR AT-RISK STUDENTS

4

Public Law 94-142 provides services for qualifying individuals with disabilities ages 3 to 21. Public Law 99-457 extended services to cover children from birth to age 2.

REFERRALS FOR ASSESSMENT

Referrals come from several sources. Doctors may refer a child at birth or shortly after if the child has a condition that will affect the developmental processes in a way that the child will predictably require intensive special education services later. Examples of such disabling conditions include Down's, Turner's and Kleinfelter syndromes; Fetal Alcohol Syndrome; cleft lip/cleft palate; spina bifida; Tay Sachs disease; cerebral palsy; deafness/blindness or one of several other conditions.

For other children, it may be the parent who first observes the child is not doing the things normally expected (see the following list of developmental milestones) and in turn brings this to the doctor's attention; then one or the other makes a referral. Some of the more common conditions here are children who are slow to talk or who are delayed in fine or gross motor skill development.

Another source of referrals is preschool teachers. When the child is enrolled in a nursery school, the teacher there observes the child is "out of step" with other children his or her age and suggests the parent seek another opinion.

The following list (compiled from multiple sources) gives the average age for the development of each skill.

Normal Child Development/Developmental Milestones

By 3 months, a baby can:
—follow movement with his or her eyes
—look at an object or person
—respond to a new sound with movement
—coo expressively
—smile
—roll from side to back
—hold head upright

Suggested Toys
—mobiles (music)
—rattles
—small stuffed animals

By 6 months, an infant can:
—reach toward something he or she wants
—turn head to follow an object or sound
—make babbling noises
—squeeze objects
—bang objects in play
—laugh
—approach image in mirror
—eat from a spoon
—hold bottle
—roll from tummy to back
—sit alone momentarily

—mirrors
—soft colorful balls
—squeeze toys
—small cardboard boxes
  covered with brightly
  colored paper
—large spoon

49

By 9 months, the infant can:
—get up on hands and knees
—sit unsupported
—respond to names (Where is the cat?)
—track and locate falling objects
—vocalize two syllables (gaga)
—stand with support
—creep on stomach
—feed self finger foods
—play peek-a-boo
—understand harsh tone
—transfer objects from one hand to the other
—grasp with thumb and index finger
—show displeasure when something is taken from him/her

Suggested Toys
—blocks
—bells, noisy toys
—toys with a suction base
—toy telephone
—push toys

By 12 months, the infant can:
—crawl
—find a hidden object
—stand by pulling self up
—look at pictures in a book
—pat-a-cake, wave bye
—stop when told "no"
—walk while holding furniture
—let go, stand alone
—make marks on paper with crayon
—bang spoon
—drink from a cup (with spilling)
—show preference for one toy
—place one block in a cup

—supported rocking horse
—drums
—pop up toys
—small books
—pots, pans, lids
—pail, handspade
—large pegs
—toy piano
—thick crayons
—metal spoons
—nest of cups
—water toys

By 18 months, the toddler can:
—walk
—recognize shapes on a puzzle board
  (put circle in formboard)
—point at an object named/wanted
—say a few words
—follow simple commands
—stack blocks (4 cubes)
—remove simple garments
—indicate wet pants

—large balls
—donut stacking toy
—large wooden puzzles
  (5 to 9 pieces)
—pull toys
—talking toys
—music boxes
—child chair
—toy box/no lid

—give a hug/kiss
—pretend to sleep/eat
—use objects or toys appropriately
—fill cup with blocks

—potty chair
—toy lawnmower
—formboard with circle, square, triangle cutouts

By 24 months, the child can:
—attend to nursery rhymes
—play house (pretend)
—point to pictures (books)
—identify parts of body (Where's your nose?)
—imitate sounds
—jump in place
—push/pull wheel toys
—turn pages in a book
—cry when mother leaves
—pay attention to other children
—use 2- 3-word sentences ("me go")
—associate toys with use
   (put spoon in cup, put pan on stove)
—run
—walk sideways and backward
—scribble with crayons
—stack five rings on stand in any order
—demonstrate the use of 6 objects
—respond to simple commands
—match 4 pairs of objects

—Mother Goose and other beginning books
—dolls
—toys with screwing action
—trucks
—climbing equipment
—large beads for stringing
—puzzles (6 to 15 pieces)
—sandbox
—plastic zoo animals, small plastic people and cars

By 36 months, the child can:
—sort objects in categories
—recognize differences in shapes
—join in singing/rhythm
—use 3-word sentences
—walk up/down stairs
—run/jump
—throw ball overhand
—ride tricycle
—make small cuts
—draw an oval
—eat by himself or herself
—toilet with some help

—toy that has holes of differing shapes and corresponding pegs
—harder books
—playdough
—safety swings
—balls
—trike
—safety scissors
—Fisher Price™ toys (barn, airport, garage)
—blocks of all shapes

—put on simple clothing
—brush teeth with assistance
—play with other children
—take roles (doctor-nurse, teacher-child, customer-clerk)
—use blocks in imaginative ways (fences, bridges)
—kick a ball
—begin to dress self
—imitate vertical stroke or V
—demonstrate understanding of terms *big* and *little*
—copy a cross

By 48 months, the child can: *Suggested Toys*
—tell a simple story   —more books
—count to five   —records
—climb a slide   —plastic ball/bat
—catch a bounced ball   —slide
—lace shoes   —lacing toys
—use sentences most of the time   —Lincoln Logs®
—hop on one foot   —coloring books
—name 4 colors   —paint/easel
—understand concepts of big/little   —Tinker® Toys
—copy a square
—color within the lines
—take care of own toileting
—share upon suggestion
—play cooperatively with other children
—throw, catch, and kick a ball
—build
—do some imaginative play
—draw a person with two body parts
—turn a somersault
—hop on one leg
—classify pictures into 3 groups
—imitate a two-step vertical paper fold

By 60 months, the child can:
—print letters (may reverse some)   —skates
—tap rhythms   —crafts materials
—understand rules to simple games   —paper/paste
—cut, paste   —Legos®

—use a needle to sew

—copy simple designs from a model

—follow 3-step commands

—skip

—make a 10-block tower

—button

—repeat several nursery rhymes verbatim

—remember simple numbers, like 911

—answer and talk on the phone

—use well-developed sentences without babytalk

—name most common objects

—draw a box

—draw a person with head, body, arms, legs, some facial features, and clothing

—associate an object with its use

—learn to tie shoes

—copy a triangle

—catch a bounced ball

—see likenesses/differences when comparing 2 pictures

—put objects into categories

—count to 10

—copy a bead pattern, alternating colors and shapes

—count sets/objects 1 to 4

ELIGIBILITY FOR SPECIAL EDUCATION SERVICES AT AGES BIRTH TO 3

To be eligible for service, the individual must:

1. be identified as having exceptional needs

2. be functioning at or below the 50th percentile for his or her age in at least one of the following areas:

    gross or fine motor development

    receptive or expressive language

    social or emotional development

    cognitive development

3. be functioning between the 51st and 75th percentile for his or her age in two of the skill levels shown in item 2

4. have a disabling medical or congenital condition/syndrome the I.E.P. team determines has a high predictability of requiring intensive special education services later

What Services Are Provided for Ages Birth to 3?

When a child qualifies for assistance between birth and age 2.9, an Individualized Family Service Plan (IFSP) must be developed within 45 days of initial referral.

For very young children (ages birth to 18 months), most districts provide in-home service. The teacher goes to the home and works with the parent on matters concerning care and development. Typically the once-a-week help given falls in the areas of feeding skills, toileting, mobility, language development, bonding between caregiver and infant, discipline, and self-help skills (for example, parents of deaf children are taught to sign).

At 18 months, the child may enter a school program. The typical program is three days a week. Parents are strongly encouraged to come to school and participate.

ELIGIBILITY FOR SPECIAL EDUCATION SERVICES AT AGES 3 TO 5

Under the provisions of P.L. 94-142, the individual must:

1. have one of the following qualifying conditions: hearing impairment; deaf-blind; speech impairment; visual impairment; orthopedic impairment; autism; other health impaired; mental impairment; seriously emotionally disturbed; traumatic brain injury; specific learning disability

2. meet the eligibility requirements by having a significant delay (1.5 standard deviation below the mean) in one or more basic psychological processes such as his or her gross or fine motor development, or receptive or expressive language

3. have an articulation disorder that interferes significantly with communication or draws adverse attention

What Services Are Provided for Ages 3 to 5?

Services provided vary from district to district and from child to child based on the severity of the child's needs.

Children with mild delays generally are served for a period of one to three hours weekly. Because they do not need intensive services, they are sometimes served by the elementary school speech therapist and/or the Resource Specialist on a regular school campus or at the nursery school they attend. They may be in Headstart programs. We want to serve them in the least restrictive environment (this requirement is explained further in Chapter 7) with their nonhandicapped peers.

Other districts choose to co-locate programs (a classroom of young children with special needs is located on the same site as a regular early childhood education or child-care program). Children with mild disabilities can spend most of the day in the mainstream with their nonhandicapped peers, while children with more severe disabilities may spend most of the day in special classes, but interact with the nonhandicapped at lunch, special events, and other activities where it would be beneficial. A second benefit of the co-location model is that regular teachers can tap into the expertise of the special education personnel as needed to meet the needs of both identified and nonhandicapped children. A third benefit is the wider variety of equipment available for use with all the children. With the trend toward inclusion, we no doubt will see more districts using this model in the future.

For children needing more intensive services, classes may be set up in a given school where specially trained staff and special equipment are available to meet their needs

ASSESSMENT OF INDIVIDUALS WITH EXCEPTIONAL NEEDS, AGES BIRTH TO 5

Assessment for young children is based on parent interviews, observation, completion of developmental scales, and the results of formal tests. Some of the most popular formal tests are described here.

The Bayley Scales of Infant Development   The *Bayley Scales of Infant Development* is an individually administered test that is given to children ages 2 months to 2.6 years with the parent present. It consists of a mental scale, motor scale, and infant behavior scale. It is norm-referenced.

The Batelle Developmental Inventory   The *Batelle Developmental Inventory* for ages birth to 8 years is also an individually administered scale based on parent interviews, observations, and structured testing. It assesses the areas of personal-social adaptive behavior, motor functioning, communication, and cognitive development—rendering age equivalent scores, percentiles, and standard scores. It is available in Spanish.

DASI-II   The *Developmental Activities Screening Inventory II* (DASI-II) is a non-verbal individually administered test for children ages birth to 5 years. It measures fine motor control, knowledge of cause-and-effect relationships, association, number concepts, size discrimination, and sequencing. It can be adapted for use with students who are visually impaired. Scores obtained are expressed in a developmental level and a quotient.

VABS   The *Vineland Adaptive Behavior Scales* (VABS) gathers information on individuals ages birth to 18 years regarding communication, daily living skills, socialization, and motor skills. Scores are expressed as standard scores, percentile ranks, stanines, age equivalencies, and adaptive levels. This test is also done in Spanish.

The Alpern-Boll Developmental Profile II   The *Alpern-Boll Developmental Profile II* takes only a short time to do with children ages birth to 2.6 years. By means of direct observation and parent interview, it measures the child's competencies in self-help, physical development, social/academic development, and communication.

The Denver Developmental Screening Test—Revised   The *Denver Developmental Screening Test—Revised* is easy and quick to give to children ages 1 month to 6 years. It measures personal/social development, fine/gross motor development, and language.

The reliability and validity of these tests are somewhat questionable and the results need to be validated by extensive observation and parent interviews. We want to look at what the child is able to do, what the child needs to learn to do, and how the child interacts with the task, setting, and other people.

WHAT DOES A PLAY ASSESSMENT LOOK LIKE?

While the nurse interviews the parent in one corner of the room, the Resource Specialist (Rsp) and child go to the play area. The child can still see the parent is in the room. The Rsp sits on the floor with the child and the speech therapist sits nearby so she can hear and record everything said. The Rsp leads the child into many different kinds of play. "Would you like to play with the blocks?" The container is placed on the floor and the observer waits to see if the child can open the container without help. The Rsp says, "Let's build something." The Rsp allows the child time to use the materials on his own, observing whether blocks are thrown, hit together, laid end to end, stacked, or if bridges are made. The Rsp may also lay out some toy cars and people. The child I observed laid out several blocks in a line but did not turn a corner. The Rsp showed him by example. The child said, "Make a hou" (house). This statement was the first of many samples that confirmed the existence of articulation problems (reason for referral). By putting out a series of items and asking the child to hand her the "big" one or the "little" one, we can see whether the child has those concepts.

The Rsp initiated some imaginative play by making the baby doll fall down and saying "Help me. I fell down." The child being observed responded by putting the doll in a stroller, and said "Go to sheep" (a second articulation error).

Awhile later the Rsp showed the child some pictures and asked him to name the objects. The child was able to name everything but the swing. The mother volunteered he had used swings but "sometimes he forgets the names of things."

The Rsp put out several plastic bears and asked, "Where are the bears?" The child pointed and said "Right dare." The child was not able to count the bears accurately, nor was he able to name colors. He was able to match things of the same color.

The Rsp asked the child to help her put the toys away, explaining that "bears go here, people in here (another container), and blocks in this box." The child helped and with only one error got things in the right places.

Markers were brought out. The Rsp drew a vertical line and said, "Can you do this?" He copied it. Then she made a circle. He did too. The assessment continued with lots of playing and talking.

Through questioning, suggestions and opportunity to play while being observed, it became evident there were some delays in speech and in understanding concepts. Activity level was normal during this sample of behavior.

The national trend in early childhood education is that both assessment and service occur in relaxed and natural settings. Play is the most natural of settings.

After a child is identified by the transdisciplinary or multi-disciplinary team, a plan for services is developed. As mentioned earlier, for children from birth to age 3, it is called the Individualized Family Service Plan (IFSP) because at this age the primary emphasis is to try to help the family adjust to the pressures of having a severely handicapped child (disbelief, guilt, anger, feelings of isolation and panic). The family's priorities (how they see the problem), resources, and concerns are identified. Parents are asked to help develop a list of desired outcomes to meet their child's needs. In other words, the IFSP is *family-centered*. The IFSP must be reviewed every six months.

When the child is aged 3 to 5, an Individualized Educational Plan (I.E.P.) is developed. This document is *child-centered*. It must be reviewed every year. At the age of 4.9, the multi-disciplinary team must meet again and assess the child's progress. If children remain eligible for services, a decision is made regarding whether they need a special day class or can go to regular kindergarten with Rsp support. *It is good practice for the preschool transdisciplinary team to involve the receiving elementary school multi-disciplinary team in information sharing and planning and the writing of the new I.E.P.*

NOTE: In our field, somewhere, somehow a myth got started to the effect that young elementary school children cannot be referred. Clearly now, the law intends serving young eligible children. Early intervention has been shown to be very effective.

THE COMPONENTS OF AN EFFECTIVE EARLY CHILDHOOD EDUCATION PROGRAM

When a program is operating effectively, you should expect to see:

1. an adult:child ratio of 1:4 or 1:5
2. a program that shows it has been extensively planned
3. a concern for parents and their involvement in the school's activities
4. careful attention to thorough and on-going assessment with development of goals that are specific to each child's needs
5. reasonable and clear behavioral expectations; effective use of positive reinforcement and principles of behavioral management
6. attention to socio-economic development; helping others establish independence/confidence/initiative and the ability to make simple decisions, to ask questions, and to exercise self-control
7. a wide variety of first-hand experiences such as field trips and examination of real-life objects
8. a wide range of activities to meet a broad range of interests
9. adults who are sensitive and responsive to the needs of children and their parents
10. a setting absent of tension among staff members and among staff and children
11. attention given to warning signs of stress in children (thumb-sucking, crying, tantrums)
12. activities that balance activity and rest; outdoors with indoors
13. provision of multiple opportunities to communicate (1 to 1 in small groups, taking turns)
14. predictability of routines and easy transition from one activity to another
15. direct teaching of some skills as well as lots of play
16. a feel for cultural diversity
17. attention at all times to health and safety issues

(Information given in this section was paraphrased from *Adapting Early Childhood Curricula for Children with Special Needs* by Ruth E. Cook, Annette Tessier and M. Diane Klein.)

MATURATION AND "READINESS" FOR KINDERGARTEN

Maturation varies from child to child and boys are more likely than girls to have maturational delays. The treatment for maturational delays is always the same—appropriate experiences and good teaching. Some children will catch up with peers of their own age in time. Children who show slow retrieval and slow response time rarely catch up. There is nothing a school can do to hurry up neural maturation but to give the brain time to develop. To push children who are not ready for formal schooling into an academically oriented kindergarten is frustrating for the child, the parent, and the kindergarten teacher. One additional year in preschool or placement in a kindergarten where the curriculum is geared more toward social development, language development, motor skills development, and pre-literary skills can be very beneficial.

TIPS FOR PARENTS OF CHILDREN IDENTIFIED FOR PRESCHOOL SERVICES

1. *Birth to 6 months:*
   —Talk and sing to your baby every day.
   —Cuddle and stroke the baby's skin.
   —By two months babies like to look at themselves in a mirror.
   —Babies like small stuffed toys, mobiles, and rattles.

2. When your baby *begins to walk,* take him or her outdoors for short walks. Stop to examine rocks, leaves, and flowers.
   —Tell the toddler the names of objects; "spoon," "ball."
   —Speak in short sentences; "Roll the ball" (demonstrate).
   —Teach body parts; "This is your eye/mouth/ear."
   —Begin to read to the toddler. *The Foot Book* by Dr. Seuss and *Mother Goose Rhymes* are good starters.
   —Toddlers like push toys, playing in their bath with water toys, blocks, balls.

3. *By 1-1/2 to 2 years old,* children can use crayons and clay under supervision. Put out a piece of paper, take a crayon and say, "Can you do this?" Draw a vertical line. Let the child imitate your movement. Next draw a horizontal line, then a circle.
   —The child will enjoy toys that can be ridden (pushed with feet), pop-up toys, toy telephones, stacking toys, toy pianos.
   —Continue to find and read simple books.
   —Continue to talk to your child. By now he or she probably can name some objects. Now you can begin teaching colors. "Your shirt is blue." "This is a red block."

4. *By 2-1/2 to 3 years,* your child will begin to attend school. It is very important that you participate and help out in the child's class a few hours each month so you can do the things at home that are being taught at school.

   By this time children enjoy building towers of blocks and knocking them down, making puzzles of 5 to 6 pieces, and turning pages in the book when you tell them to.

THE ROLE OF THE STUDENT STUDY TEAM

MAKING A PRELIMINARY STUDY

It is a natural thing for a regular class teacher to make a preliminary study of the class at the beginning of the school year. Within the first week, most teachers have a pretty good idea of what their students can do. Out of thirty children, you can spot between four and six children whose progress is a matter of concern—they are "out of step" with their grade-level expectancy—either socially, academically, or both. This is as true in secondary school as in elementary. At the secondary level these may well be the youngsters who will soon drop out unless someone intervenes in a meaningful way.

There is no single child who is typical of all other learning disabled youngsters. Each child must be viewed in terms of his or her strengths and weaknesses and a plan must be developed to meet that child's needs. We can clearly recognize that the following conditions are likely to result in school failure: (a) frequent absence; (b) failure to satisfactorily complete assignments on a regular basis; and (c) behavior that requires excessive teacher attention.

To begin this process, it is suggested that you start a folder on each of these students and document your concerns with daily entries, samples of student work, and all efforts made to intercede. If you have a classroom aide, that person can begin the interventions and do the documentation under your guidance.

The documentation log becomes the source of valuable information if correctly done. If the log merely says "read pages 23, 24" or "did ok," that is not helpful. Show the aide the sample completed log given in Figure 5-1. This will help that person understand what kinds of comments are pertinent. (You'll find a blank documentation log in Figure 5-2.)

It is also a good idea to apprise your principal verbally and in writing of those children in your class whom you deem to need extra one-to-one help. There are several reasons for doing this:

- Many principals feel they have a better understanding of what goes on in your room if you let them know. If they are your evaluator, it is good for them to realize you are providing extra help to struggling students. (One of the most effective ways to use the classroom aide is to help struggling students.)

- Letting the principal know who is struggling alerts the principal so that if parents call, the principal has some prior knowledge about the child and your efforts to remediate the problem. What seems to be happening more and more is that at the time of the first parent conference, you must explain the child is having difficulties. A day or two later, the parent calls the principal wanting the child moved to another room because they have concluded you just don't know how to teach.

- One final advantage of letting the principal know is that if volunteers are available, you stand a great chance of getting one if the principal knows you have several children needing that extra help.

TALKING WITH PARENTS AND GETTING THEIR SUPPORT

The goal of meeting with parents is to establish a cooperative working relationship between school and home. As soon as you realize a child is in trouble, it is wise to begin some interventions whereby the child will clearly have some extra one-to-one help. Wait

Figure 5-1. Sample of a Completed Documentation Log

Student _Young, Boy_

date-time	# of minutes / size of group	Activity	Comments
9-6-95 2:15	30 min. 1:1	Reading Multiple Skills B-4 #3-6	—where "There" —being "begin" —very antsy; wiggling; pencil dropped 2X —Pace of reading is OK, but he makes multiple errors. —Reads much better using a marker.
9-7-95 11:00	15 min. 1:1	Math - long division	—errors in subtraction step counts multiplication facts on fingers —While teacher was doing example on board, he neither looked nor listened (whispering to friend) $3\overline{)205} \begin{array}{c}6\\-18\\\hline 85\end{array}$
9-8-95	absent		
9-11-95	20 min 1:1	Multiple skills #7-10	Called calm "clam" but self-corrected. "Very tired," "up late watching TV" "out of town with parents on Friday"
9-12-95	20 min. 1:1	Multiple skills #11-15	Very chatty—asking lots of questions; finally said he "didn't want to read." When encouraged, he did. He frequently misses question 4 (inferential information).

Figure 5-2. Documentation Log

Student _____

date- time	# of minutes/ size of group	Activity	Comments

about three weeks after you have begun the interventions (it takes a child that long to settle into a new situation and for you to gather the information you need to have an effective conference) before scheduling the parent conference. In setting the appointment time and place, the parent's schedule and wishes must be considered. You can ask the child when his or her parents are home or what time they go to work or get home. Mail a letter home offering the parent a choice of times and asking them to contact you to let you know which one best fits their schedule. (A sample is shown in Figure 5-3.) The most convenient hours are just before school in the morning, the noon hour, or later afternoon such as 4:00. You may want to offer a choice of place. Some parents feel more comfortable if the principal and teacher come to their home. (This option should never be offered if there is danger involved.) Some parents feel better if they may bring a friend. Conferences should be "scheduled" rather than happening on the spur of the moment—unless the parent has a history of nonattendance, in which case you must just "catch as catch can." Likewise, with the parent who rarely comes to school or is difficult to handle, it is wise for you to have the principal present.

Figure 5-3

Dear Mr./Mrs. _____,

I am Sabrina's teacher. I would like to talk with you at your earliest convenience. Sabrina is having trouble with reading. You may already be aware of this. If you and I can sit down and talk about it, I feel we can find ways to help her. I could meet with you at 8:00 A.M. on Monday, September 17 or at 12:00 on Tuesday, September 18, or at 4:00 P.M. on Wednesday, September 19. We will need about an hour to get acquainted and work out a plan. I don't want you to feel rushed. We need adequate time to share ideas. Please feel free to bring a friend or relative to the appointment.

<u>Call me and let me know when you are coming</u>. If none of these times are good, call and we'll try to find one that will work for you.

Sincerely,

When you talk with a parent, tell it like it is. Be factual, but not judgmental. Be honest, but not brutal. If you "soft pedal" your concern, the parent may not hear your concern.

Instead of saying "Sabrina is lazy," describe what she does. "When I give an assignment, Sabrina does not start to work. She looks around to see what others are doing. She loses about 10 to 15 minutes time at the start of each period."

Instead of "Sabrina is a little behind in reading," try "When Sabrina reads, she misses about two out of every five words. When you listen to her, what kind of errors have you seen?"

It is sometimes wise to take notes while talking to the parent. Tell parents you need the notes because your memory is poor; offer to make a copy of the notes for them.

Upon learning that a child is having problems at school, parents may show a variety of reactions. These reactions may or may not be voiced and they vary in intensity among individuals. Figure 5-4 is offered to help you develop an understanding of common reactions.

Figure 5-4

Shock/Denial
The parent wants to deny the seriousness
  of the problem.

"All kids fight."
"I was like that too but I did all
  right in life."
"It's just a phase."

Anger/Guilt/Blaming
Parents admit there is a problem
  but . . .

"It's the school's/teacher's/ex's
  fault."
"If only . . . hadn't occurred
  when I was pregnant."
"Why me?"

Resignation

"It runs in the family."
"It's my rotten luck."
"It's God's will."

Depression
Some parents become isolated;
  others call out for help.

"I can't bear this. How can I go
  on?"
"What will people think?"

Acceptance
At this point the family can function in spite of the problem.

It is also not uncommon to see a person vacillate back and forth between two stages. Occasionally a parent will tell you not to give the child extra help. In this case you need to say, "We respect your decision, but we want you to sign a statement that shows we apprised you of the problem and you declined the extra service."

Most parents will be happy to have you assist their child. At this initial meeting, you will want to inquire about their expectations for their child. Do they want the child to go to college/trade school or what do they see in the child's future? Ask where and how homework gets done and whether the child is cooperative. Tell them what you need for them to do at home and work out a system for daily two-way communication. You need to provide a way for them to indicate daily they are getting the information. You may want to give them your home phone number; if so, you need to tell them what time you ordinarily go to bed and get up. Parents usually feel you are truly trying to help the child if you give out your home phone number. They also usually do not abuse the privilege.

If, after a period of eight to twelve weeks, you are not seeing improvement in the child's performance, you will want to initiate a request for assistance from the Student Study Team (SST). Each school has one, although there is no consistency in what it is called—it may be called the Guidance Team, the Child Study Team, or the Intervention Team.

For children who come to you so far behind that they are not within the instructional range for the grade (can do none of the classwork), you will want to involve this team at the same time you begin intervention.

Initiating a Request for Help

Each school has a procedure for scheduling its Student Study Team meetings. Usually this begins with completion of a written form. This document requires general information about the student, but there is a space for you to write your concerns. The more specific you can be, the better. See Chapter 1 for a list of symptoms. List the ones that apply to your student and be prepared to back up your statements with work samples wherever possible.

Instead of saying "Sabrina is behind in reading," it is more informational to say "When given a grade-level reading passage of 100 words, Sabrina correctly read 71 words. When she comes to a word she doesn't know, she skips over it. When asked to read a passage of 100 words at grade level 3, she read 97 words correctly. She is confused by words that are similar, for example: *though* and *through, these* and *those.* When asked to read a grade 4 passage, she was able to satisfactorily answer 3 out of 5 questions on the grade 4 level passage, but answered 5 out of 5 correctly on the grade 3 passage." Instead of saying "Sabrina has trouble getting along with peers," you might say "Sabrina has gotten four referrals for fighting on the playground."

The Student Study Team Process

The Student Study Team meeting is the proper forum for discussing all types of problems—academic, social, attendance, behavioral, and health.

Each school needs a sufficient number of teams to handle the requests in a reasonable amount of time (three weeks from referral date). *SST is a regular educational function;* therefore, the teams should be constructed from the regular education staff. It is recommended that persons such as the psychologist, Resource Specialist, and nurse attend only those meetings where their expertise is required. It is also recommended that the chairpersons of these teams be regular education staff.

A Student Study Team ordinarily consists of:

1. An administrator who generally acts as facilitator. This person introduces the team members and sets the purpose of the meeting, sees that all participants get to talk, and that no single participant "takes over"
2. SST chairperson who generally records the minutes of the meeting
3. Referring teacher
4. One other teacher—good choices are the child's last teacher or, if the year is nearing an end, his or her next teacher
5. Parents and the child if over 8 years old
6. Other personnel as appropriate

Prior to the meeting, it is desirable that someone has done an observation and read the child's cumulative folder. A copy of the attendance record is also helpful.

If the parent does not attend, the meeting is not going to produce the desired results (information gathering, planning joint cooperation, and getting parent agreement on the plan). A follow-up meeting with the parent will then be needed.

The Student Study Team does the following:

1. Gathers data about the child
2. Plans strategies to assist the student in the regular classroom
3. Monitors the student's progress

It is a group problem-solving process. The parents and the student will feel more comfortable if they are truly a part of the process; therefore, the completion of their questionnaires is recommended. It is also recommended that all members sit in a semi-circle during the meeting because this arrangement seems less confrontational.

Data is written on a large sheet of paper (3' x 8') called a group memory sheet. Following the meeting, this sheet is rolled up and stored until the time of the second SST meeting when it is brought out and displayed. At this second meeting, it serves to remind the committee of what was said at the first meeting. At the second meeting you may update the group memory sheet (using a different color of marker for each meeting held).

To make the parent and student less tense, begin with the student's strengths. The referring teacher should come up with a list of at least five or six. Next ask the teacher to list his or her concerns, prioritizing them. Next you will gather as much data as you can.

Here is a sample list of questions to ask at the first Student Study Team meeting.

Strengths
- What does ____ like to do?
- Is ____ an easy or difficult child to raise? Tell me more.
- Has the school attendance been good? How many absences this year?
- Is homework turned in? What is its quality? Is it easy to get homework done?

Concerns
- Ask the teacher for the list of concerns and prioritize them.
- This is often a good time to review the child's portfolio.

Known Information

- List the child's date of birth/chronological age.
- Determine the child's school history—how many schools attended. Begin with kindergarten.
- Look at report card comments for each school year. Note where the first mention was made of difficulty.
- Was there any significant health history?

    —Was the pregnancy of normal length?

    —Was the pregnancy/delivery normal? Did the baby leave the hospital at the same time as the mother? If not, why not?

    —What was the weight at birth?
- Have there been any high fevers?
- Have there been any serious accidents, especially accidents to the head?
- At what age did _____ begin to walk? Talk?
- Does _____ have allergies, asthma?
- When _____ was very young, were there ear infections? How often? How were they treated? When did these begin and when was the last?
- Is _____ a good eater?
- How does _____ get along with others? (This is a good time to talk about who lives in the home.)
- What kind of sleeper is _____?
- Are there two parents exercising parental rights? If separated, when did the separation occur? How did the child react to it? Do the parents see the child? What is the quality of the interaction of the parents now?
- Has anyone else in the family had trouble in school? If so, who? Nature of the problem? How resolved?
- Is the child taking any medications? If so, what? when?
- List any formal test scores that are available.

When you reach this point, you will want to brainstorm strategies for use in helping the child. Choose two or three, and list them. Decide who will be responsible for carrying them out. (It is best if it is someone who was at the meeting.) Decide on a follow-up date to meet again to see what progress has been made.

NOTE: When the team decides on a strategy, it needs to write it in measurable terms. For example, if "reading aloud" is a goal and the parent is responsible, give the parent papers on which to document his or her work with the student. A sample goal might read "_____ will orally read aloud to his/her mom for 15 minutes each night." Ask the mother to document exactly what was done by giving the date and the materials read and what kinds of errors were made. The child is then instructed to bring the parent's comments and materials to the teacher each day.

By requiring this, there are three benefits. It is far more likely the parent will follow through on the intervention. You will be aware immediately if the intervention process broke down and can contact the parent to find out why. The parent will be encouraged to be involved in the child's education.

Figures 5-6 through 5-9 offer you samples of forms to use at an SST meeting.

Figure 5-5
Flow Chart—Student Study Team

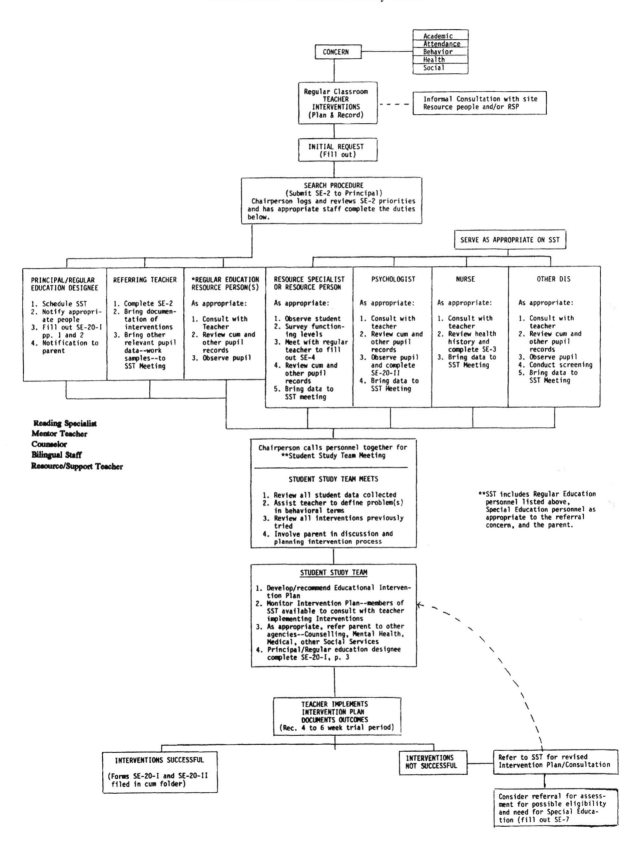

Figure 5-6

PARENT PREPARATION FOR SST

Note: Please complete this sheet and bring to the SST meeting.

1. Things I really enjoy about my child (his/her strengths) are:

   _____

   _____

2. Activities I think my child likes best are:

   _____

   _____

3. My concerns about my child are:

   _____

   _____

   a. At school

   _____

   _____

   b. At home

   _____

   _____

4. Types of discipline I find to be most effective with my child are:

   _____

   _____

5. Expectations I have for my child are:

   _____

   _____

Source: Marcie Radius, Pat Lesniak Collaborative Associates, Oakland, California (510-632-1178)

Figure 5-7

STUDENT WORKSHEET

1. At school, activities I really like are:

   _____

2. The activities I like most away from school are:

   _____

   _____

3. The subjects I am best at are:

   _____

   _____

4. I learn best when: _____

   _____

5. I want more help with these school subjects:

   _____

6. If I could change one thing about school, it would be:

   _____

7. My teacher, the principal, my parent(s), and I are having a meeting about me because:

   _____

8. When I do things well, I like to do or get:

   _____

9. When I grow up, I would like to be:

   _____

At home:

1. My family (the people who live in my house) consists of:

   _____

2. I get along best with:

   _____

3. The person I like to talk to most is:

   _____

Source: Marcie Radius, Pat Lesniak Collaborative Associates, Oakland, California (510-632-1178)

Figure 5-8

STUDENT STUDY TEAM SUMMARY

NAME OF STUDENT _____

DATES OF MEETINGS

TEACHER _____ SCHOOL _____

_____

STUDENT _____ PRIMARY LANGUAGE _____ GR. _____ BIRTH _____

_____

M _____ F _____

TEAM _____

PARENTS _____

Strengths	Known Information	Concerns (choose)	Questions	Strategies Brainstorm	Actions (choose)	Responsibility
	Modifications					Who? When?
						Follow-Up Date

Source: Marcie Radius, Pat Lesniak Collaborative Associates, Oakland, California (510-632-1178)

72

Figure 5-9

STUDENT STUDY TEAM SUMMARY
(Typical Column Topics)

NAME OF STUDENT _____

TEACHER _____ SCHOOL _____ TEAM _____

STUDENT _____ PRIMARY LANGUAGE _____ GR. _____ BIRTH _____ PARENTS _____

M _____ F _____

DATES OF MEETINGS _____
_____
_____

Strengths	Known Information	Modifications	Concerns (choose)	Questions	Strategies Brainstorm	Actions (choose)	Responsibility Who?	When?
Academic Social Physical What student likes Incentives Career potential Activities Hobbies	School background Family composition Health Performance levels	Changes in program Reading specialist Tutoring Counseling Repeating grade	Academic Social/ emotional Physical Attendance	Questions that can't be answered at this time	Team brainstorms multiple creative strategies to address top concerns	Two to three actions chosen from strategies brainstormed	Any team member, including the parent and student	Specific dates
							Follow-Up Date 3-6 weeks	

*Source: Marcie Radius, Pat Lesniak Collaborative Associates, Oakland, California (510-632-1178)

Instructional Interventions for SST Meetings

- Evaluate hearing and vision
- Change seating/preferential seating near teacher
- Adjust grouping
- Write directions/have student repeat directions/discuss
- Peer buddy or peer tutor
- Test orally
- Carrel out of traffic pattern
- Shorten or modify assignments
- Student-teacher contract with reward attached
- Additional one-to-one help from teacher or aide
- Remedial program within school (goes to another classroom for instruction at a lower level; this is particularly useful with math/learning cursive)
- Remedial program outside school (some parents do offer to take students for private tutoring at their own expense)
- Use alternative materials that are at student's functional level
- Classroom change
- Counseling
- Extra time to complete assignments
- Provide immediate feedback of results
- Daily/weekly teacher-parent conference, with parent giving rewards or aversives based on student's performance
- Visual charting that encourages self-monitoring
- Use of concrete teacher devices—calculators, computers, math manipulatives such as counters

Specific Interventions by Subject

Reading

- Assign student a specific section of the text he or she will read aloud to the teacher. Allow student time to study that section before reading it.
- Record selection on tape. Allow student to listen to tape several times before attempting to read it.
- Have student make notes of important parts and read those notes back to you; if student can draw a picture to depict the actions, encourage this (see "marginalia" in Chapter 11).
- Introduce new vocabulary words daily for several days before asking student to read them.
- Have student use a marker to keep his or her place.

- If the reading text is impossibly beyond the student's ability, have student read from materials at the appropriate level.
- Help student learn how to syllabicate long words.
- Have student use the Student's Reminder for Decoding (found in Volume II) to analyze words.

Spelling

- Reduce number of words to be learned; let students choose words from the list.
- Have another student dictate those words to him or her each day; student makes corrections and writes each word missed in color (vowels red, consonants green).
- Make student a copy of the 500 most used words (found in Volume II) to keep in his or her desk and teach student to locate a word from that list.

Mathematics

- Allow student to use counters or to count on his or her fingers.
- Teach only two or three skills to mastery; continue daily practice of these while adding one new one (examples: writing and saying numbers 1-100; counting by 5's; adding simple facts to make sums under 10).
- If assignment involves several processes, have student use color coding to call attention to the process (red for plus; blue for subtract, etc.).
- If task completion is the problem rather than lack of skill, have someone else copy problems for the student.
- If student has some idea about what he or she is doing, allow student to check each answer with a calculator provided he or she agrees to come to you if he or she cannot figure out where the error was made (student must show all steps on paper); seat child near you so you can keep a better eye on the work progress.
- Reduce/shorten assignment.
- Give alternate assignment at lower level.
- Allow student to use graph paper if columns tend to drift.
- If student's progress is being adversely affected because facts are not committed to memory, try to arrange for a volunteer to teach the facts; or encourage parent to do so (you may need to show parent how to teach them).
- If word problems are the problem, have student draw pictures.
- Allow student to use manipulatives.

Social Studies/Science

- Tape lectures so student can relisten.
- Reduce assignments.
- Allow student a choice of projects to demonstrate understanding.
- Assign a peer tutor to help student locate important facts and concepts.

- Provide student with list of study questions in preparation for exams.
- If writing is a barrier to success, allow student to take oral exams; use matching tests and multiple-choice tests as opposed to essay and total recall tests.
- Teach older student to use the Multi-Scan Strategy described in Chapter 11.

Illegible Handwriting

- Allow oral testing or other alternative testing or project.
- Allow student to use computer or word processor.
- Allow student to dictate to another who will write it.

Attentional Deficits

- Minimize distractions.
- Shorten tests.
- Provide extra time to complete tests.
- Give tests in small increments; this student often will give up if the task looks too long.
- Help student get organized, nothing but necessary materials at hand; extraneous stuff out of work area.
- Offer alternative assessments or projects.
- Carrel away from traffic pattern.

LIST OF ACADEMIC AND BEHAVIORAL INTERVENTIONS BY SPECIFIC PROBLEM

Visual Perceptual Deficits

DEFICIT: Reverses/inverts letters or numerals
INTERVENTIONS:
1. Make and attach a visual strip to the student's desk and notebook so there is a model for those symbols that give trouble. Help the child build the habit of looking at the model each time he or she needs to.

2. Have the student go to the board. Take only one troublesome symbol and draw it about a foot high. Have the student trace over it 25 times a day until he or she no longer reverses it. As the student is going over the symbol, say "Feel the way your hand is going" to speed acquisition.

DEFICIT: Loses place/skips lines/rereads lines/omits words
INTERVENTIONS:

1. Encourage the student to use a bookmark during reading. Set the example by using one yourself. Being engaged with moving a bookmark is helpful to inattentive and fidgety students as well as those with perceptual problems. It also allows you to quickly and quietly monitor whether a child is following along. When you find a child is out of place, you are able to move the bookmark to the correct place without a verbal reprimand.

   The best bookmarks are about six inches long, one inch wide with a one-inch dark line in the center. This dark line is placed under the word the child is reading as he or she moves the marker left to right.

2. Reproduce material to be read. Have the student underline it with a pencil as he or she reads.

DEFICIT: Yawns/blurry vision/itchy eyes during reading
INTERVENTIONS:

1. Suggest a professional eye examination to be sure the student has normal acuity and that the eyes converge properly. Encourage students who need glasses to wear them.

2. Enlarge printed material if you can.

3. When the student begins to have trouble, tell the child to close his or her eyes and rest them for 30 seconds. A damp paper towel helps with itchy eyes. Some students find they can solve these problems by reading with only one eye at a time.

4. Flourescent lights on white paper produce a glare. Use reproduced copies, not dittoes, and do them on blue, tan, or green paper. If the student must read from white paper, reduce the amount of light by shutting off some of the lights, or allowing the student to cover the paper with a transparent nonglare plastic theme cover or even wearing lightly tinted sunglasses.

DEFICIT: Cannot copy accurately
INTERVENTIONS:

1. Make sure the child has normal vision.

2. Seat the student near the board if copying from the board.

3. When copying from a book at his or her desk, show the student how to use the index finger of the free hand to hold the place on the material to be copied while copying.

4. Train the student to remember groups of letters so that he or she does not have to look back at the model after each letter. The ideal number of letters to train would be those in a syllable.

DEFICIT: Poor letter formation/handwriting illegible
INTERVENTIONS:

1. Teach the student the touch-typing system and how to use a word processor.

2. Teach or reteach printing or cursive. Make the student aware that legibility of his or her writing must improve. Begin by showing the student how to place the paper correctly on the desk, how to hold the writing implement (erasable pen makes a good one), and how to form each letter. When working with students who need reteaching, keep the number of students in the group small enough so you are able to be certain each person is starting the letters in the correct place. Begin with letters that have similar strokes. Go slow. Have the student repeat directions such as "Begin on the line and move up and around."

3. When working with a pencil, some students will benefit from a plastic pencil grip that forces them to place the fingers correctly.

DEFICIT: Slow, laborious handwriting
INTERVENTIONS:

1. On long assignments, let the student dictate to you or use the tape recorder.

2. Allow the student to sometimes take oral tests.

3. Allow the student to take the assignment home (extra time).

4. Shorten the assignment.

5. Allow the student to use the word processor.

DEFICIT: Messy papers
INTERVENTIONS:

1. Make the student aware of the fact that research shows pretty papers get better grades. This fact is easy to drive home. Just show the student two papers (*not* his or her own—one that is neat with margins, etc., and one that is messy) and ask the student which one he or she thinks will get the better grade. Point out that while it may not seem fair, teachers begin to judge the paper by its looks and have been known to reject a paper without even reading it just because it is messy.

2. Tell the student he or she may not erase. If a mistake cannot be corrected by writing over, he or she is to cross it out with one line and go on.

3. Allow the student to use the word processor.

Auditory Perceptual Deficits

DEFICIT: Does not understand conversation at normal speed
INTERVENTIONS:

1. Have the student sit close to you.

2. Make sure he or she is attending before you speak.

3. Speak slower. Use short sentences. Repeat if necessary.

4. Tape record lessons so the student can stop the machine and relisten.

5. Assign a capable and patient student-buddy to repeat directions and information.

6. Provide the student with written notes regarding major points covered in the lecture.

7. Encourage the student to give you some sign when he or she is not following what you are saying. Students are usually too self-conscious to raise their hand, but will agree to pull on their ear to let you know.

8. Stop frequently to check for and clarify understanding.

9. Use lots of visuals and board notes to support aural input; notes contain key words, definitions, questions.

10. Refer the child to the speech therapist for evaluation of receptive language.

DEFICIT: Not able to distinguish between spoken sounds
INTERVENTIONS:

1. Have hearing acuity checked. If normal, ask the speech therapist to check the child's auditory discrimination.

2. If the child is not hearing final consonants, exaggerate the sounds you want him or her to hear; write the word, pointing out the sound you want the student to hear.

3. Show the student where to place the tongue and lips, and how much air is involved to make the sounds he or she does not hear.

DEFICIT: Is not able to filter out extraneous noises
INTERVENTIONS:

1. Have the student sit near you.

2. Be sure you have his or her attention before speaking.

3. Tell the student to watch your lips.

4. If the problem continues, suggest a professional hearing test.

5. Write important points on the board.

6. Try to keep the classroom as quiet as possible during instruction.

7. Tape the lesson in a totally quiet setting. Let the student use earphones to listen.

8. During independent work periods, use "white music" to mask distracting noises.

DEFICIT: Does not benefit from auditory input
INTERVENTION:

Give student a copy of important information that is being done auditorily; this way he or she can see the words while you are talking. At the end of the lecture, have the student highlight important points. Check for the student's understanding.

Spatial Awareness Deficits

DEFICIT: Gets lost in ordinary surroundings
INTERVENTIONS:

1. Send a buddy with the student.
2. Take the student on jaunts around the area asking him or her to observe stable visual data, i.e., ask the student to count how many rooms he or she will pass on the way to the bathroom.
3. Have the student draw maps of the school and neighborhood noting distinguishing features of the landscape.

DEFICIT: Cannot remember left-to-right sequencing
INTERVENTIONS:
1. Put an arrow on the student's desk that looks like the one shown in the illustration. The student lays his or her paper just below the arrow. Tell the student to begin on the side where the dot is and proceed in the direction of the arrow.

2. Put five rows of masking tape on the floor and play "typewriter." The student is guided to move as the typewriter does, stepping left to right on the tape; when he or she reaches the end of the row, the student doubles back to the next line.
3. Teach left and right. For most students you can say, "You **write** with your **right** hand."

DEFICIT: Cannot write in a given amount of space/no space between words
INTERVENTIONS:
1. Ask the student what he or she plans to write. Have the student repeat his or her sentence two to five times. You will draw enough spaces on the paper so he or she can write one letter in each space. For example:

The boy went for a walk.

— — —   — — —   — — —   — — —   — —   — — — —.

2. Teach the student to use the word processor.
3. Use large-square graph paper. The student places one letter in each square and skips a space between words.

DEFICIT: Disorganized
INTERVENTIONS:
1. Show the student how to organize a task; show him or her several times. Get the student to repeat what actions were involved, i.e., "Clear my desk." "Put out my book, pencil, and paper."
2. Pull periodic inspections. Give rewards for clean desks.
3. Teach the child to keep an assignment calendar.
4. Teach the student to organize his or her papers—margins, headings, and indenting.

5. In math, have the student fold the paper to produce squares and put only one problem in each square.

6. Enlist parent help in organization: keep a neat room at home, regularly using the old adage "A place for everything and everything in its place."

Conceptual Deficits

DEFICIT: Cannot read social situations/body language
INTERVENTIONS:
1. Role-play social situations in class. (You can have students act out scenes from a story just read or movie watched, or act out some of the social skills listed in Chapter 14.) Stop frequently and discuss possible feelings. Model ways to get through these situations and have students role play what you modeled. Be sure to talk about people's need for personal space and the fact that when someone unfamiliar gets too close (invades the other's personal space), it makes the other person feel uncomfortable.

2. Whenever a situation arises naturally that calls for understanding of body language—such as confrontation between two kids—begin to explain what a look/stance means and what is a proper response. Oddly, doing this often diffuses the combatant's anger while serving as a lesson to others.

3. Using the face pattern shown on the next page, have students draw what different emotions (bewildered, depressed, etc.) look like.

DEFICIT: Cannot see relationships between similar objects/poor inferential thinking
INTERVENTIONS:
1. Have two objects that are similar for students to examine and describe. After describing them aloud and writing ideas on the board, the students then write a paragraph describing and comparing the two similar items for both similarity and difference. Examples are:

cup/mug   avocado/pear   briefcase/overnight case   picture of a cradle/crib   fork/spoon

2. In Volume II you will find a series of exercises for improving inferential thinking.

DEFICIT: Does not understand the concept of "hurry"
INTERVENTION:
Model "hurry." Have students watch and describe the difference in the rate of speed (walking, getting out materials, or putting materials away).

DEFICIT: Reads words but does not convert them to mental images
INTERVENTIONS:
1. Use activities found in Volume II.

2. Have cooperative groups turn a story they have read into a playlet and act it out.

3. Demonstrate yourself what it means to see something in "your mind's eye." For example:

> Mary built a snowman. Later she laughed because her cat was sitting on the snowman's head.

I ask the kids, "What color was the cat?" They scurry back to reread it. I say "I saw a gray striped cat like my cat at home. What do you see?" They catch on and volunteer different colors of cats. I tell them it's okay for us to see cats of different colors in our minds unless the story tells us what color the cat is.

Memory Deficits

DEFICIT: Cannot remember what was just seen/spelling words
INTERVENTIONS:

1. Play memory games. Show the student 10 objects in a box for 30 seconds. Close the lid and have the student name as many objects as he or she can. Vary the objects and repeat the game. Tell the student the tricks you use to remember what's in there. (What colors did I see? What is it used for? In what room is it found?)

    Play the same kind of games using a short vocabulary list, such as:

am	be	can	do	do	is
are	been	could	did		
			does		

    Students can use a formula: 2 <u>a</u> words, 2 <u>b</u> words, 2 <u>c</u> words, 3 <u>d</u> words, and 1 <u>i</u> word.

    "Concentration" is another game that stimulates memory. On one card, print the word. On the other, draw the picture. Make about 10 matches and arrange them so pairs are not together. Have the child name each word and point to the picture. Then turn all the cards upside down. Time the child. As the child turns a card up, he or she must find its mate. Play often enough that the child can see he or she is showing improvement.

2. Teach older students to highlight, outline, and summarize information.

3. Teach note-taking skills and use advance organizers.

4. Teach children to use resources (encyclopedias, dictionaries, indexes) to locate needed information and to relocate the same information later.

5. See Chapter 12 for ways to help students remember spelling words. By all means, teach them to use verbal rehearsal when learning spelling. For example, in a word such as *satisfy*, the student's self-talk should go something like this: "I can hear the *s*, I can hear the *a*, I can hear the *t*—*sat* spells *sat*. I see the word *is*. I can hear the *f*. The *y* sounds like an *i* but it's spelled with a *y*. Hmmm . . . s–a–t–i–s–f–y spells *satisfy*." This activity is modeled daily with different words until students internalize it. Self-talk done out loud will help them learn and retain spelling.

6. Teach kids to use mnemonic devices or associative clues to assist memory. For example, if the student is trying to learn the names of the Great Lakes, the mnemonic **HOMES** will help. **H** is for Huron, **O** is for Ontario, **M** is for Michigan, **E** is for Erie, and **S** is for Superior.

7. Use the board/facts sheet to remind students of main ideas.

DEFICIT: Cannot remember what was just heard
INTERVENTIONS:
1. Write list of questions to be answered as lesson proceeds.

2. Tape-record session.

3. Encourage note taking.

4. Repeat. Assign a peer buddy who is willing to repeat the information.

DEFICIT: Cannot remember what was just seen or heard. (Severe memory deficits. Scores on the Visual Aural Digit Span Test [VADS] fall at or below the 10th percentile.)
INTERVENTIONS:

1. Decide what information *must* be acquired. Weed out less essential stuff.

2. Give parent and student a list of what must be learned and show parent how to work with the child.

3. Commit yourself to the task. I hear colleagues say, "He just can't learn it." In my experience, I have never met a student who could not learn—it just takes incredible amounts of time and effort to get the job done. This is why it is so essential to carefully screen what must be learned, i.e., survival words. In addition to committing yourself to the task, be aware that you must work on the task *every day*! So keep it small. If you don't get results in a few weeks, do it twice a day. Once learned, this material will still need to be reinforced regularly.

4. Allow the use of calculators in math.

5. Allow students to take open-book tests (easiest), matching tests (easy), or multiple-choice tests (harder) rather than tests involving pure recall (hardest). If it is really important knowledge, you may want to give all three kinds of tests on the material. As the child masters one kind of questioning, go on to the next.

6. Use concrete examples and experiences in teaching. (The child sees it, hears it, does it.)

DEFICIT: Loses things; cannot remember homework assignments
INTERVENTIONS:

1. Label belongings with student's name.

2. Limit what must be carried from place to place to what can be placed in the child's pocket or backpack. The child puts it there while you are looking and the parent knows to ask for it when the child gets home. One of these things is a spiral notebook containing the homework assignments (checked for accuracy by the teacher before the child leaves school).

DEFICIT: Cannot remember to capitalize, punctuate, indent; has trouble spelling
INTERVENTIONS:

1. In the pre-writing stage, help the child make a brief outline of what he or she wants to say. The cluster works well (described in Volume II). Have the child number his or her ideas in the sequence he or she will write them. Next, allow the child to write, not worrying at this point about mechanics. Help the student learn to edit, using the editing checklist also found in Volume II.

2. Allow the student to use a word processing program that has an editing program built in.

Attentional Deficits

DEFICIT: Does not attend to directions
INTERVENTIONS:

1. Use a signal to indicate directions will follow. At camp we used to sing "Announcements . . . announcements . . . announcements!" This signal got everyone quiet and ready to listen. You could substitute the word "Directions."

2. Have the students come to the front during the input part of instruction.

3. If directions are given orally, hold them to no more than three. Hold up one finger, give the first direction, and have students repeat it. Hold up the second finger, give the second direction, and have students repeat it. Follow the same procedure for the third direction. Then ask at least two students to repeat all three directions.

4. Put directions on the board.

5. Teach students to read directions and underline/circle words that tell them what to do. For example:

   <u>Look</u> at each set of words. On the blank line,

   <u>write</u> the word that best fits the sentence.

6. Circulate early into independent work periods to see if students are proceeding according to the directions, clearing up any misunderstandings as quickly as you can.

DEFICIT: Does not begin assignments
INTERVENTIONS:

Circulate early. Get stragglers working by having them sit near you or near a study buddy who will help them keep going.

DEFICIT: Difficulty sustaining attention
INTERVENTIONS:

1. When a youngster starts out listening but loses concentration midway, work his or her name into the lecture. "And as Anna knows . . ."

2. Reduce distracting stimuli. For example, if you see the student begin to fiddle with an object, have it put away. If it comes out again, take it, but tell the student you will return it later.

3. Require students to make notes. They will get more out of a lecture and attend better.

4. Break an assignment into segments with a reward for each segment accomplished.

5. Use a peer buddy to remind a student to stay on task.

DEFICIT: Distractibility
INTERVENTIONS:

1. Eliminate all possible distractions during independent work periods (including distracting objects). Use "white music."

2. Assign a student to a carrel or a corner out of the area of movement.

DEFICIT: Low frustration tolerance/explodes
INTERVENTIONS:

1. Constantly monitor the stress levels of your students. Encourage parents and students to let you know when they are having a "real problem."

2. Make provisions for *timeout*. There are times when a student must escape. It is well to have an ongoing arrangement with a colleague whereby a student who needs timeout can go to the colleague's room for the balance of the period.

3. For students who do okay in the room but get in trouble at recess and lunch, you need to arrange a supervised place where the student goes. Call a conference with the parent, explain what you are going to do, and why. Obtain the parent's agreement and write it as an I.E.P. special review.

4. If a student regularly explodes, parents will want to consider seeing a physician.

DEFICIT: Rushes through work/"hurry up and do"
INTERVENTIONS:

1. LD kids who are ADHD often "hurry up and do" their work usually because as soon as they can hand it in, they can go to some other activity they find more enjoyable. They may even write all wrong answers just to be able to tell the teacher they are "through." Knowing that a student does this, talk to the student before he or she begins the assignment about what standards you will expect—and check the work before allowing the student to go to the more enjoyable activity. If you keep the assignment short, the student is more likely to try to meet your standards.

2. Arrange a daily two-way communication (notebook or phone call) system with the parent. Keep parents apprised of daily behavior, progress, and assignments with which they may need to give help.

3. Arrange for the parent to give a reward to the child when work is properly done the first time. (See the section on money therapy in Chapter 9.)

4. Allow the child a choice of assignments whenever possible.

DEFICIT: Incomplete assignments
INTERVENTIONS:

1. Shorten assignments or modify the way the child does the assignment; for example, half written, half oral.

2. Allow extra time to complete the assignment.

DEFICIT: Makes inappropriate noises/incessant talking
INTERVENTIONS:

1. Many ADHD students make mouth noises and, many times, they are not even aware of it. You must first make the student aware of the mouth noises, and then motivate the student to want to try to eliminate them. You may want to discuss this problem with the student in the presence of his or her parents; you will need their support to make any plan work.

2. Move the student to an area where his or her noises/talking are less disturbing to others.

3. Use a behavior modification chart and a parental reward to eliminate unwanted behavior. On the chart, give a "smile" face for each period the child avoids making noises. Decide with the parent how many "smiles" must be obtained for a reward. (I usually suggest 25 cents for each 10.)

4. If the behavior appears to be deliberate and for the purpose of calling attention to himself or herself, talk with the student and offer a positive way to get attention if he or she abandons the inappropriate behavior.

5. Remember that mouth noises may be a symptom of Tourette Syndrome. If the noises continue, a referral to a physician is recommended.

DEFICIT: Bothers others who are trying to work
INTERVENTIONS:
1. Place the child in a different grouping or seating arrangement to see where he or she functions best.

2. Talk to the child and explain he or she is not to touch others or their things or to talk to them when they are working.

3. Sometimes kids behave like this when they are starved for a friend. Lacking the skills to make a friend, they prefer to have others angry at them instead of being ignored. So you may have to help the child learn how to make a friend.

4. During work periods, have the child work at a carrel or sit near you.

Excessive Absence

DEFICIT: Child misses or is projected to miss more than 20 days of school this year (no obvious cause)
INTERVENTIONS:
1. Send a letter to the parent pointing out that the child's absences are adversely impacting on learning. (Keep a copy in the cum folder.)

2. If absences continue, talk with the student about the situation and explain why he or she needs to be in school every day. Ask what the student does when he or she stays home. If you find the student is being kept home to babysit, you may need to involve your district's attendance review team. If the student tells you school is boring, inquire for more specific feedback of his or her likes and dislikes.

3. Select one or two people on the faculty/staff who will agree to pay more attention to this child—make a point of being friendly, talking to the child about things that interest him or her and, when the student is absent, letting the child know he or she was missed.

4. Meet with the student's other teachers. Review and revise your expectations of the student. Modify curriculum so the child can feel successful. Avoid embarrassing the student. If assignments are not done, find someone else who will help the student get the work done.

5. These children are often feeling isolated, so you may need to help them make a friend. One of the easiest ways to do that is to invite two students to eat their lunches with you. Choose a child who is somewhat like the isolated child—one who also needs a friend. It is not a good idea to choose the most sociable or brightest child

because he or she will have little in common with the shy child (reinforcing the shy child's feelings that there is something wrong with him or her). After lunch, sit with them while they play checkers or work with some art materials. Be near at hand in case an awkward situation develops. At the end of the period, it is okay to tell the students why you wanted them to eat with you. "I noticed that both of you seemed to need a friend and I hope now you feel like you know each other." If this does not work, ask the shy child to choose who you will invite next. Try again.

DEFICIT: Student "cuts" the same class over and over
INTERVENTIONS:
1. Talk with the student; find out why.
2. If it is possible to change the student's program and give him or her another teacher, ask the student which teacher he or she wants and grant the wish if possible. If not, explain to the student why you can't change the program; ask what it is that bothers him or her and then try to modify that.

Poor Work Habits

DEFICIT: Assignments not turned in
INTERVENTIONS:
1. Many students do not understand how teachers evaluate a student's progress. They may even be unaware that teachers keep an ongoing record of grades. Let students watch you enter a grade on several occasions. When a student who ordinarily does poorly has a good score, grab your grade book and announce loudly, "It is a pleasure to record such a good job." This kind of remark dignifies the student receiving it but also motivates others because they also want that kind of recognition. Likewise, you need to show students how a zero adversely affects their overall average, whereas a 50 percent may not be quite so devastating. Many students think they cannot hand in a paper that is not complete. There are some teachers who will not accept an incomplete paper. The only true way one can tell what a student has learned is to accept all papers—done or not completely done.
2. Many LD students will remain reluctant to hand in their work, particularly if they feel it is not well done. If they ask to keep it and hand it in later, it is extremely unlikely you will ever get it. Unless you keep asking for it, the student rarely completes it; therefore I suggest having *one* monitor to pick up papers at the end of each period. The paper remains on the desktop until the monitor gets it. If it is not there, the monitor will ask the student for it; if it is not forthcoming, the monitor will let you know quietly but immediately. You can then talk to the student.
3. If homework is not returned, contact parents. Sometimes they will say, "I didn't know he had any. He said he did it at school." In this case a parent conference *with the student present* needs to follow with development of a plan for how to handle this. (I suggest a packet of alternative assignments that the parent can use if the child claims he or she had no homework.)

   If the parent says "I know he did it," try to make the parent feel responsible for seeing to it that the child turns it in. When parents begin to use restriction for failure to turn homework in, it usually comes in.

DEFICIT: Does not use time wisely
INTERVENTIONS:

1. Talk with the student regarding the problem. Many times the student is not aware of the problem.

2. If the student is a fast worker, offer him or her a choice of things to do (pleasure reading, computer time, act as a helper with slower students, work on an ongoing project, have art*) when he or she finishes the assignment. Let students know that their time is too valuable to waste just looking around. *One art project that "keeps on giving" is mosaics. At the beginning of the year, have volunteers cut brightly colored construction paper into 1/2″ x 1/2″ pieces; place them in shoe boxes (one color to each box). Do one or two art lessons so students understand how they can make stunning pictures with the pieces by gluing them to the paper. You can set up an ongoing display board. Enjoyed by students aged 7 to 19, this project is relatively mess free and allows for quick clean-up.

3. Allow students to begin homework in class if time permits. If they finish it, make a big deal over "how they really used their time wisely and can now go home and do the things they want to do." It is wise to have them take the paper home with a note from you saying the homework is done.

DEFICIT: Does not participate in classroom discussions
INTERVENTIONS:

1. LD students have met with failure so often that they decide not to "risk" participating. To overcome this, you must insure success on repeated occasions. See the techniques for overcoming failure syndrome described in Chapter 8.

2. Decide whether the child's lack of participation is truly a problem before making an issue of it. If it is, start praising/rewarding students who sit near the reluctant student.

3. Tell the student ahead of time you plan to call on him or her so you want the student to listen carefully and be prepared to give an answer. You can even tell the student what you plan to ask him or her, giving the student time to prepare an answer. When the answer is offered, be prepared to say, "Thank you for your contribution. Let's see what others are thinking." Try not to embarrass the shy child.

DEFICIT: Does not stay seated/does not sit in the chair properly
INTERVENTIONS:

1. Talk with the child about your expectation that he or she will stay in his or her seat/sit properly in the chair.

2. Arrange a signal that you will give if the student forgets to stay in the seat/sit properly.

3. Use a behavioral modification chart (one "smile" for each period the student can comply, with a parent reward for every 10 "smiles").

Poor Social Relationships

DEFICIT: Poor peer relationships that lead to name calling or fighting
INTERVENTIONS:

1. Be alert. Always intervene because name calling leads to fights on the playground and parental complaints. (These behaviors are often seen in ADHD/ADD students.) Make reciprocal arrangements with a colleague that if this occurs, you may send the student to the colleague's room with work to do. The student stays there for the balance of the period and also gives up the next recess.

2. Talk in private with the two students involved as soon after the incident as possible. Try to get to the bottom of the problem—why do they get into it? They may have been doing this for so long they can't remember or they may find out it began due to a misunderstanding.

3. Be sure the participants understand that there will always be negative consequences for these behaviors. If the name calling happens a second time, tell the students their parents will be asked to come in. A fight should result in parents being informed the first time. If it is necessary to call the parents in, develop a Behavioral Contingency Plan (see Chapter 3).

4. Some students cannot handle unstructured time (playground). You may have to make special arrangements for them to spend their recesses under supervision in a quiet setting such as the nurse's office, library, etc.

5. Seat the student where he or she will be visible at all times.

PROBLEM: Student is physically aggressive with teacher or staff
INTERVENTIONS:

1. If a student has had an episode involving a teacher or member of the staff, a Behavioral Contingency Plan should be in place. If not, move swiftly toward getting one. (Students who are aggressive may also be ADHD/ADD.)

2. Both parents and student should be informed that if the student assaults a teacher, a complaint will be filed with the police department.

3. Try to prevent frustration and anxiety-producing situations; if a situation develops that must be handled, have the principal summoned (without letting the student know).

4. Never embarrass or tease the student.

5. Avoid competitive situations.

6. Talk with the student. Let the student know you want him or her to be successful. Develop a way the student can let you know if he or she is upset. Allow a timeout (student goes somewhere else until he or she feels he or she can return).

7. Take rumors about possession of a weapon seriously and summon the appropriate authority to investigate.

8. If the student is threatening you, try to speak in a quiet, calm voice. Say "I can see you are upset. I'm really sorry. What did I/we do to cause this?" Do not threaten the student or make little of the circumstances.

PROBLEM: Responds inappropriately to teasing
INTERVENTION:

Some students do not have the social skills to rebuff teasing. Students need to learn things they can say when they are being teased. For example, if someone says something about your mother and that person doesn't know the mother, the proper response is

"That's ridiculous. You don't even know my mother." If someone says. "That's an ugly dress. Did you buy it at Goodwill?" Teach the child to respond, "I may have an ugly dress, but I have a good heart." These are the kinds of situations that can be role-played during social skills training.

PROBLEM: Student is not accepted by other students
INTERVENTIONS:
1. Allow the student to be the leader in a group of your best-adjusted, kindest students.

2. Observe the student and try to learn why the others don't accept him or her. Don't be afraid to ask "How do you feel about . . ." Listen carefully to their answers. They usually have merit. Then try to help the students alter those things.

3. Sometimes these children get others in trouble. Be careful not to punish everyone in the group. Punish only those students you are certain are guilty.

4. If obnoxious behavior occurs under competitive circumstances, let this student leave the group.

5. Do not try to force interaction.

PROBLEM: Student blames other people/does not take responsibility for own acts
INTERVENTIONS:
1. In private, calmly confront the student with the facts. The child probably will go into his or her pattern of denial and projection. Calmly tell the student you are happy that the student expressed himself or herself, but the facts simply do not support his or her point of view. Levy punishment if it is a serious offense.

2. Try to get to know this child better and give him or her support. This behavior sometimes masks great insecurity. The parents may be harsh in punishment, so denial is used in order to avoid the punishment. Try to let this child know he or she does not have to be perfect to please you. In your counseling with students, it is sometimes helpful to relate stories of your own childhood in which you relate how you were not a perfect child either and got punished. For instance, "When I was little my mom had this beautiful vase. I just loved it. She told me not to touch it, but I loved it so much I touched it anyway. It fell and broke. My mom was very upset and asked how it got broken. I said my little sister had broken it. Then I really got yelled at because my little sister was only a year old and there was no way she could have reached that vase. When my dad got home, mother told him about my lie. From then on, my little sister got out of everything because, even when she was guilty, they thought I was lying." In your social skills role playing, set up some scenarios and help the students practice the most palatable responses. Teach them to say, "I did it but I'm really sorry. How can I make amends?"

3. In cases where you are less certain about what happened, try to get the truth. Say to the student or students involved, "We can solve this right here and now—but if you continue to deny it, you will have to talk to the principal, which means you will miss recess and your parents will be called." Once the truth is out, ask the students to come up with at least three punishments they feel are appropriate; you will choose one of those (or if they do not seem appropriate, you will come up with one of your own).

4. If the child is under 12, counseling may be needed if denial and projection are frequently used. In older students, these mechanisms may be a sign of conduct disorder, in which case, they are not likely to be extinguished.

PROBLEM: Cheating/stealing
INTERVENTIONS:

1. Cheating and stealing among young children under 10 is not so serious as it is with students over 10. Talk with younger students about why they should not cheat. Tell them, "I want to see what you can do. I don't expect you to get it right all the time. You don't have to be perfect. I need to see what kind of errors you make so I know what I need to teach you."

   If a younger child steals, say "That belongs to Jane. It's nice and I can understand why you wanted it but she wants it too so we have to give it back." Tell the child that you will need to call his or her parent if the cheating or stealing happens again.

   If an older student steals, an office referral, parental involvement, and possibly counseling are in order.

   If the student is over 10, try to help the child get prepared for tests so he or she does not feel compelled to cheat. I had a colleague a few years ago who thought herself clever if she could ask a question that no one in her class could answer. She also started tests by reminding her students that if they didn't do well, they probably would flunk. The stress level in her room was out of sight! So were the clever ways her students worked out to cheat. The best tests are those for which all the students are fully prepared. Wouldn't it be grand if every student got 100%? There is no rule that there must be a curve. It is even okay for students to know ahead what the questions will be on teacher-made tests. It would be unethical to tell them the questions on standardized achievement tests.

2. If it happens again, do let parents know and ask them to talk with the child about it while you are present.

3. In your social skills group, have the children give their views on these subjects. Start by asking, "What is cheating? What is stealing?"

4. Keep a closer eye on the student.

5. Proper storage of tempting and expensive items is essential.

PROBLEM: Student has temper tantrums
INTERVENTIONS:

1. Temper tantrums may be a sign of ADHD and with medication might be eliminated. Sometimes tantrums are attention-getting behaviors, so if you can eliminate the audience, the tantrum stops shortly.

2. When a student has repeated tantrums you need to talk with the class when the student is not present. Ask them to brainstorm things the class might do to help. Hopefully they will come up with the following list: They will refrain from laughing, ignore it, or give negative feedback, such as "You're acting like a small child."

3. If the tantrum seems to come because of frustration or anxiety, try to prevent future ones by neutralizing or avoiding situations that will cause them.

4. Temper tantrums are a power trip. The child feels helpless so he or she has a tantrum to get out of the situation. If the child gains some knowledge, he or she may not need to have a tantrum. Work that is commensurate with the child's level of knowledge helps. Testing the student one to one in a totally quiet situation may help. Giving the child a choice of activities also sometimes works.

5. If tantrums are a regular occurrence, counseling may be needed.

PROBLEM: Student makes sexually inappropriate comments/displays sexually inappropriate behavior
INTERVENTIONS:

For a Younger Child
1. If a younger child talks a lot about sex, and/or seems to have knowledge beyond others of the same age, the child may have been molested. Take time to get to know the child better, and watch for other signs that may indicate abuse. Do not be alone with the child for your own protection. Check to see what is your reporting obligation.

2. It is not uncommon for younger children to engage in self-stimulation of their genitalia. If this happens, calmly take the child aside and explain that this kind of behavior is not appropriate at school and not to do it anymore.

For an Older Student
1. If an older pupil is sexually inappropriate, it may be an offense requiring referral to the principal. Sexual harassment has become a hot issue and cannot be tolerated in school. Parents are filing lawsuits against schools who allow this to occur.

2. Do not allow the student out of class unless you are sure there is supervision wherever that student goes, including going to and from.

3. Talk with the student's parents (with the principal present) about what behaviors are of concern.

4. Seat the student near you in order to monitor conversation.

PROBLEM: Student refuses to obey reasonable directives
INTERVENTIONS:
1. You know your request was valid, so evaluate how it was delivered. Sometimes under time pressure we are abrupt with students. If you decide you sounded like a drill sergeant, say, "I'm sorry, Jon. I think I barked that like an order. Please forgive me. Let me rephrase that. I would really appreciate it if you would . . ." Walk away at that point and give the student time to reconsider your request.

2. If the request was reasonable, delivered respectfully but is still ignored, calmly and quietly ask the student why it is not being honored. If the student complies, fine. If not, decide whether it is really important for the student to comply. If it isn't, let it go. If it will negatively affect the student's grade, quietly tell him so.

If the request is important, concerns school rules or treating other people with respect, you may need to make an office referral.

PROBLEM: Cannot work cooperatively or in a group
INTERVENTIONS:

1. Change the group the student is in.

2. Talk with the student about why he or she misbehaves at these times.

3. Allow the student to work alone; do not force him or her to participate in a group activity.

PROBLEM: Has difficulty maintaining eye contact with others
INTERVENTION:

Discuss with your students the importance of eye contact. Explain that if you do not look some people in the eyes, they question your honesty. Employers, for example, may eliminate you from consideration for a job. Have students play a game, the aim of which is to maintain eye contact with their partner no matter what happens. Have students pair up, choosing their first partner. Give them something to talk about. They are to gaze steadfastly into each other's eyes. If the partner looks away, the other partner says "Beep." Students continue for the entire period (or length of time you've determined). There is so much beeping at first, that it is quite funny! Make the activity fun with lots of laughing. As students get better at maintaining eye contact, they can hear the beeping decreasing and interpret this as success.

PROBLEM: Student does not respond to positive reinforcement
INTERVENTIONS:

1. Once in a while you will find a student who does not work for positive reward. Talk to the student about this observation. Ask "Why?" Older students may not want to be perceived as a teacher's pet; a "macho" image, for example, may be undermined by positive strokes from a woman teacher.

2. These students may work to avoid loss of privileges.

3. Have a conference with the student and the parent. Explain the problem and ask for guidance.

STORAGE OF SST INFORMATION

At the end of the SST meeting, the chairperson sees that the parent has a copy of the group memory sheet, that another copy is placed in the student's cumulative file, and that the teacher has a copy. The parent is also given documentation sheets and an explanation of what to write.

The large group memory sheet is rolled up and stored until the next meeting.

FOLLOW-UP SST MEETINGS

From the 1970s through the 1980s, teachers were encouraged to get students who were having difficulties formally assessed and identified for special education services as quickly as possible.

Under the General Education Initiative's influence, the thrust is to bring all of regular education's resources to bear on the situation to see if the student can begin to make progress within the regular program. Special education referral is not considered until after the school has demonstrated it cannot meet the student's needs through regular education.

Each school has different resources. Schools in areas of low income tend to have greater resources, including special labs for reading improvement, extra aide time, extensive materials, and extra support personnel. These extra services are funded in large part through federal grants that seek to provide the disadvantaged student with an opportunity for learning. Schools in more affluent areas may have fewer resources. Therefore, it is up to each school to determine what resources are available for meeting student needs.

At follow-up SST meetings, it is *not* customary to make a referral for formal assessment if the student has begun to make progress as a result of the SST interventions. The interventions are continued for another period of time. The team may also decide to add additional goals.

If documentation shows that the strategies recommended by the first Student Study Team were routinely carried out but the student is not making progress, the team may recommend formal assessment, especially in those cases where it is fairly obvious there is a learning disability.

The SST should make every effort to be sure the child has been or will be checked for such things as hearing and vision problems. When an attentional deficit is clearly the problem, if the parent takes the child to a physician and gets the student medicated, sometimes that alone often leads to improvement in learning. While districts cannot force parents to give their children medication, parents seem much more likely to follow through on a physician referral during the SST process than after the child is accepted for special education services.

Likewise, attendance problems must be resolved before special education is considered. It is obvious that poor attendance impacts negatively on learning.

When all these issues have been taken into consideration, the team may proceed. A referral is made for assessment by the multi-disciplinary team, sometimes called the I.E.P. team.

THE ROLE
OF THE MULTI-DISCIPLINARY
TEAM IN ASSESSING THE
NEEDS OF STUDENTS

When P.L. 94-142 was passed, the role of the multi-disciplinary team was created. The team consists of the psychologist, the resource specialist, the nurse, an administrator, the child's teacher, and other personnel such as the adaptive physical education teacher, speech therapist, occupational therapist, and counselor if appropriate. The parent and student (if over 8) are an integral part of the team. Each person on this team has a part to play in pulling together the information needed to determine eligibility for special education service and in developing a plan for meeting the student's ongoing needs.

- The psychologist conducts the assessments and observations necessary to determine intellectual capacity and the existence of a learning disability.
- The resource specialist collects work samples and gives individualized academic tests to determine the child's current academic status/needs and may also observe the student.
- The nurse interviews the parent regarding the student's health history and gathers information regarding the student's early development and current health status including vision and hearing.
- The classroom teacher has important information regarding the student's behavior, motivation, and work habits.
- Parent and student input is solicited so that the final list of objectives developed for the student reflects the best thinking of all team members. Under both the collaborative-consultative Rsp model and inclusion, it is the classroom teacher who will be responsible for helping the student achieve the objectives. (The classroom teacher may ask for assistance from other special education personnel to do so.) If your school has not made the transition yet to these models, the Rsp may still be responsible for seeing the student works on the objectives.
- The administrator is in charge of allocating funds and overseeing the whole I.E.P. process.
- If the student appears to need services from the speech therapist, adaptive PE teacher, etc., these personnel conduct an assessment of the child's needs in their area of expertise and recommend additional goals.

It is important to mention here that a parent can request formal assessment, bypassing the SST process. As soon as the request for formal assessment is dated by the Student Study Team, or is requested in writing by a parent, timelines go into effect. Figure 6-1 shows a flowchart and those timelines.

Within a few days, the psychologist will meet with the parents to explain what assessment documents will be needed and answer questions about the assessment. If the parent gives written permission, the assessment proceeds. Once in a while a parent refuses permission and the request for assessment dies at this point. (This is far less likely to happen, however, when the parent has been a full participant in SST meetings.)

THE PURPOSE OF ASSESSMENT

The purpose of assessment is to help identify the student's strengths, needs, and learning characteristics. Assessment includes both formal and informal procedures. *Tests are samples of behavior;* they do not tell you how a child performs daily under classroom

Figure 6-1

FLOW CHART - REFERRAL

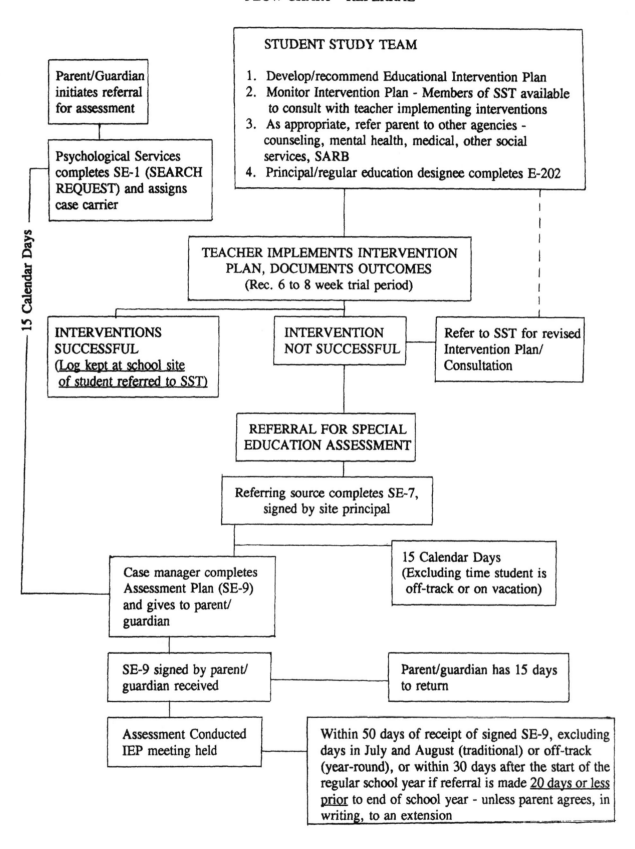

STUDENT STUDY TEAM

1. Develop/recommend Educational Intervention Plan
2. Monitor Intervention Plan - Members of SST available to consult with teacher implementing interventions
3. As appropriate, refer parent to other agencies - counseling, mental health, medical, other social services, SARB
4. Principal/regular education designee completes E-202

Parent/Guardian initiates referral for assessment

Psychological Services completes SE-1 (SEARCH REQUEST) and assigns case carrier

15 Calendar Days

TEACHER IMPLEMENTS INTERVENTION PLAN, DOCUMENTS OUTCOMES
(Rec. 6 to 8 week trial period)

INTERVENTIONS SUCCESSFUL
(Log kept at school site of student referred to SST)

INTERVENTION NOT SUCCESSFUL

Refer to SST for revised Intervention Plan/ Consultation

REFERRAL FOR SPECIAL EDUCATION ASSESSMENT

Referring source completes SE-7, signed by site principal

Case manager completes Assessment Plan (SE-9) and gives to parent/ guardian

15 Calendar Days
(Excluding time student is off-track or on vacation)

SE-9 signed by parent/ guardian received

Parent/guardian has 15 days to return

Assessment Conducted IEP meeting held

Within 50 days of receipt of signed SE-9, excluding days in July and August (traditional) or off-track (year-round), or within 30 days after the start of the regular school year if referral is made 20 days or less prior to end of school year - unless parent agrees, in writing, to an extension conditions. We must consider test scores in relation to other indicators, such as observations, work samples, and teacher judgment. Assessment also allows us to determine whether the student is eligible for services provided for under P.L. 94-142 (special education).

ELIGIBILITY FOR SPECIAL EDUCATION SERVICES

Eligibility for special education is dependent upon:

1. the existence of a learning disability or other handicapping condition
2. the existence of a severe discrepancy between ability and current achievement
3. the student's clear need for over/above services in order to make progress

The intellectual assessment reveals whether the child meets the conditions specified in #1 and the academic assessment deals with #2. The collective judgment of the SST decides issue #3.

THE INTELLECTUAL ASSESSMENT

Assessing IQ

The psychologist may choose from a variety of instruments to get a measure of an individual's intellectual functioning. The device chosen should be appropriate for the age of the student and free of cultural bias. Some of the more popular individually-administered instruments are explained here.

Stanford-Binet Intelligence Scale   The *Stanford-Binet Intelligence Scale* is the oldest of the tests mentioned here. It is well-standardized with acceptable levels of validity and reliability for ages 2 to adult, and renders standard scores. There are 15 subtests measuring vocabulary, bead memory, quantitative skills, memory for sentences, pattern analysis, comprehension, absurdities, memory for digits, copying, memory for objects, matrices, number series, paper folding and cutting, verbal relations, and equation building.

Wechsler Intelligence Scale for Children—Revised   The *Wechsler Intelligence Scale for Children—Revised* is probably the most widely used intelligence test for ages 6 to 16. It has been considered to have good standardization, coupled with adequate reliability and validity. The test has two sections:

1. *Verbal*—Subtests measure the student's knowledge of general information, similarities (ability to perceive the common trait in two words; for example, in what way are an apple and a banana alike?), arithmetic reasoning and computation, vocabulary (given a word, the student must define it), comprehension (the student is asked questions that require moral, social, and ethical judgments such as "What are you supposed to do if you find someone's wallet in a store?"), and digit span (the student is given numbers to repeat both forward and backward).

2. *Performance*—Subtests measure the student's ability to complete a picture that has something missing and to put a series of pictures in proper sequence. The block design subtest has a student look at a certain design and then build the design. The object assembly test involves solving jigsaw puzzles. The coding subtest requires the student (within a certain time limit) to copy geometric symbols that are paired with other symbols. Mazes require a child to visually plan in order to complete the mazes.

Kaufman Assessment Battery for Children   The *Kaufman Assessment Battery for Children* (K–ABC) is a newer device for children ages 2.6 to 12.6. There has been some concern about validity. In the 16 subtests the child is asked to perform tasks involving repetition of hand movements, number recall, recognizing and naming an object from a picture that is only partially drawn, spatial memory of several pictures, identifying letters and reading words, following directions that are read, and solving arithmetic problems.

Woodcock-Johnson Psychoeducational Battery   The *Woodcock-Johnson Psychoeducational Battery* (for ages 3 to 80) is divided into three sections. Section 1 measures cognitive ability. Students with learning disabilities tend to score lower on this cognitive section of the test than on the WISC–R. Subtests include identifying objects and actions, identifying pieces that go together to make a shape, memory for sentences, answering questions about arithmetic and symbols, and demonstrating a knowledge of synonyms, antonyms, and analogies. (Sections 2 and 3 of the *Woodcock-Johnson* are described later in this chapter.)

Columbia Mental Maturity Scale   The *Columbia Mental Maturity Scale* is a nonverbal assessment of the cognitive ability for children ages 3.6 to 10. Psychologists sometimes use this scale when they are not able to test youngsters with the preferred tests due to a physical or language impairment.

Learning Potential Assessment Device   The *Learning Potential Assessment Device* is a new nonverbal measure that uses a test–train–retest format.

Assessing Visual Perception

Visual perception is not to be confused with visual acuity. *Visual acuity* is how well the eyes *see*; *visual perception* refers to how the brain *interprets* what the eyes saw.

The most commonly used visual-perception tests are:

- *Bender Visual Motor Gestalt Test* (ages 5 to 11)
- *The Developmental Tests of Visual Motor Integration* (ages 2.11 to 14)

Each of these easy-to-give individualized tests involve having students look at a design and then copying it. While it is interesting to look at a given student's performance on these tests (a student's drawing sometimes shows remarkable errors in rotation, shape, integration, and perseveration), their value must be questioned. The tests show low reliability and validity. Since this is one of the areas that we use in determining eligibility for services, most psychologists continue to use these tests in spite of that recommendation.

Those who are observing students can frequently find observable evidence of the disability. When a child shows several or all of the following symptoms, it is reasonable to suspect a visual-perception deficit:

1. sloppy work (poor legibility/poor spatial planning, lots of erasures, difficulty when asked to draw a picture from a picture)
2. reversals of numbers (2, 3, 4, 5, 6, 7, 8; reversals of letters (b/d, p/q, s, c), and inversions of letters (u/n, w/m); these occur well past the age of 8
3. poor spelling; these students often show sequencing errors (all the correct letters but the wrong order)
4. poor directional sense (confuses left and right)
5. does not enjoy books
6. slower work production with no evidence of being off-task
7. needs more time to name known objects
8. some students have trouble planning/organizing in math; cannot copy problems accurately or arrange them neatly on paper; numbers in columns are misaligned; when using manipulatives to count, they will miscount unless they are taught to line items up linearly and to touch them as they count
9. poor motor coordination (awkward and clumsy)

Assessing Auditory Perception

Tests of auditory perception have come under the same kind of criticism as visual-perception tests. They are used less often than visual-perception tests.

Here are some of the most used tests:

- *The Auditory Discrimination Test* (ages 5 to 8)
- *Goldman-Fristoe-Woodcock Test of Auditory Discrimination* (ages 3.6 to 80)
- *Lindamood Auditory Conceptualization Test* (preschool to adults)

The assessment of a student's ability to process auditorially is often made informally. The psychologist carefully observes and records the student's responses on other tests. If a student asks for questions to be repeated, says "What?" or "Huh?" frequently, it may mean there is an auditory processing problem. When a child is asked to repeat a series of numbers and cannot, it may signal a processing problem.

The classroom observation gives clues as to whether students listen. Do they look at the speaker? Can they answer questions regarding the information just presented? Ask, "What was your teacher just talking about?" With LD kids, you usually get a shrug and have to probe with "Can you tell me any word that was said?" You will find that most LD students get almost nothing out of a lecture unless it is supported with pictures or word clues on the board or overhead. Other common difficulties include:

1. trouble repeating (mispronounce) words like chimney, spaghetti, particularly, magnificent, resonance

2. when given four spoken words such as *seed, need, peel,* and *feed*, they are not able to tell which word does not belong

3. their knowledge of phonetic elements is weak (cannot give you the sound of the short vowels, *c, g,* and blends such as *ou, oo, er*; may omit final consonant from spoken words, "ca" (cat)

4. if they come to an unfamiliar name in their reading, you tell them what it is and retell them each time they come to it, but they still continue to mess it up

5. slow auditory processing time; cannot follow ordinary conversation delivered at the regular rate

6. have difficulty recalling names of known objects ("you know, the round thing you eat" when he meant an orange)

7. may talk very slowly; slow to respond

8. fails to hear verbal directions

9. does not enjoy being read to

Assessing Memory

Psychologists sometimes look within the tests given to determine IQ for scores that reflect memory. For example, the *Stanford-Binet* contains a section for memory of sentences. The examiner reads a sentence, then the student repeats it—a task of auditory short-term memory. The test for bead memory asks the student to look at a picture of beads of various sizes and colors and then to reproduce it—a visual memory task. Likewise, the *Wechsler* subtest of digit span reflects auditory memory while the coding taps into memory. Although assessing memory is done within certain tests, it is not so good as giving a separate test, such as the following:

- *Visual Aural Digit Span Test* (VADS) (ages 5.6 to 12.11) is an easy-to-administer test of short-term visual and aural memory.
- *Learning Effectiveness Test (LET)* (ages 6 to adult) takes longer to give.

When a child displays several or all of the following behaviors, we must suspect memory deficits:

1. does not know personal information such as birthdate, address/phone number, what kind of work parent does

2. knows parts of nursery rhymes but not the whole rhyme

3. makes mistakes counting

4. cannot remember oral directions

5. loses things or forgets things that result in a problem for the child; for example, parent gets angry when coat is left at school, teacher takes a toy but the child forgets to reclaim it at the end of the day

6. teacher reports the student appears to know something but has forgotten it by the next day

7. fails to commit simple and frequently used words such as "is," "are," "come" to memory by the end of grade 1; fails to commit arithmetic facts such as 3 + 4 = 7 to memory by the end of grade 2
8. cannot remember the names of common objects
9. misspells his or her own name at the end of grade 1
10. still does not say alphabet correctly at end of grade 1 or cannot name all letters when presented randomly

Assessing Language

Research has made it very clear that students identified as having learning disabilities often have language deficits. If you ask teachers of LD students, they will tell you that roughly half of their LD students have deficits in semantics (knowledge of word meaning), syntax (how to put words together to form sentences) and pragmatics (getting the subtle meanings by skillful manipulation of language). Written expression is particularly difficult for the LD child.

It is puzzling to me that we do not routinely do a formal language assessment, particularly in the face of extensive research that shows this to be such a common problem. For example, it is at the heart of the dyslexic's problem.

It would be wonderful to see speech teachers working on language development with primary (grades K, 1, 2, 3) children—teaching them to listen more effectively, to follow directions, to use correct verb tenses, etc.

The observation of a student is very important in determining language. You want to look at:

1. *Work samples*—What is the nature of the response: Word? Phrase? Complete sentence? Compound/complex sentences? Check spelling and mechanics. Is syntax correct? What is the average length of the response?
2. *Observe utterances*—How many words? Syntactically correct? Are tenses of verbs correct? What is the extent of vocabulary? Does it exceed the most basic 500 words on a regular basis?
3. *Listening*—After the student listens to the teacher, ask "What did your teacher say?" You usually get a shrug. Probe by asking, "Do you remember any word she (he) used?" The child usually can repeat some of what was said.
4. *Student's informal conversation with peers*—Is it different than their conversation with adults? How?

The following are among the most widely used language assessment documents.

Peabody Picture Vocabulary Test—Revised The *Peabody Picture Vocabulary Test—Revised* (PPVT–R) is an old but popular measure of receptive language for ages 2.6 to 40.

Test of Adolescent Language—2 The *Test of Adolescent Language—2* (TOAL–2) has subtests that cover such areas as listening/vocabulary, listening/grammar, speaking/vocabulary, speaking/grammar, reading/vocabulary, reading/grammar, writing/vocabulary, and writing/grammar. It is for ages 12 to 18.6.

Test of Language Competence   The *Test of Language Competence* (TLC) is specifically designed to be used with students ages 9 to 19 who have language disabilities. Subtests measure understanding of ambiguous sentences, making inferences, recreating sentences, and understanding metaphoric expression.

Tests of Language Development—2   The *Tests of Language Development—2* (TOLD–2) come in two parts and hold great promise:

1. The primary test (ages 4 to 8) covers vocabulary, sentence imitation, word discrimination, and articulation.
2. The intermediate test (ages 9 to 12) covers constructing sentences, vocabulary, grammatic comprehension, and correcting nonsensical sentences.

Test of Written Language   The *Test of Written Language* (TOWL) allows us to evaluate students' written language at ages 3 to 8. It can be administered individually or to a group. It measures a child's knowledge of mechanics, spelling, thought units, and style.

Assessing Adaptive Behavior

In the course of your work you may be exposed to adaptive behavior scales. In California, they are sometimes used in lieu of intellectual testing. In 1979, as a result of a court decision known as the Larry P. case, districts were forbidden to give an IQ test to a black child. In order to assess cognitive functioning of some students, adaptive scales were used. They are also useful in assessing children who do not speak English, the mentally retarded, and the emotionally disturbed. They attempt to measure independent functioning and social maturity.

Some of the most frequently used are:

- *The Adaptive Behavior Inventory for Children* (ABIC) (ages 5 to 8)
- *The AAMD Adaptive Behavior Scale* (AAMD) (grades 1 to 8)
- *Vineland Adaptive Behavior Scale* (VABS) (ages birth to 18)

In all three tests, the child's functioning is assessed by asking pertinent questions of persons who are extremely well acquainted with the student. The ABIC is an interview with the mother that asks questions such as "Does the child bring notes home?" "Does he (she) get along with neighborhood children?" On the AAMD, the evaluator may question the student, the parent, or the teacher and will ask questions about the child's daily living skills. In addition, there is a section to evaluate maladaptive behavior that asks questions such as "Does (child) damage property?" The VABS interviews teachers and parents with questions similar to those presented.

A teacher's behavioral logs can also provide much information.

Assessing Emotional/Behavioral Problems

Many LD students have emotional problems. If the psychologist becomes aware of this in the course of the assessment, it is important for planning to know what seems to be happening. Some of the devices used to pursue this type of information are:

Burks Behavior Rating Scale The *Burks Behavior Rating Scale* is given to someone (teacher/parent) intimately acquainted with the child. It asks questions about attention, impulse control, social interaction, identity, aggressiveness, dependency, intellectuality, and academics. The *Burks* is used in grades 1 to 8.

Child Behavior Checklist The *Child Behavior Checklist* is filled out by parents of children aged 4 to 16. The checklist looks for serious emotional problems such as depression, social withdrawal, somatic problems, schizophrenia/obsessive tendencies, or aggressive tendencies.

The Devereux Scales The two *Devereux* scales are completed by the teacher and cover work organization, creative initiative, attitude toward teacher, and need for direction. The scales also ask for opinions regarding peer cooperation, anxiety, and more. The *Devereux Elementary School Behavior Rating Scale—II* is for grades 1 to 6; the *Devereux Adolescent Behavior Rating Scale* is for ages 13 to 18.

Piers-Harris Children's Self-Concept Scale The *Piers-Harris* is administered to students in grades 4 to 8 asking questions regarding behavior, intellectual/school status, physical appearance and attributes, anxiety, popularity, happiness, and satisfaction.

Minnesota Multiphasic Personality Inventory The *Minnesota Multiphasic Personality Inventory* is for students ages 16 to adult to help ferret out serious emotional problems.

Personality Inventory for Children The *Personality Inventory for Children* is one of the best instruments for interviewing parents to get an overall idea of the child's functioning. The inventory is for ages 3 to 16.

Conner's Scale The *Conner's Scale* has two parts: a rating scale that is filled out by the parent and a rating scale that is completed by the teacher. Scores obtained often pinpoint attention deficit, hyperactivity, conduct disorder, somatic problems, and anxiety.

The Academic Assessment

Normally, it falls to the resource specialist to do the academic assessment and observations of students referred to the multi-disciplinary team. It is relatively easy to do an observation; the hard part is finding time to do three or four observations. Under the collaborative-consultative Rsp model, you will be doing less teaching and tutoring, thereby freeing time to do more elaborate observations.

Classroom Observations

You will want to observe the student under a variety of circumstances, such as during a listening session, during a writing session, and at least once while participating with other students in an activity either on the playground or in a cooperative learning group. Generally, an observation will take no more than 15 minutes. It is a good idea to schedule observations ahead with the teacher through a personal contact. If the student is aware that he or she is being observed, it is unlikely you will get a true picture of his or her everyday performance; therefore, it is important that the teacher not "give it away." Let the teacher acknowledge your presence in the classroom by saying, "I asked Ms. Harwell to stop by and see what we are doing today. She may want to talk to you individually about what you are doing. She will make some notes about how we are doing this lesson." If I do not know the student whom I came to observe, at this point the teacher will assist me by laying her hand casually on the observee's shoulder as she ends her remarks. All of this can be done so naturally that students do not catch on.

You will want to appear to look at several students and their work, circulating around the room for a few minutes. Once the students have more than likely forgotten you are there, you may concentrate on the students in the vicinity of the observee so that every few seconds you can check what he or she is doing.

On an observation sheet, you will record what was observed. (See Figure 6-2 for a sample.) While I am in the observation classroom, the student's name is not put on the observation sheet; I add it as I leave. That way if I am careless and a student sees my clipboard, the student does not immediately know what I was doing.

In the observation writeup, you want to:

1. tell what the lesson was

2. tell what the student's responsibility was during the lesson

3. detail the student's degree of participation in the lesson and state how his or her participation compared with that of other class members

4. stick to the facts (i.e., if a student tears up his paper and throws it on the floor, you say "student tore up his paper and threw it on the floor" (a fact) rather than saying "student became frustrated and tore up his paper" (an opinion)

5. record verbatim any answers, questions, or comments made by the student

6. ask the teacher to evaluate/"grade" the student's work and give you a copy of the student's paper to attach to your report

7. ask teacher if today's performance was typical of usual performance

8. include a time-on-task report

Observable data may include:

- Statements about the way a student organizes his or her work. Did the student begin immediately or take time to make a preliminary draft? Did he or she look at what others were doing? Did he or she understand and follow the directions or need 1:1 teacher assistance to begin? Was paper spatially organized or messy as compared with those of others nearby?

- Statement regarding handedness and fine motor control.

- Statement about verbal fluency/signing fluency. Was the student able to communicate satisfactorily with peers/teacher?

- Statement of activity level. Was the student in his or her seat, sitting appropriately? Did the student complete the task?

- What skills were demonstrated in the lesson? If you sit between the observee and another student and ask what they are getting out of the activity, you have a pretty good gauge of what the observee comprehended as compared with a peer's comprehension.

Figure 6-2

SAMPLE OBSERVATION SUMMARY

Student ___Shelley Cute___ Grade ___2___

Date ___11-15-95___ Time ___9:15___ Length of Observation ___20 min.___

When I entered the room, the teacher was reading a story to the class. The students were supposed to follow along in their books using a book marker.

Shelley sits in the back of the room. When I walked by her, I noted she was not even on the right page. During the balance of the reading, Shelley looked around—not at the book. (As I circulated, 26 students were in the right place, 5 were not, including Shelley.)

The teacher told the students to pair up and "Buddy read." They were to reread the section just read to them. Shelley's partner had to tell her at least 50% of the words. Shelley shut her book and said to her buddy, "You read it to me. It's too hard." The buddy read to her slowly, pointing at each word as she read it. Shelley looked at the book as her partner helped.

I asked Shelley to retell the story to me. She said, "Some elves made shoes." I asked, "What else happened?" Pointing at the picture of the shoemaker, she said "They made clothes for the elves."

I asked her why she said the story was too hard. She said, "I don't read very good." I asked if she would read a bit to me. (See attached sheet for her miscues. She got 98 out of 153 words right—64%.) When Shelley comes to a word she doesn't know, she usually guesses something that begins with the same initial sound but that may not make sense. She goes ahead instead of trying to self-correct. She did seem to try harder when reading to me than when reading to her buddy.

The teacher reports this is typical of her daily performance and that her spelling is "atrocious." She showed me the paper and it was totally dysphonetic. (See spelling paper—see right hand column for what words were dictated.) The teacher reports the mother is a single working parent who works P.M.s (gone 2:00-11:30). The two children get themselves up and dressed for school. Shelley does not always comb her hair and sometimes looks totally disheveled. Shelley says the babysitter, who is 16, helps her with homework. On days off, Shelley reports her "mom goes to see her boyfriend." Shelley and her brother are left home with a babysitter or at the grandmother's house. When asked if anyone reads to her, Shelley said "No." The teacher is concerned about the poor quality of the homework that is returned. The classroom aide works with Shelley 1:1 for 15-20 minutes a day "because Shelley never understands the verbal directions and just sits until someone shows her what to do."

Questions to be answered:
— Does Shelley have an adequate grasp of receptive language?
— What can be done to increase time she spends reading to someone?
— What is parent's expectation of Shelley?
— Is Shelley adequately supervised/can parent help at home?
— Why is Shelley so frail? Pale?

- Clues about level of language functioning (quotes), knowledge of previously taught skills, and general information level.

- Perceptional speed. Does the student respond quickly or slowly? Are responses on target or off base?

- Statement concerning the status of grooming, allergies, etc. Be careful about what you say. Instead of saying, "The child is filthy" or "She stinks," you can say "His hands and face were dirty" or "She had an odor." The latter statement, when shared with the parent, may lead to information, such as she wets the bed or the child hates to bathe. If the problem is something that can be worked on, such as teeth brushing or hair brushing, ask the parent if it would be helpful for the school nurse to work with the child daily on grooming skills. Parents will sometimes tell you they aren't home when the child gets up to supervise the grooming and would appreciate the nurse's help.

While the primary purpose of an observation is to look at the student in the learning setting, occasionally you will pick up other helpful information. For example, we had a boy in kindergarten who was driving the teacher "nuts" by displaying inappropriate behaviors—dropping his pants, pretending he was urinating by his stance, and making mouth noises. Unconsciously, the teacher was reinforcing these behaviors by stopping her lesson when the boy did these things and saying "Look at that!" Immediately, the child became the center of everyone's attention. This was a child who adored attention—good or bad. We had to work with the teacher on ignoring the behavior. (The aide would whisk the child out of the room to the principal's office where he would be isolated for 30 minutes, with absolutely nothing to do. Except for a periodic reminder that it was not proper to pull his pants down in class, he was ignored.)

Doing a Time-on-Task Assessment

Using two strips of paper marked off into ten slots, you observe two students (the observee and another student [the controlee] whom the teacher reports as an average student.) *Time-on-task is defined as time engaged (looking at) with the task.* Look at the observee for ten seconds. If he is looking at the job, mark +; if not, make a note as to what he is doing. For the next ten seconds, watch the other student and mark her strip. Now, using slot #2 watch the observee again for ten seconds and mark his strip. Do the same for slot #2 of the controlee's strip. Continue until you have done all ten slots for both students. If the student has 4 pluses, the time-on-task behavior for the sample observation is 40% (4 x 10). Figure 6-3 shows a sample time-on-task observation sheet.

A final word about observations. It is a good idea to do each observation on a different day and to vary the time of day as well, because student performance varies from day to day. Sometimes a child is fine in the morning but falls apart after lunch.

Formal Testing for Academic Assessment

Public Law 94-142 states that more than one measure of performance will be obtained. It is suggested you do two tests each in math, reading, and spelling and get at least two writing samples.

If your training did not prepare you to give academic tests, contact your local program specialist or special education director. Public Law 94-142 says that testing will be

Figure 6-3

SAMPLE TIME-ON-TASK SHEET

Time-on-task observation   1:15 P.M.   3-13-95   Joe Doe, grade 3

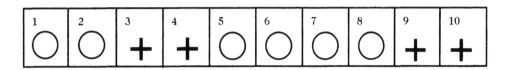

1. looking around
2. sharpening pencil
3. wrote name and one problem
4. on task
5. talking

6. rummaging in desk
7. erasing
8. talking
9. on task following teacher redirect
10. at end of 10 minutes, Joe had completed 3 problems (2/3 correct—1 copying error)

Time-on-Task Rate 40%

Time-on-task observation   1:15 P.M.   3-13-95   control student

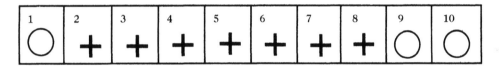

1. looking around
2. wrote name/heading
3. on task
4. on task
5. on task

6. on task
7. on task
8. on task
9. raised hand, waiting
10. at end of 6 minutes, student had completed all 10 problems (9/10 were correct)

Time-on-Task Rate 70%

done by "trained" staff, so your local support staff will find someone who will show you how to give the tests. Do not be embarrassed to ask; many new Rsps and special day class teachers have never had this training.

Read test manuals carefully and completely. They provide essential information about what you can do and what things you should not do. To become a good tester, you will need to watch someone give the test, and then have at least two opportunities to give it yourself under supervision. Watch how they handle the materials. Make notes of what they say to students and the speed at which they talk. If you have questions about what they did, write the questions and ask the testers after they finish the test. Be certain you learn how to score the tests properly. If not scored accurately, it could harm the student as well as make you look careless.

There are many tests from which to choose. (See Figure 6-4.) The most frequently used tests are described here. All of these tests are individually-administered tests.

Wide-Range Achievement Test—Revised   The *Wide-Range Achievement Test— Revised (WRAT–R)* measures the student's ability to spell (total recall), recognize words presented in isolation, and to compute. Its weaknesses lie in the fact it doesn't measure a student's reading comprehension, ability to reason in math, or to express him- or herself in writing. Its value is that it is quick to administer, requires little testing skill, and the grade-level scores it renders fairly accurately reflect a student's functional academic level. The WRAT–R is for ages 5 to 74.

Peabody Individual Achievement Test   You will want to validate the scores obtained on the WRAT–R by giving other tests that do give a more comprehensive picture of the student's functioning. One such test is the *Peabody Individual Achievement Test* (PIAT), which tests the areas missed on the WRAT-R. Scores obtained on the PIAT tend to be somewhat higher than on the WRAT-R or the *Woodcock-Johnson* described next. This may be due in part to the PIAT's mutiple-choice format. The PIAT is used for grades K to 12.

Woodcock-Johnson Psychoeducational Battery   Section 2 of the *Woodcock-Johnson Psycoeducational Battery* offers a comprehensive look at a student's skills in letter/word identification, word attack, passage comprehension, calculation, math applications, science, social studies, dictation, and proofing. Section 3 delves into the student's interests. For ages 3 to 80, this test comes with a computer program for scoring.

The Brigance Inventories   *The Brigance Comprehensive Inventory of Basic Skills* is for children in grades K to 9 and *The Brigance Inventory of Essential Skills* is for students in grades 4 to 12. Both are very comprehensive measures of student achievement that, when analyzed for errors, provide much information about what a youngster needs to learn.

Informal Reading Inventories

There are several ways to informally assess a child's reading level. One method is to take a graded word list such as the Dolch List or Fry List and give the child a copy of the same list. Sit so the child cannot see how you are marking the list (+ for a correct answer, — for an incorrect answer). Ask the child to say each word. You can help the child stay in the right place by furnishing a marker and having the words numbered. If the child gets the first half of the list right, you can try him or her on the next (harder) list. Periodically say "Good" or some other form of encouragement so the student does his or

Figure 6-4

CHART OF ACADEMIC ASSESSMENT INSTRUMENTS	
Oral Language	• language sample • Gilmore Oral Reading Test • Diagnostic Assessment Battery
Listening Comprehension	• Spache Reading • Diagnostic Assessment Battery
Written Comprehension	• Test of Written Language (TOWL) • work samples • Kaufman Test of Educational Achievement 2 (K–TEA) • Woodcock-Johnson (spelling) • Wide Range Achievement Test (spelling) • Peabody Individual Achievement Test (spelling) • Diagnostic Assessment Battery
Basic Reading Skills	• Peabody Individual Achievement Test (PIAT) • PIAT—Revised • Woodcock-Johnson • Woodcock-Johnson—Revised • Brigance Inventory of Essential Skills • Brigance Comprehensive Inventory of Basic Skills • Durrell Analysis of Reading Difficulty • Gilmore Oral Reading Test • Gray Oral Reading Test—Revised • K–TEA • WRAT–R
Mathematics	• Key Math, Key Math—Revised • WRAT–R (computation only) • Brigance • Woodcock-Johnson • Woodcock-Johnson—Revised • PIAT, PIAT—Revised • K–TEA

her best. If the student seems perturbed because he or she realizes a word has been missed, say "I don't expect you to get every word right." If a student cannot get a word after looking at it for 10 seconds, say, "Try the next one." If the child misses the word on the first try, it is counted wrong even though the child self-corrects. The reason for this is the student may be reading your face and realizing when he or she is wrong.

You can have a student read 100-word passages (do not count proper names as part of the 100 words) from the text for his or her grade level. Circle any word missed unless the student self-corrects. Do not mark proper names as being missed. When a student misses a word, you want to write what the student actually said above the circled word. In analyzing a student's errors, we can frequently discover clues to where his or her understanding of the reading process breaks down. A reader has the following three levels:

- *Independent Level/Comfortable Level*—the student gets at least 95 percent of the words correct.
- *Guided Level/Instructional Level*—the student gets between 80 percent to 94 percent of the words correct.
- *Frustration Level/Failure Level*—the student identifies less than 80 percent of the words correctly.

If the student is identifying less than 80 percent of the words, you can locate the student's comfortable reading level by moving to a slightly lower grade level. Keep moving down a grade level at a time until you find one where he or she is reading at the 95 percent level.

If the student is going to work alone, you will need to assign the student materials at his or her comfortable reading level. If the student will be working in a group with the teacher or a peer teacher, you may give him or her materials at the guided level. If the material that must be used is at the student's failure level, someone will have to read to the student.

THE HEALTH ASSESSMENT

As part of the assessment process, someone must discuss the student's health status with the care-giver. This function is often assumed by the school nurse, who checks the student's vision and hearing acuity. If health problems exist that will markedly affect the student's ability to benefit from extra assistance, the optimal time to work on these is during the assessment process. Once children have begun to receive services, parents sometimes feel less compelled to follow up on recommendations. This is especially true in the case of attentional disorder. The question always arises, "Can a district insist on a parent following through on getting or giving medication for this condition?" As the law currently stands, the answer is *no*.

THE SOCIAL ASSESSMENT

This area needs to be consistently addressed at I.E.P. meetings. Often, if there are no glaring signals, it is overlooked. The parent, child, and teacher are the primary persons to consult on these issues.

SAMPLE MULTI-DISCIPLINARY ASSESSMENT REPORT

Figure 6-5 offers a sample psychoeducational assessment report.

Figure 6-5

PARADIGM UNIFIED SCHOOL DISTRICT
MULTI-DISCIPLINARY TEAM PSYCHOEDUCATIONAL ASSESSMENT REPORT

Name: Ronnie Gladson
Birthdate: 9/24/86
Age: 8.6
Grade: 2
School: Panacea Elem.
Student#:00000001

Parents: Aunt Merry Gladson
Assessment Date: 3/95, 4/95
Primary Language: English
Language Used for Assessment: English
Ethnicity: White
Examiner: James Forthwright

Reason for Referral
School History
The teacher reports that Ronnie is low in all academic subject areas. He may have memory deficits. He is slow in retrieval of known information. He may have visual perception deficits. He may have attentional deficits; his body is in constant motion. He is usually well-behaved at school and is accepted by his peers.

Summary of Interventions and Modifications of Regular Education Program
The school staff reports they have made the following interventions and/or modifications of the regular educational program:
—retention in kindergarten, placed in grades 1 and 2
—parent/teacher conferences
—extra one-on-one help from teacher and aide on letter recognition in grade 1
—worked in "at-risk" program for reading under Rsp supervision; daily one-on-one assistance for 20 minutes using materials at his functional level in grade 2
—peer buddy
—3 Student Study Team meetings
Although many interventions have been attempted within the regular education program, little or no changes in Ronnie's skills have been evidenced.

Effects of Environmental, Cultural, or Economic Factors
English is spoken in the home. Current ethnic designation for this student is white. The family has adequate financial resources to meet basic needs. No adverse environmental, cultural, or economic factors are apparent at the present time. Ronnie lives with his maternal aunt, Merry Gladson. Ronnie has attended one school in this district. He has been at Panacea School for three years. He was retained in kindergarten. School experience has been normal. School attendance has been regular. Ronnie has a history of slow progress in school. During grade 1, Ronnie had five discipline referrals for name calling and pushing kids around. He has had no referrals this year although he still engages in this behavior occasionally.

Health and Developmental Information
3/30/95   The school nurse reports that vision was 20/30 in both eyes and hearing was passed at 25dbl.

3/30/95 The aunt reports that health and developmental history was unremarkable. Ronnie has lived in her home since birth. He weighed 8lbs 4oz. Developmental milestones were within normal limits. Adaptive behaviors appear to be average. The aunt reports him to have average social/emotional behaviors at home.

According to the aunt, Ronnie's mother abandoned the family when he was two months old and has not been heard from since. Additionally, she believes Ronnie's mother was using drugs on and off during the pregnancy. The aunt says no one is sure who the father was.

Previous Assessment Results

5/94   Underline: First Grade I.T.A.S.

Reading comp.	55 percentile
Reading total	26 percentile
Language total	13 percentile
Math problems	35 percentile
Math total	34 percentile
Reading/Language	15 percentile
Total Battery	19 percentile

Observation Results

4/6/95

When I entered the room, a cooperative learning project was going on. Students were to draw a kind of light and tell what the light was "good for." Ronnie and his partner were talking. Ronnie drew a sports shoe with lights on the back. (See attached drawing.) The shoe is well-drawn, proportional with good attention to detail, i.e., laces, grommets, and sole. Ronnie was not able to read any of the words his partner wrote to explain what the lights were good for.

As I circulated to ask several students about their work, I noted the teacher had put notes on the board. The class had had a discussion about what kinds of things they might write. One of the words on the board was "light." Ronnie's partner had used it more than once. When I asked Ronnie how he would spell the word, he said "lit." He did not realize it was still on the board.

The teacher had students get up and orally talk about what they had done. Ronnie got through it largely because his partner stood behind him telling him what to say. While other students were explaining what they had done, Ronnie sat staring off into space, rocking his chair on 2 legs.

The classroom aide called Ronnie to the back of the room to do the spelling test. He got only 3 out of 10 words right despite having written them 5 times each on Monday night, putting them in alphabetical order on Tuesday night, and using each in a sentence on Wednesday night. Ronnie is tested one-on-one as an accommodation because "he needs more time than most kids to take the test."

The Rsp has seen Ronnie 20 minutes a day (in the morning before school) four times a week, one-on-one for a year. Even under these conditions, Ronnie is quite distracted. He is a fidgeter, constantly fooling with objects. If you remove all objects, he will go to cracking his knuckles. He has had extensive training in phonics, yet when confronted with a new word, he does not approach it phonetically until reminded to do so. Ronnie makes it very clear he does not want to read: "Do I have to?" When told yes, he does so but negotiates throughout the reading session, "Can I go now?"

The teacher reported to the observer that Ronnie is in a "dreamlike state." Homework is done sporadically.

Test Behaviors

Ronnie was friendly, cooperative, active, restless, fidgety, off-task, and slow to respond to the examiner's requests during the evaluation. Ronnie has average oral communication skills in English. He was polite and well behaved. He has average social skills. Ronnie was observed to have great difficulty on paper-and-pencil tasks. On the Bender Gestalt Visual Motor Test, Ronnie rotated the paper, counted and recounted the dots, erased designs again and again, and was impulsive with his responses to the task. These behaviors are indicative of a neurological involvement and possible ADHD-type behaviors.

Tests Administered

Intelligence Measures

4/6/95   Stanford-Binet Form L-M
         C.A. 8.6   M.A. 9.0   IQ 101

Achievement Measures

4/7/95   *Wide-Range Achievement Test—Revised (WRAT–R)*

Test	Raw Score	St. Score	%ile	G.E.
Reading	35	57	.5	1B
Spelling	26	63	1	1M
Math	23	93	32	3B

4/8/95   *Peabody Individual Achievement Test*
         Administered by Rsp Connie Dogood

Test	Raw Score	G.E.	%ile	S.S.
Math	25	2.3	19	90
Reading Rec.	24	2.0	17	89
Reading Comp.	20	2.0	7	87
Spelling	23	2.0	12	82
Gen. Info.	15	1.6	1	65

4/8/95   *Writing Samples*
         Estimated grade level range: 1B-1M

Memory Measures

4/6/95   *Visual Aural Digit Span Test (VADS)*

Aural-Oral	25	Aural Input	25
Visual-Oral	50	Visual Input	25
Aural-Written	50	Oral Expression	25
Visual-Written	25	Written Expression	50
Total VADS	25	Intrasensory Integ.	25
VADS A.E.	7.0-7.5	Intersensory Integ.	50

Perceptual Motor Measures

4/6/95   *Bender Gestalt Visual Motor Test*
         C.A.: 8.6   A.E.: 6.0-6.5
         Emotional Indicators Detected: B.I. = 8

Language Measures

4/6/95	Receptive Language	8.0 (CABS)
	Expressive Language	8.0 (CABS)
	Expressive Vocabulary	8.0 (Stanford-Binet)

Adaptive Behavior Measures

4/6/95 *California Adaptive Behavior Scale (CABS)*
C.A.: 8.58   Adaptive Age: 9.83

Emotional/Behavioral Measures

4/7/95 *Piers-Harris Children's Self-Concept Scale*
R.S.: 69   %ile: 91   Total test: Above Average

4/6/95 *Bender Gestalt Motor Perceptual Test*
E.I.: 2
1) poor impulse control
2) possible acting-out behavior

4/7/95 *House-Tree-Person (H-T-P)*
E.I.: 2
1) poor impulse control
2) immaturity

3/31/95 *Conner's*

CPRS-48 (T scores)		CTRS-28 (T scores)	
Parent Form		Teacher Form	
Conduct Problem	50	Conduct Problem	69+
Learning Problem	80*	Hyperactivity	65
Psychosomatic	55	Inattentive/Passive	58
Anxiety	50	Hyperactivity: Index	67
*referable score		+nonreferable score	

Discussion of Assessment Results

Cognitive/Developmental/Intellectual

Current cognitive skills were assessed using the Stanford-Binet, yielding an overall IQ score of 101. AMA of 9-0 was obtained based on a chronological age of 8.6. A basal was obtained at year 8, and a ceiling at year 11. Expressive vocabulary falls at a year 8 level.

Academic Skills

WRAT–R scores reveal the following standard scores: 57 Reading, 63 Spelling, 93 Arithmetic. Phonic skills appear not to be developed, and letter-sound associations appear not to be developed. Ronnie is basically a non-reader. He is able to identify correctly all the letters of the alphabet and read a few simple one-syllable words such as "cat," "see," "to," "big" using a whole-word recall approach rather than any word attack skills.

Ronnie can print his first name correctly but is unable to print his last name. He can spell a few simple grade 1 words such as "boy," "in," and "will." Ronnie can print a sentence using four words. "I like to play" with the letter p reversed. Ronnie's area of strength is math. He can do 3-place addition and subtraction with regrouping.

Perceptual and Motor Skills (gross and fine)

Gross motor skills appear to be within normal limits. Visual motor integration, based on the Bender Gestalt, are at a 6.0 to 6.5 age level. Errors were noted in the areas of rotations, distortions, integrations, and perseveration. Ronnie took 10 minutes to finish the test; average time is 5 minutes. Fine motor skills appear to be below average for Ronnie. He reverses letters and is inconsistent in forming his letters, ranging from a small presentation to a large presentation of letters.

Processing and Memory Skills

Ronnie does have weak short-term auditory and visual memory processing skills, yet is not significantly delayed. Overall test scores place him at the 25th percentile in these skills areas or with an age equivalent of 7.0 to 7.5 years (VADS). Ronnie does have some intra-individual memory strengths in Visual-Oral and Aural-Written with scores at the 50th percentile or normal level.

Language Skills

Ronnie has clear speech. He has average oral communication skills. He has average vocabulary skills.

Adaptive Behavior (home and school)

Current adaptive behavior was assessed using the CABS, yielding an adaptive age of 9.83, falling within normal ranges.

Social/Emotional (home and school)

Ronnie's social and emotional functioning falls within normal limits. Current projective testing does not reveal any significant emotional indicators for his age. Self-esteem is considerably above average with no significant deficits in his profile. The Conner's Scales indicate the aunt believes Ronnie to have a learning problem more than possible hyperactivity. The teacher reports no significant referable scores on his report; however, he does have near significant scores in the area of attention and hyperactivity. Both aunt and teacher do not see Ronnie as a conduct problem. Ronnie can be inattentive, off task, impulsive, restless, and have poor test competition. These behaviors may be related to possible ADHD and his learning disability.

Prevocational/Vocational Skills

Ronnie has age-appropriate personal information about himself and other family members. He knows how to write his first name correctly. He can say his address, the days of the week, his age, grade, and the month and day of his birthdate. He performs routine chores at home.

Summary

Ronnie is a second-grade boy with average potential, yet has significant delays in his reading and language arts skills with respect to expected levels of achievement. His strength subject area is in math. When he chooses to do his work, he is able to experience academic success in this skill area with current skills at or above his current grade placement. Ronnie has significant delays in his visual perception and fine motor skills that are currently impacting adversely on achievement. Ronnie's memory-processing skills—while weak—are not significantly delayed, but need to be kept in mind by the school staff. Ronnie does have some behaviors of a child with attentional deficits that may be adversely affecting his performance in the classroom. Ronnie has normal adaptive behaviors, language development, gross motor skills, and normal social/emotional functioning for his age.

Currently, there is a severe discrepancy between his potential and his achievement. This discrepancy exists in the areas of written expression, basic reading skills, and reading comprehension. The specific learning disability appears to be in the areas of visual processing and sensory motor skills.

Statement of Eligibility

This discrepancy is not primarily the result of limited school experience or attendance. This discrepancy is of such a severe nature that it cannot be remediated completely in the regular classroom. Ronnie meets California State Department of Education guidelines for placement.

Recommendations

1. It is recommended that the multi-disciplinary team needs to determine educational services needed.

2. Additional recommendations include:
   —modify assignments
   —extend time to complete his assignments
   —preferential seating
   —oral presentation of assignments and tests
   —a multisensory approach to teaching new tasks
   —more drill on spelling words at appropriate level
   —repetition of directions
   —immediate feedback regarding assignments
   —auditory-visual presentations of directions and assignments when possible
   —use concrete manipulatives
   —be consistent in behavioral expectations; make sure the student understands the natural consequences of inappropriate behavior (less freedom, loss of privileges, referrals, staying after school)
   —allow student to be a leader of a group/peer tutor when he has mastered a skill
   —try to provide student with as many social/academic opportunities as possible
   —refer to the family physician for possible ADHD

School Psychologist, Report Coordinator

7

THE ROLE
OF THE MULTI-DISCIPLINARY
TEAM IN DEVELOPING
THE I.E.P.

When the assessment process is complete, the members of the multi-disciplinary team convene to review the information garnered with the parents and the teacher and to look at the resources available to meet the student's needs. The meeting usually begins with the various team members giving the results of their observations and assessments. Sometimes it sounds like everyone is talking in a foreign language as terms such as standard deviations, standard scores, percentile ranks, and grade/age equivalences are thrown around—to say nothing of such other terms as norm-referenced tests, criterion tests, and curriculum-based assessment.

Understanding the Jargon

When test scores are discussed in an I.E.P. team meeting, if you are not sure what they mean, ask the psychologist for an explanation. Others in the meeting may not understand either and will be glad you had the courage to ask.

When a child takes a test, it is customary to count the number of correct responses. The number obtained is called the *raw score*.

If the assessment given was a *norm-referenced test*, such as PIAT–R or WRAT–R, the student's performance on the test will be compared with the performance of other students who have taken the same test. The student's performance may be described in terms of *percentiles*, grade or age equivalents, or standard scores. On a norm-referenced test, a score of the 50th percentile is average (meaning that half of the children scored higher and half lower). A child with a percentile rank of 50 is doing average work for his or her grade or age. Those children who qualify for special education services tend to have scores below the 10th percentile.

If the score is given as an *age-equivalent*, what does it mean? Let's say that on the Bender Gestalt Test, a child who is actually 9 years old receives an age-equivalent score of 5.6 years. This means the child is functioning on that skill like a child at age 5.6. With learning disabled children it is not uncommon to find a child with a discrepancy of one to three years in the areas of memory, language development, or visual perception.

On the PIAT–R Achievement Test, for example, a child's performance will be given as a *grade equivalent*. The student may be in sixth grade but he or she made a 3.2 score. This means the student is able to perform at the level expected of a child in the third grade, second month of school.

You may come across a test that produces *stanine* scores. Stanines are ranked from a low of 1 to a high of 9 with 5 being average.

Intelligence tests produce scores that are plotted along the normal curve. The *mean* is obtained when the scores of a large group of students of the same chronological age are added together and then divided by the number of students in the group. It is the average score of the group. The mean for IQ is 100. Statistically, 68% of students will obtain scores that fall between +1 or -1 standard deviation (15 points) of the mean. (See Figure 7-1.)

Figure 7-1

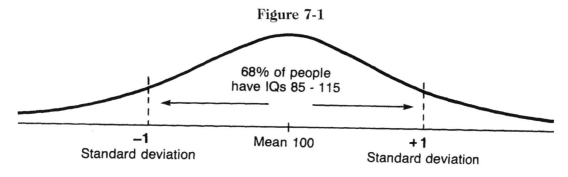

123

Figure 7-2

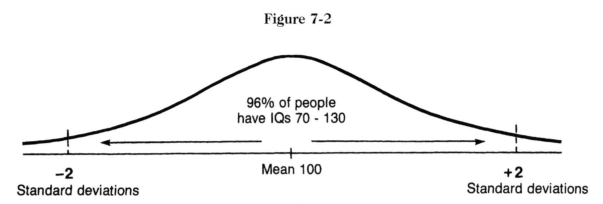

96% of people
have IQs 70 - 130

−2
Standard deviations

Mean 100

+2
Standard deviations

Ninety-six percent of people have IQs that fall between -2 standard deviations and +2 standard deviations of the mean (IQs of 70 to 130). (See Figure 7-2.) Thus, we classify IQ ranges as shown:

130+	Very superior	about 2% of the population
120-129	Superior	about 7% of the population
110-119	High average	about 16% of the population
90-109	Average	about 50% of the population
80-89	Low average	about 16% of the population
70-79	Borderline	about 7% of the population
Below 69	Mentally retarded	about 2% of the population

Some tests have scores that express the student's performance in *standard scores*. The WISC–R, and the Woodcock-Johnson batteries (all have a mean of 100 and a standard deviation of 15) are easily compared. *How much must the discrepancy be between IQ and standard score for a student to qualify for special education services?* If a student gets a standard score of 85 on an achievement test and the child's IQ is 100, the child is one standard deviation below his or her expected level. Does that student qualify for assistance from special education? To answer that question, the following explanations must be offered.

THE DISCREPANCY MODEL

Federal regulations state there must be a severe discrepancy between ability and achievement for special education eligibility to exist. The amount of that discrepancy, however, varies somewhat from state to state because federal regulations do not spell it out. In general, it seems to be 15 to 20 points.

Naturally, since it is not spelled out, there are some inequities. For example, a child in West Virginia with a 12-point discrepancy may be receiving services while a child in Georgia is denied services because Georgia requires a 20-point discrepancy.

EXCLUSIONARY SITUATIONS

QUESTION: Can a child who is mentally retarded be learning disabled? ANSWER: Technically, no. Mental retardation is a handicapping condition in its own right. You will often find children who are having much difficulty in school; they are two or three years behind grade level, but they do not qualify for special education because their IQs fall between 75 and 84 (too high to qualify for service under the mental retardation category). Their achievement is low, but it is not significantly below what would be expected based on their lower potential and they do not qualify for services under P.L. 94-142. They may, however, fall under the umbrella of Section 504.

QUESTION: Can a student who is mentally gifted be learning disabled? ANSWER: A resounding yes. These students may qualify for assistance from special education if their achievement is not commensurate with their ability. Unfortunately, if they are able to meet minimum grade standards, they never get referred, never get identified, and often remain underachievers for life.

QUESTION: Can a student who is emotionally disturbed be learning disabled? ANSWER: There are youngsters who are both LD and disturbed. Emotionally disturbed youngsters who show no learning disability should not be placed in LD classes.

QUESTION: Can students with medical conditions be learning disabled? ANSWER: There are students who have medical conditions and learning disabilities. In these cases, the I.E.P. team must carefully analyze where and how the student needs to be served.

QUESTION: Can a student who is culturally deprived or who is a low achiever be served? ANSWER: There are no clear guidelines. These students may show the severe discrepancy and may have low receptive/expressive language due to environmental influences. I.E.P. teams must carefully look at each child's situation. The decision lies with the team and the policies of the school district.

ASSESSMENT SCORES AND THEIR IMPLICATIONS FOR LEARNING

When younger, I put more stock in assessment scores than I do now. I have seen students with high IQs and mild disabilities (who should be expected to do well with extra help) make minimal progress, and I have seen kids who appeared to have every strike against them surprise all of us. Student motivation and parental involvement can work miracles.

Assessment scores represent an approximate baseline. We predicate our expectancy for the student on them. We teach and work with the student, parent, and classroom teacher as diligently as possible; we eagerly await the result of the annual assessments/triennial assessments, and teacher and parent feedback to let us know what progress the student is making. Once in a while, a student will astound everyone and get caught up. More often, though, our students—once identified—continue to need assistance for the remainder of their school years. The research suggests that most LD students show less than a year's gain for each year of instruction, which results in a cumulative deficit (Deshler, Schumaker, and Lenz, 1984).

For most LD students, achievement patterns look like Figure 7-3. Note that the achievement of LD students does not rise much in the last three years of high school.

Figure 7-3

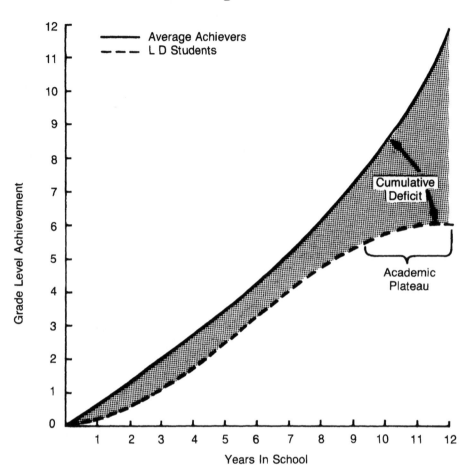

Chart from W.N. Bender, *Learning Disabilities, Characteristics, Identification and Teaching Strategies* (Boston: Allyn & Bacon, 1992) Reprinted by permission of Allyn & Bacon.

There are some details of the WISC–R of which you need to be aware. The WISC–R uses *scaled scores*. Scaled scores run from 1 through 19, making 10 the average. Scaled scores above 13 represent a superior ability; scaled scores below 8 indicate the student will probably not be able to keep up even with extra help. The profiles in Figures 7-4 and 7-5 will help you interpret what scaled scores tell you.

The profile shown in Figure 7-4 is that of a learning disabled student. Note the scatter of the scores, ranging from a low of 7 to a high of 13. In the classroom, the teacher often picks up on the student's strengths and weaknesses. The teacher may think that because the student is so capable in some areas, the child is just not trying in others. LD students typically have normal IQs and this intertest scatter.

Figure 7-4

Verbal		Performance	
Information	7	Picture Completion	13
Similarities	10	Picture Arrangement	10
Arithmetic	8	Block Design	10
Vocabulary	8	Object Assembly	10
Digit Span	10	Coding	10
Verbal IQ = 94	Performance IQ = 104		Full Scale IQ = 98

The profile shown in Figure 7-5 belongs to a youngster who has a severe language disability. This student can run the classroom projector and computer even when the teacher can't, but he has trouble expressing himself orally and on paper. He is miserable in school and, at the age of 12, says he will quit as soon as he can. Fortunately, his father owns an automotive shop and is already teaching his son to change oil and do simple automotive repairs.

Figure 7-5

Verbal		Performance	
Information	6	Picture Completion	12
Similarities	5	Picture Arrangement	8
Arithmetic	6	Block Design	11
Vocabulary	3	Object Assembly	11
Digit Span	4	Coding	13
Verbal IQ = 68	Performance IQ = 106		Full Scale IQ = 85

If you see a profile where all scores are in the 6, 7, 8 range, the student probably is a slow learner. Unlike the learning disabled, there are no areas of strength. If all scores are below 5, the student is retarded. If all scores are above 10 and many are over 14, the student may be gifted.

In assessment we do not confine ourselves to norm-referenced tests. There are *criterion-referenced* tests that frequently prove valuable in what the student needs to learn. These tests compare a student's performance to a set of skills to be mastered. For example, can the child correctly add two digits to two digits? The Brigance inventories are examples of criterion-referenced tests.

By using a process called *task-analysis*, the teacher can determine where the student's understanding broke down. For example, in the addition problem below, the teacher notes the child can add problems that do not involve regrouping, but misses problems involving carrying because the child doesn't know which number to carry. The teacher may want to use manipulatives to teach place value.

$$\begin{array}{r} \overset{3}{2}6 \\ +\ 37 \\ \hline 81 \end{array}$$

Finally, the newest assessment device is the *portfolio*. The teacher collects samples of student work over a period of time, thereby showing the student's progression in understanding. The portfolio is an example of *curriculum-based assessment*. It may contain daily papers, commercially made tests such as those in social studies and science books, or teacher-made tests. In curriculum-based assessment, the student's performance is not measured against that of other students; rather, it reflects the gains the child makes.

THE INDIVIDUAL EDUCATION PLAN

If the student qualifies for special education assistance and the parent agrees to a placement, a legal document called the I.E.P. is developed. It will:

1. give a statement of the student's present levels of educational performance based on norm-referenced and criterion-referenced tests
2. contain a statement of annual goals and short-term objectives stated in behavioral terms
3. contain a statement of the specific education and related services that will be provided
4. state the extent to which a child will be able to participate in the regular education program and the support services needed within the regular program

If you cannot carry out the plan as written, you are obligated to call the parents in for a special review and together to revise the plan in writing.

"Delivery of Services" Models

Once the I.E.P. team determines a student is eligible for special education services and *needs* them in order to make progress, then it must decide how the child's needs would be best served. This truly is a very individualized decision requiring the best professional judgment of the entire team. Each school and each district has different services available; try to do what will most benefit the child.

Keeping in mind the "least restrictive environment" requirement, the I.E.P. team must recommend a placement. The parent then will either agree to that placement or reject it. The placement options include:

1. Student is placed in a regular classroom with a consultative teacher providing assistance to the classroom teacher.
2. Student is placed in a regular classroom for the majority of the day, but attends a resource room pull-out program for specialized instruction in deficit skill areas.
3. Student is placed in a special education classroom for the majority of the day, but is "mainstreamed" out for subjects he or she can adequately manage.
4. Student is placed in a full-time special education class in a regular school.

5. Student is placed in a special school (may include residential facilities for handicapped).

6. Student is homebound or hospitalized with hospital instructional services provided.

NOTE: Most students can be served in settings #1 and #2.

The "Least Restrictive Environment" Decision

One of the most crucial decisions made by the I.E.P. team is where to place a student. Many factors must be looked at. We want to choose the setting that will be motivating, meaningful, and pleasant for the child. When children are initially identified, we tend to try to keep them in the mainstream. In choosing a classroom, we need to consider teacher acceptance, teaching style, teacher training, teacher flexibility, and behavioral management skills. The team must discuss its recommendation with the parents and child. It is critical that they agree with the recommendation for it to work.

The "Number of Hours" Issue

After deciding where a child would be best served, a decision must be made about the number of minutes or hours the child will need direct assistance from special education personnel.

When children are being served in regular class, you must consider how much help is available in that room, the talents of the staff, and how much the child requires from special educators to begin to make progress. The best way I found to estimate the number of hours is to address each objective separately, deciding who is responsible for that goal and how much time it will probably take daily to meet each objective. Then you can total up the minutes that will be required from special education.

If an Rsp student is seen in pull-out, his or her time in pull-out may not exceed 49 percent of the school day. Most Rsp students can be served adequately in programs of one to two periods a day (50-minute periods).

When placing children in special day class, you want to consider what portion of the day they could spend in the mainstream; the classes most often mainstreamed include art, music, P.E., science, and social studies. Be sure to cover this subject on the I.E.P. forms.

Writing Objectives

The type of objectives written will be influenced by the setting where the student is placed, by whom the student will be served, and by the student's needs. If the student is in setting #1, the objectives will strongly resemble the regular class curriculum. In other words, the student should be capable of benefiting from the skills taught there without making excessive demands on the regular teacher's time or the time of the Rsp. If the student's skills are below the instructional range of the grade (for example, in a fourth-grade class, the instructional range is about 3.0–3.5), then the student will probably need some resource room help because he or she lacks the prerequisite skills to do the regular classroom assignments; therefore, objectives would reflect skills found in the curriculum at a lower grade (the child's functional level). We want to do whatever we have to to get the student into making steady progress.

Academic Objectives It is customary to write short-term goals and long-term goals. (See the sample I.E.P. in Figure 7-6 at the end of this chapter.) An example of a short-term goal might be:

> By 1-31-96, on 3 consecutive days, Andrea will recognize and name 50 words not known on pretest when they are presented randomly.

The long-term goal might read:

> By 6-10-96, on 3 consecutive days, Andrea will recognize and name 100 words not known on pretest (including the 50 named above) when they are presented randomly.

NOTE: Andrea might move before the objective is achieved, so put a list of the words in her folder for the new teacher's information.

As you will note, the I.E.P. objective states clearly:

- a time line for achievement
- an easily measurable goal
- the accuracy expected
- how the goal is to be measured; i.e., orally or written
- who is responsible for teaching the goal
- what materials will be used

You want to write your objectives so carefully that anyone else looking at them knows exactly what to do.

Here is an example of an ambiguous goal:

> Andrea will get 75% of her spelling words right.

You don't know if this means once every week. You don't know if Andrea takes the regular class words or a modified list. Is she to write them or can she spell them orally?

You want to write a sufficient number of goals so the student will make progress. There have been lawsuits won because too few objectives were written. If reading and writing are deficit areas, they will impact negatively on the student's ability to complete assignments in other areas, such as science and social studies, so you may need to write goals for these areas. For example:

> By 1-31-96, Andrea will take 3 social studies chapter tests orally achieving an average score of 70%. Andrea may have a copy of the test to study at home for a period of 15 school days before each test.

A possible objective in science might read:

> By 1-31-96, Andrea will write the answers to 3 chapter tests (open book) by using key words and the index to locate the answers. She may have the help of the classroom aide or teacher who will read the material to her once she locates the correct page.

Some teachers do not want to make accommodations and modifications for special education students. These teachers will insist that every student must take the same test under the same conditions. These teachers have sometimes lost in court and been required to pay damages.

If your district wants the I.E.P. to reflect a vocational objective, the one that follows is an excellent example:

> By 1-31-96, when given a set of 3 oral directions, Andrea will be able to repeat them in the order given.

Behavioral Objectives

There are many students whose I.E.P.s will require behavioral goals. If a student has a Behavioral Contingency Plan, these goals are a must. It is important to write goals that are measurable and, if possible, do not rest on the subjective opinion of the classroom teacher. One such goal might read:

> By 1-31-96, Michael will decrease the number of office referrals he gets by 50%. (September, 1995 baseline was 8 referrals.)

Behavioral objectives are a bit more difficult to write, but help is available in a book entitled *The Source Book: Behavioral I.E.P.s for the Emotionally Disturbed* by Sherry Crane and Judy Reynolds, published by Crane/Reynolds, Inc., 10203 Oak Point, Houston, Texas 77043; 713-984-0688. Many of the objectives are relevant to the behavior of LD students. *The Source Book* will assist you in clarifying the nature of the problem and then give you a list of several behavioral goals/objectives. You can choose one that best seems to fit the situation.

Modifications and Accommodations

By making modifications or accommodations to help students succeed, we should be able to maintain more students in the regular classroom and prevent them from dropping out. Some of the students now being served in special classes can be moved back into the mainstream. The I.E.P. has a great deal of latitude in recommending adjustments to what we will teach and how we will teach it as well as what standards a student must meet to be considered successful. In the area of discipline every effort is made to accommodate the youngster and help him or her adjust satisfactorily. The classroom teacher and special education staff will need to work hand-in-hand to find what works for each student.

The services that the collaborative-consultative Rsp and special education staff in inclusion settings can provide to the regular classroom teacher include:

1. providing alternative assignments/materials at the student's functional level; alternative homework if needed
2. observing the student and offering suggestions
3. teaching learning strategies to the class
4. training peer tutors
5. using one-to-one feedback to identified students on results of their work as time permits
6. training parents in ways to help
7. coordinating services for a student
8. alternative testing of students (giving oral tests, helping with open-book tests)
9. offering crisis-intervention services if a behavioral problem erupts
10. diagnosing and prescribing
11. assisting the classroom teacher with special projects as time permits
12. assisting "at-risk" or LD students (tutorial mode)

NOTE: Other suggestions for modifications and accommodations will be offered in the later chapters regarding the teaching of subject matter.

In education today, we seem to be moving away from rigid standards/methods and discipline to which students must conform to a position where students progress at their own rate and pursue education from their own interests and strengths. The emphasis is definitely on the individual. Signs of this shift are the current emphasis on the thinking curriculum, discipline with dignity, curriculum-based assessment and portfolio assessment, changes in retention policies, dropping of proficiency standards for promotion, and the recognition of multiple intelligences. Will these changes improve the results we get? Will students be better prepared for their roles as adults? Will they be more tolerant of individual differences? Of course, these are the outcomes we hope for. The future of public education is on the line.

Dissenting Opinions

Occasionally, a member of the I.E.P. team does not agree with the recommendations made and feels so strongly about it that that person does not want to sign the I.E.P. If this occurs, it is this person's right to state his or her objection in writing. This is called a dissenting opinion, which becomes part of the student's record. *Do not agree to something you have no intention of doing.*

Differential Standards—Promotion, Placement, and Retention

This is probably one of the least understood parts of the I.E.P. On the I.E.P. we write objectives the student is to achieve. If the student achieves them, he or she is "promoted on differential standards." If the student does not meet them, the I.E.P. team (with parent present) needs to be reconvened. The team reviews the student's progress and program. This is a *special review* and minutes of the team's deliberations are recorded on the forms normally used for I.E.P. meetings. The team can decide to "place" the student in the next grade or retain him or her. Research on retention shows retention in kindergarten and grade 1 may be beneficial when there are maturational delays, excessive absence, or a divorce; however, rarely does retention help after that. If retention is to occur, it is beneficial to counsel parents (fathers seem to have more problems with retention than mothers, so talk with dads) to the effect that the child did not "fail" but rather needs an opportunity to be re-exposed to the curriculum because he or she "was not ready" the first time. It is absolutely essential that if retention is decided upon, provision be made by the school for extra one-to-one help during the second exposure. Retention in later grades can be very detrimental to a child's self-esteem. Therefore, the team will generally recommend placement unless the parent is adamant that the child be retained. At this meeting, it is wise to review and possibly write new objectives.

Once in a while you will have a student make enough progress to meet regular standards. If this happens, the wording used is "promoted on regular standards," even if the student did not complete all I.E.P. objectives.

THE ANNUAL I.E.P. REVIEW AND THE TRIENNIAL REVIEW

After being identified for services, the child's progress will be reviewed every year and a meeting held with the parents. Generally, the whole I.E.P. team is not involved. Usually the special education teacher reviews the student's progress by giving the same formal tests used for the original placement, reviewing the child's portfolio. Attendees at the annual meeting minimally are: an administrator, the special education teacher, the parents (and child if over 8), the regular class teacher (if there is one), and any other special education personnel giving services to the child, such as speech therapists, etc. The same paperwork is completed as at the first meeting with parents receiving copies. The parent is told what objectives were met and new objectives are written for the next year.

The Law provides that every three years, the full team be involved in reassessing the student's progress and eligibility at a triennial I.E.P.

EXITING A STUDENT FROM SPECIAL EDUCATION SERVICES

If a child no longer qualifies for assistance (there is not a severe discrepancy between achievement and potential), the full I.E.P. team is reconvened. Exiting paperwork addresses why the student is being exited with good supporting documentation (such as test scores, a statement from the regular class teacher, etc.) and whether there is eligibility under Section 504 regulations. (If so, the SST receives notice of its responsibility to provide future service.)

Figure 7-6

INITIAL PLACEMENT [ ]	TRIENNIAL [ ]	**INDIVIDUALIZED EDUCATION PROGRAM**	MIS NUMBER

INITIAL PLACEMENT [ ]   TRIENNIAL [ ]   **INDIVIDUALIZED EDUCATION PROGRAM**   MIS NUMBER `O O O O O O`

INTERIM [X]   SPECIAL / REVIEW [ ]   [X] RESIDENT SCHOOL **Panacea**   ATTENDING SCHOOL **Panacea**

ANNUAL [X]   TRANSITION [ ]   DATE OF MEETING **10-17-95**

PUPIL NAME **Helpful, Andrea**   D.O.B. **10-2-85**   AGE **10.0**   SEX **F**   GRADE **4**   ETHNICITY **W**

ADDRESS **207 Any Street #A, Somewhere, Calif**   HOME PHONE / BUSINESS PHONE **none**

NAME OF [X] PARENT/ GUARDIAN [ ] SURROGATE PARENT [ ] FOSTER PARENT   **Sharon Helpful**

ENROLLMENT DATE `1 0 0 6 9 4`   ENROLLMENT CODE `1 2`   ANNUAL IEP DATE `1 0 1 7 9 5`   NEXT REVIEW `1 0 9 6`   3 YEAR `1 0 9 7`

PUPIL LANG. **English**
HOME LANG. **"**

FLUENCY [ ] LEP / NEP [X] EO
[ ] FEP [ ] U

[ ] NEED INTERPRETER
[ ] OTHER MODE OF COMMUNICATION

PROFICIENCY STANDARDS
[ ] REGULAR STANDARDS
[X] DIFFERENTIAL STANDARDS (CHECK BELOW)

	READING	LANGUAGE	MATH
ELEMENTARY	X	X	X
JUNIOR HIGH			
GRADUATION			

ALTERNATE MODE OF ADMINISTERING MINIMUM PROFICIENCY
[X] READ TEST TO STUDENT
[ ] SIMULATED PERF
[X] EXTENDED TIME PAPER & PENCIL TEST
[ ] ORAL
[ ] DIRECT PERFORMANCE
[ ] BRAILLE
[ ] OTHER

TRANSPORTATION
[ ] 1 [ ] 5
[ ] 2 [ ] 6
[ ] 3 [ ] 7
[X] 4

LOW INCIDENCE [ ]

HANDICAP		
090 - SLD [X]	060 - SED [ ]	030 - DEAF [ ]
111 - EMR [ ]	080 - OHI [ ]	050 - VI [ ]
010 - MR [ ]	110 - MH [ ]	130 - TBI [ ]
040 - SLI [ ]	070 - OI [ ]	120 - AUT [ ]
	020 - HH [ ]	100 - DB [ ]

DESIGNATED INSTRUCTIONS

	BEGIN	EXIT	BEGIN	EXIT
SPEECH 50		PARENT / INFANT - 61		
HOME HOSPITAL 51		OTHER		
APE - 52		OTHER		
VOC ED - 63		OTHER		

RECOMMENDATION FOR INSTRUCTIONAL SETTING BASED ON STUDENT NEEDS

ANTICIPATED DURATION OF IEP: **1 yr.**
PROJECTED DATE OF INITIATION **on-going**
HRS/WK

PRESENT	CONSIDERED		PLACEMENT
420	**420**	410 — DESIGNATED INSTRUCTION & SERVICE	**420**
		420 — RESOURCE SPECIALIST PROGRAM	
		430 — SPECIAL DAY CLASS	
		440 — NON-PUBLIC SCHOOL / AGENCY	
		450 — HOME / HOSPITAL	
		— EXTENDED YEAR	

1 - 3

GENERAL ED. PROGRAM **27 - 29** HRS / WK

EXIT DATA

EXIT DATE _____

[ ] 70 - RETURNED TO REGULAR CLASS
[ ] 71 - REG STAND GRADUATION
[ ] 72 - DIFF STAND GRADUATION
[ ] 73 - MAXIMUM AGE REACHED
[ ] 74 - DROPPED OUT
[ ] 75 - EXPELLED
[ ] 78 - PARENT WITHDRAWAL
[ ] 80 - MOVED

ANTICIPATED SERVICES
[ ] [ ] [ ] [ ] [ ]

PRESCHOOL ONLY (3 - 5 YEARS)
[ ] INTENSIVE   [ ] NON-INTENSIVE

☒ Meets   Title 5 eligibility criteria for Special Education.
☐ Does not Meet

BUSSING RATIONALE: **Walks**

For Specific Learning Disability Identification Only

	YES	NO
1. Child has a Specific Learning Disability?	[X]	[ ]
Child qualifies for Special Education?	[X]	[ ]
Child needs Special Education?	[X]	[ ]

2. The IEP team finds that a severe discrepancy exists between ability and achievement as a result of a disorder in:
☐ Attention   ☐ Visual Processing   ☐ Auditory Processing   ☐ Sensory-Motor Skills   ☐ Cognitive Abilities
(including association, conceptualization and expression). This is not the result of limited school experience
or poor attendance and is not correctable without special education and related services.

3. Educationally relevant medical findings present (if any specify): _____   [ ] [X]

4. Effect of environmental, cultural, economic disadvantage (if "yes" specify): _____   [ ] [X]

5. Relevant behaviors based on observation and relationship of that behavior to academic functioning _____
needs encouragement to "try", reluctant to take risks

Figure 7-6 continued

UNIFIED SPECIAL EDUCATION LOCAL PLAN AREA

INDIVIDUALIZED EDUCATION PROGRAM

NAME Helpful, Andrea   BIRTHDATE 10-2-85

DATE 10-17-95

IEP SUMMARY AND RATIONALE FOR PLACEMENT IN SPECIAL EDUCATION PROGRAM:

IEP Team met this date for annual review of Andreas progress and to review needs. Results of assessments were reviewed. Andrea met all her 1994-95 goals. She has made good progress w/ Rsp support. She has been seen 45-60 min a day 4x a wk in a pull out program (Resource Rm) for development of basic skills in the areas of reading, writing and math. She can now function w/ some help within the instructional range of her grade so for the 1995-96 school year she will receive service primarily in regular classroom. Pull-out service will be reduced to less than 2 hours per week.

Mother reports Andrea is beginning to read for pleasure.

The classroom teacher modifies her assignments by either shortening them, altering them to fit her functional level, allowing her to take oral or open book tests. The teacher reports Andrea still needs one-to-one help to get started on assignments (she doesn't always understand directions). She is well-behaved in class.

Andrea remains eligible for sp. ed. services Rights were explained. New goals were written

PARENT CONTACT FOR IEP CONFERENCE

10-1-95	letter
M/D/Y	METHOD
10-8-95	ph call
M/D/Y	METHOD
M/D/Y	METHOD
M/D/Y	METHOD

I certify that this report reflects my conclusion.

Tom Wakefield 10-17-95   _Sally Nice_ 10-17-95
SPECIAL ED. TEACHER   M/D/Y   REGULAR ED. TEACHER   M/D/Y

Georgia Stern 10-17-95
ADMINISTRATOR   M/D/Y   OTHER - SPECIFY   M/D/Y

OTHER - SPECIFY   M/D/Y   OTHER - SPECIFY   M/D/Y

PARENT APPROVAL
My signature indicates that I consent to the individualized Education Program placement, and my rights to appeal have been explained to me

X _Mrs. Sharon Helpful_ 10-17-95
SIGNATURE OF PARENT   M/D/Y   SIGNATURE OF PUPIL   M/D/Y

135

Figure 7-6 continued

INDIVIDUALIZED EDUCATION PROGRAM
UNIFIED SPECIAL EDUCATION LOCAL PLAN AREA

NAME _Helpful, Andrea_ BIRTHDATE _10-2-85_

DATE _10-17-95_

SUMMARY OF PRESENT LEVELS OF STUDENT PERFORMANCE AREAS

ACADEMIC SKILLS (Reading, Math, Spelling): _WRAT-R 10/95_
Reading 2m   Spelling 2m   Math 2E
BAT-R 9/95
Read. Rec. 2.7   Read Comp 2.8
Spelling 3.2   Math 2.6
Writing Sample approx. 2.0-2.5

PSYCHOMOTOR SKILLS (Auditory/Visual Perception, Fine/Gross Motor):
Visual perceptual delays
memory deficits - visual memory
is somewhat better than auditory.

Language, Communication: _Andrea can communicate_
adequately orally. Her written
communication is delayed (errors
in syntax, mechanics, spelling)
Low in semantics (wd meanings & use)

PRE-VOCATIONAL & VOCATIONAL SKILLS
(Awareness of Self, Exploratory Information, Work Experience): Knows personal
information, can count $, tell time
Says she wants to be a nurse
or an animal doctor

HEALTH-PHYSICAL DIAGNOSIS:
Acc. to mother, Andrea's
general health is good.
Attendance is good
Vision & hearing are normal

SELF-HELP SKILLS (Functional Skills, Independent Skills, Activities & Daily Living):
Grooming - done independently
Chores - " w/ encouragement
Homework - requires 1:1 supervision
of parent to get it done.

SPECIAL ADAPTATION SKILLS (Cooperation, Attention, Organization, Social Acceptance, Responsibility):
Cooperative; quiet
Socially accepted
Responsible - takes notes home, tries
Mild attention problems

PHYSICAL SKILLS (Motor Performance, Fitness):
adequate for reg. PE

OTHER:

GENERAL P.E. [X]   ADAPTED P.E. [ ]

MODIFIED P.E. [ ]   ADAPTED P.E./COLLABORATION [ ]

SPECIALLY DESIGNED P.E. [ ]

Description of Activities to Integrate Pupil Into Regular Education Program:

Specific Activity &/or Instructional
Delivery Model   Hours Per Week/Day

Collaborative -   20 min in reg M-W-F
Consultative Rsp   Classroom 3x a wk
Pullout Resource Rm   45min -60min 2x T-Th

Describe Activities Provided to Support Transition of Pupil From Special Education to Regular Education Program: Classroom teacher reviews assignments
daily. Andrea gets regular assignments (shortened/extended time) if she can
do them. Alternate assignments are given at her functional level
for homework

136

Figure 7-6 continued

UNIFIED SPECIAL EDUCATION LOCAL PLAN AREA

INDIVIDUALIZED EDUCATION PROGRAM   NAME _Helpful, Andrea_   BIRTHDATE _10-2-85_

DATE _10-17-95_

Short Term Objectives	Person(s) Responsible For Implementation	Hours Per Week	Methods, Materials and Activities	Evaluation
By _1-31-96_ the student will demonstrate an increased competency in: GOAL – _reading_ OBJ: _After listening to a story read and discussed, Andrea will write a summary of the story (at least 5 sentences)_	_Reg teacher_		_Houghton-Mifflin Gr 4 test. Andrea will read her summary aloud to teacher_	Achieved ___ Not Achieved ___ METHODS OF MEASUREMENT ☑ Observer ☐ Teacher Made Test ☐ Standardized Test ☐ CR Test ☐ Other
By _1-31-96_ the student will demonstrate an increased competency in: GOAL – _reading_ OBJ: _Andrea will orally read aloud 15 min daily to her mom and 15 min 2x a wk to Rsp at her functional level_	_Parent/Rsp. 3_		_Library books, Multiple skills, any appropriate material, immediate feedback if she makes errors_	Achieved ___ Not Achieved ___ METHODS OF MEASUREMENT ☐ Observer ☐ Teacher Made Test ☐ Standardized Test ☐ CR Test ☒ Other _Parent/Rsp read material read_
By _1-31-96_ the student will demonstrate an increased competency in: GOAL – _voc. dev._ OBJ: _Given 15 words taken fr. classrm reader, Andrea will match them w synonyms w 100% acc and use 10 correctly in oral sentence_	_Reg teacher classrm aide_		_flashcards, daily practice_	Achieved ___ Not Achieved ___ METHODS OF MEASUREMENT ☐ Observer ☒ Teacher Made Test ☐ Standardized Test ☐ CR Test ☐ Other _check word usage in sentence_
By _1-31-96_ the student will demonstrate an increased competency in: GOAL – _Social Studies/Science_ OBJ: _Andrea will write the answers on each chapter test to 5 questions w 80% acc_	_Classroom teacher_		_open book test may use class notes. If not able to read may have help from aide or teacher_	Achieved ___ Not Achieved ___ METHODS OF MEASUREMENT ☐ Observer ☐ Teacher Made Test ☐ Standardized Test ☒ Other _test decoding or teacher_ ☐ CR Test
By _1-31-96_ the student will demonstrate an increased competency in: GOAL – _multiple predict math_ OBJ: _Given 20 problems of the type practiced daily (including 4 story prob) Andrea will write the ans w 70% acc on final test_	_Reg teacher_		_daily practice_	Achieved ___ Not Achieved ___ METHODS OF MEASUREMENT ☐ Observer ☒ Teacher Made Test ☐ Standardized Test ☐ CR Test ☐ Other

137

MAKING THE CHANGES
REQUIRED BY THE REGULAR
EDUCATION INITIATIVE

Whenever there is a major shift in special education philosophy, it is always followed by a period of uncertainty, frustration, and experimentation. If you are feeling a bit unsure of yourself concerning the implementation of the collaborative-consultative Rsp model or the Inclusion classroom, you are not alone. In this chapter, I will describe how it is happening in my local area (California).

IMPLEMENTING THE COLLABORATIVE-CONSULTATIVE MODEL

Resource specialists (Rsps) met and were encouraged to move into the collaborative model. The model was briefly described; i.e., Rsp youngsters would be served primarily in regular classrooms with pull-out reserved for only those youngsters who absolutely could not make gains in the regular classrooms. (Figure 8-1 shows a copy of the suggestions we received at that meeting.)

Rsps returned to their schools and began to work with principals on a local site plan. The most successful programs seemed to develop in those schools where the principal exercised a leadership role by actively inservicing teachers about the change, encouraging teachers to work with Rsps and providing release time for Rsps and classroom teachers to jointly plan.

Figure 8-1

ON-SITE PREPARATIONS FOR THE COLLABORATIVE-CONSULTATIVE RESOURCE SPECIALIST MODEL PROGRAM

1. Confer with site administrator to plan a workable site program.
2. Initiate an awareness of the collaborative-consultative model with parents and staff.
3. Describe your school site's plan to teachers at a regularly scheduled staff meeting.
4. Contact each teacher for a needs assessment (any services teachers desire).
5. Develop a workable draft schedule with input from teachers. (Remember to be flexible.)
6. Implement program:
   — start gradually
   — select one agreeable teacher and expand as the level of success increases
   — plan with classroom teacher the most appropriate days, time slots, and services
   — be aware of on-site procedures and scheduling of other school support programs
   — whenever possible, stay within classroom for the complete lesson
   — remember to consult requirements of I.E.P.

The Roles of the Rsp and the Regular Classroom Teacher

After working in this model, most districts now realize there is a need for some fine-tuning to make the program work more effectively. There are two areas of recommended change.

First, we need to have classroom teachers assume primary responsibility for the progress of *all* the students assigned to their class. This will mean rewriting many I.E.P.s so they reflect what is actually being taught in the classroom and shifting the responsibility for the teaching of most objectives to the classroom teacher and aide. When regular teachers do accept responsibility, it is likely the following things will naturally occur:

1. They will truly see SST meetings as problem-solving sessions.
2. There should be less push to get kids identified and a greater willingness to work with "at-risk" students.
3. Teachers will welcome any help the Rsp can give to help them get the job done.
4. Teachers will want to learn special techniques to use with these children.
5. Teachers will include handicapped children more fully in all classroom activities, giving more thought to how to reach them through each lesson.
6. Teachers will thoughtfully share in the development of the I.E.P. objectives.
7. Better results will be obtained because the written objectives will more nearly match the regular class instruction, curriculum, and expectancies.

Second, across the nation Rsps have functioned like tutors. This needs to be changed because it is not the best use of their training and time. Rsp tutors can assume this function, freeing the Rsp to observe students; diagnose and prescribe for their needs; demonstrate for classroom teachers strategies that work (coaching them until they feel comfortable); teach students strategies for educational success; consult with parents and community workers; provide inservice to staff; train peer tutors and other tutorial persons; work with students who have difficulty adjusting to regular standards or who have learning deficits that require the skills of a specialist; and keep up with the paperwork required by P.L. 94-142 and Section 504.

With these two changes, the roles of the Rsp and classroom teacher become complementary rather than parallel. They are working toward the same end, but there is no duplication of services. In their joint planning, the old adage of "Two heads are better than one" should provide for a broadening of ideas for helping students. Because the Rsp is not confined to teaching, that person can take care of things that have in the past required teachers to work evenings (for example, conferencing with parents or making alternative assignments).

IMPLEMENTING THE INCLUSION MODEL

Starting an inclusion program requires a longer period of preparation than the shift in the Rsp model because the Rsp students are already in regular classes and their handicaps are somewhat milder.

Districts across the country are wrestling with the question, "Should all special day class students be candidates for inclusion or should this be done on a case-by-case basis?" The Council for Learning Disabilities (CLD) issued this statement in April, 1993:

> "The Council supports the education of students with LD in the general population when deemed appropriate by the Individual Education Program (I.E.P.) team. Such inclusion efforts require the provision of needed support services in order to be successful. One policy that the council CANNOT SUPPORT is the indiscriminate full-time placement of *all* students with LD in the regular classroom, a policy often referred to as 'full inclusion.' CLD has grave concerns about any placement policy that ignores a critical component of special education service delivery: Program placement of each student should be based on an evaluation of that student's individual needs. The Council CANNOT SUPPORT any policy that minimizes or eliminates service options designed to enhance the education of students with LD."

Despite this note of caution, many districts are moving forward into full inclusion. In an article entitled "On the Nature and Change of an Inclusive Elementary School," the authors describe how one school district decided that every class would eventually be an "included" class. The school began by integrating eight students with disabilities into kindergarten. The second year, first grade and kindergarten became inclusion classes and so on until all the classes were inclusion classes. The kindergarten teacher described the first year as being "overwhelming" despite having the assistance of the special education teacher and her aides (Salisbury, 1993).

Other schools have begun by fully including special education students in regular classes for one to three hours a day. If it is to be one hour, the subject most often chosen seems to be science. Students are usually paired or work in teams with regular students to do hands-on experiments.

Some districts ask for teacher volunteers to take inclusion classes. Other districts simply assign special education students to a class and then inform the teacher that the child is coming. As you can imagine, the assimilation seems to be easier for everyone when the teacher volunteers.

How many children can be integrated into an inclusion class? Here, again, there are no set guidelines. The number ranges from a single student to as many as half the class. In speaking with teachers of these very integrated classes, they say the most important variables are who is in the class and how well do they adapt. The students who are most easily assimilated, they say, are those who have appropriate work habits, respect others and their property, follow school rules, and do not have severely disruptive behaviors. This reply suggests that inclusion is not an appropriate model for all students. These teachers report also that it is essential the special educator be on-hand and serve as a co-teacher.

The steps given in Figure 8-2 might be helpful in implementing inclusion.

Inclusion teachers say they do a lot of cooperative-learning activities and assignments where students have a wide choice of ways to express their learning. In one class where half of the students are handicapped, the teachers do a lot of peer-buddy instruction, whereby each nonhandicapped student is a mentor for one handicapped student.

Figure 8-2

On-Site Preparation for the Inclusion Model

1. When you want to volunteer to begin an inclusion program, confer with the site administrator.
2. The site administrator will notify the special education department.
3. Locate a partner with whom to team.
4. Work out the details of the program with your site administrator, team partner and special education department. Order any special supplies needed.
5. Initiate an awareness of the model with staff at several regular staff meetings.
6. Hold meetings with parents and students who will be involved. Be sensitive to their feelings. No child should be compelled to participate in the class. Rewrite I.E.P.s, if needed, to reflect change of setting.
7. Hold meetings with auxiliary staff—aides, counselor, librarian, computer lab, yard duty personnel—who will be involved with the program.
8. Implement the program.

Teachers take two weeks to prepare students for how this model should look and to role play how to work cooperatively, giving encouragement. (Two students in this particular class who did not wish to be mentors were moved to another room.)

In talking to regular class teachers who have done inclusion, they express a need for more information on handicapping conditions and special techniques, and for daily release time for planning with special education staff. They express great concern for special education youngsters who lack basic skills (barely reading or writing, or functioning far below grade level in math) and feel special education staff must teach these skills because the students need so much one-to-one help.

Where pairs are used (one handicapped to one nonhandicapped), they suggest you try to pair students who will complement each other skill-wise; if this is not possible, they should have something in common (two shy kids working together or two who live near each other). The teachers caution against overusing the nonhandicapped students to help the special education students lest their educational growth be compromised.

The teachers also feel that when they agree to work in an inclusion situation, class size must be adjusted downward.

The Role of Special Education Personnel in the Inclusion Classroom

Again, there is no set way to do this. What transpires depends on the style of the individuals involved. The most frequently seen pattern is where two teachers share the teaching duties based on their perceived strengths and interests. Usually, one aide floats to watch for and prevent misbehavior while the other aides or helpers give help to individual students. Some teachers ask for students who want to serve as peer assistants and who are assigned one or two special education students to assist.

Sometimes the class breaks into groups to do different assignments together. The number of students in each group may vary depending on who needs to learn what. For example, you might have one group learning to recognize a complete sentence from a sentence fragment, another group learning to find nouns embedded in sentences, a third group working on writing sentences, and a fourth group categorizing words into nouns versus verbs. Each group has an adult to oversee the activity. As many as six activities can go well when you have four to five adults to supervise.

Recently, I talked with an Rsp who is involved in an inclusion program. At her school, she and the special day class teacher are cooperating to serve all LD students. They divided the class in half, placing half of the students in each of two rooms. In addition to the six special class students, each room contains three Rsp students. She serves all the LD students in one room while the special education teacher serves the other room all morning, regardless of which program the child is in (Rsp or special day class). In the afternoons, they hold a lab (not in the regular classroom) for the LD students and the special day class students.

At this point, you seem to be free to develop a program of inclusion that is tailored to your school's resources and needs.

THE STATUS OF THE REGULAR EDUCATION INITIATIVE TODAY

The debate regarding Regular Education Initiative rages on. There are those who will tell you almost every handicapped child can be served in regular classes and will benefit from being served there. There are those who cite "miracles" that have occurred with these children. Other teachers are not so sure; they worry about how they will meet the needs of so many children.

It is easy to understand why teachers feel unprepared to teach a profoundly handicapped child. Some of these students need services such as diapering, catheterization, gastric feedings, and suctioning of the windpipe. The question arises as to who will do that and what liability does the teacher assume. Hopefully, districts will provide trained health personnel to take care of these services.

Parents of identified students have the right to decide where their child will be served. Even when the child is profoundly handicapped, they do not have to agree to place their child in a special education setting. Some are opting to have the child served in the regular class to which the child would be assigned if he or she were not handicapped. If it develops that the child cannot progress in the least restrictive environment or creates so much disruption that other students' learning is disrupted, the team may reconvene and suggest that the appropriate placement for the child is in a more restrictive environment. Every effort should be made to engage the parents' cooperation and agreement. If, however, an impasse is reached, the decision is then referred to a mediator under the due process procedure guaranteed by P.L. 94-142.

Successful inclusion programs seem to begin with all participating teachers agreeing on the importance of including disabled students and expressing a willingness to adapt curriculum and procedures so these children can be in regular classes. In schools where teachers have been railroaded into inclusion, there has been confusion, resentment, and tension. Sometimes this has disappeared after a period of time, but it was stress producing until the teachers involved began to feel more comfortable and capable of working with disabled youngsters.

Figure 8-3 offers material that can be used to familiarize regular class teachers with regard to students with learning disabilities. Make copies of it for the teachers in your school and present it after teachers have "bought into" the inclusion philosophy.

Figure 8-3

CHARACTERISTICS OF LEARNING DISABLED STUDENTS AND THEIR IMPACT ON TEACHING

The following characteristics of LD children will impact on how you prepare and deliver lessons.

Linguistic Deficits are common among LD students. Many of these children do not learn much when the lecture format is used.

Suggestions

1. Increase what they learn by putting notes on the board or giving them a summary of the major points to keep in their notebook so they can refer to it later.

2. Have materials on tape if students are allowed to listen to the tape several times.

3. Since most LD students show deficits in semantics and pragmatics, we have to make a concerted effort to teach vocabulary in all subject areas. Students need to keep lists of vocabulary words worked on for later reference, so provide looseleaf binders for adding pages.

When vocabulary is introduced, present it in syllables, i.e., *com/fort/a/ble*. LD students often do not see the relationship of the spelling of one word to another. Show them that once they have the *com* in their head, it will be used in other words such as *com/ply, com/plete, com/mit, com/pre/hend*. Similarly, the *ply* in *com/ply* finds its way into other words, such as *sup/ply, im/ply, re/ply*. For several days bring up other words with the *com* in them until the students recognize this syllable and notice it when it is embedded in a word.

4. For some LD students listening-processing speed is so slow it is almost as though they are from a foreign country. Those kids require a lot of patient one-to-one help in order to get anything. Peer buddies can help the handicapped student get the major ideas. Research has shown it is often valuable to both students for a student who understands to teach it to one who doesn't. In choosing a buddy, you may be tempted to use your brightest students. This sometimes is not the best choice because they consider the LD students to be a drag. It usually works better to choose students who are more middle of the stream because it bolsters their self-esteem and they tend to be more accepting of the LD child's problems.

Deficits in arousal, sustaining attention or in ignoring competing stimuli affect 20 to 33 percent of LD children.

Suggestions

1. When beginning a lesson, it is necessary to get the students' attention.

2. Students get more from the lesson when sentences are kept short and frequent stops are made to check understanding.

3. During instruction, ask students to turn to the person next to them and explain what was said. The other student acts as a sounding board to say, "Yes. That's right!" or to clarify what was said.

Figure 8-3 continued

4. Require students to make notes (adults circulate checking to be sure they are), which often improves listening. Requiring students to regurgitate what was said in some form (orally, writing, or art) discourages their natural tendency to space off.

Memory deficits occur in most LD students. They have deficits in their short-term memory, *and these deficits result in deficits in long-term memory.* While LD students have difficulty learning spelling words and times tables, it is usually due to insufficient practice.

Suggestions

1. Teach students to use *verbal rehearsal* to help themselves. When required to write a word five times, they need to say the letters as they write; for some reason, LD students do not do that. They must be trained to use verbal rehearsal to learn. Peer buddies can supervise this activity.

2. Allow them to read notes aloud before a test or repeat times tables orally as they write them.

Loss of control is an issue among LD students. For the most part, these students do not feel they have any control over their learning or what occurs in the classroom. They view bad grades or being disciplined as either bad luck or unfair treatment. They rarely see that what they do (the quality of their effort/action) determines the outcome. Feeling they cannot do what others do results in withdrawal behaviors and lowered task-completion efforts.

Suggestions

This is an issue that must be constantly addressed. If a student receives a poor score, it is helpful for someone (aide or volunteer) to talk with the student about how he or she could have improved his or her score. Here is a sample dialogue.

"Gloria, do you remember the directions for this assignment?"

"No."

"You were to write at least five sentences about the story. Let's look at your paper. How many sentences did you write?"

"Three."

"Your score was not satisfactory because you did not write five. Do you remember why you didn't do that?"

"I ran out of time."

"Did you talk to Mr. Sabati about that?"

"No."

"If you had told him that, he would have allowed you to take this home to finish. You can take it home tonight to finish. Bring it back tomorrow and Mr. Sabati may raise your grade. Will you do that?"

(student shrugs)

"Gloria, it is up to you. If you finish it and bring it back tomorrow, Mr. Sabati will raise the grade to passing. If you don't, he will make a note in his book that you chose not to do that and may contact your mom. You can fix this."

Figure 8-3 continued

On the next day ask the student for the assignment. If it is done say: "I'm so glad you took charge. Good for you." It is important for Mr. Sabati to let Gloria watch as he changes the grade in the grade book and to say, "See. Your extra effort did that." If the student does not do the assignment, say "You decided to fail. Mr. Sabati was fair. He offered you the opportunity to pass. Why did you choose to fail?" Wait for an answer. Gently ask the question several times. Try to get the student to face the fact that he or she didn't make an effort.

A second example of this phenomenon might be when Sam gets caught stealing, taking something from Mr. Sabati's desk drawer. Sam wanted to transfer the blame from himself to the teacher.

When confronted, Sam yells, "You are just picking on me because I'm black." (I am not responsible; you are the one who is wrong.)

Mr. Sabati ignores the ploy with "No, I'm picking on you because you stole something from my desk drawer and two people saw you do it."

Self-esteem of LD students is an area that has been extensively studied. Some studies showed that LD students had lowered self-esteem; other studies found the self-esteem of LD students was similar to that of nonhandicapped students except in one area—their feelings about their academic prowess. Lack of confidence translates into lower levels of effort exerted; lowered levels of frustration tolerance (give up more easily); lowered willingness to take a risk (do not volunteer answers = do not participate = withdraw).

In studies that looked at how LD students were perceived by their peers, it was found that LD children were less popular and were more rejected by their nonhandicapped peers (Siperstein, 1985). According to its proponents, the current movement toward inclusion and regular class service will positively influence how these children are seen by their peers.

Failure syndrome is a phenomenon frequently seen in LD children. The child with failure syndrome has experienced more failure in his or her efforts than success. Children in this position usually take one of the following stances: To withdraw and not try (*learned helplessness*) **or** to be angry/frustrated and refuse to try (*active resistance*).

To improve self-esteem, it is essential for the LD student to experience success (to be able to do most assignments).

Suggestions for Eliminating Failure Syndrome

1. Give short assignments that are at the student's functional level.
2. Be on hand to give immediate *positive* feedback. "Wow!" "Great!" If there is an error, you will very quietly sit down and show the student how it is done and stay with the student as he or she goes through the process.
3. Give encouragement. If you sense a student is weary, say, "You did fine today but I can see you have had enough for today. We'll work on it some more tomorrow. I really appreciate what you did today. I know this is difficult for you."
4. Avoid overkill. Divide long assignments into shorter segments, giving feedback, instruction, and encouragement after each segment.
5. Do not put a grade on the paper until most of the errors are corrected—until you can put at least a satisfactory grade. Teachers are not compelled to put a grade on every paper. They *do* need to give the student some feedback: "This was a good point." "Can you write more about this point so I can understand how you feel?" "The way you want to say this is . . ." (show them how the sentence might be worded).

Figure 8-3 continued

6. Some students experience test phobia. In some cases, use a well-done daily paper as proof of the child's progress.

7. If it is important that a student memorize certain facts, give the facts to the parent several days before the test and make provision for the student to study them in class.

8. Give the students daily work that is in the same format as the test.

9. When a child who previously did not try begins to try, make a big deal out of it. In front of the class, you can say, "Keep trying. You are getting it!" Write a good note home or call. Pat the student on the back and say, "Good for you!"

10. Above all, understand and be compassionate. Think of how you feel when you're overwhelmed or don't understand. Tell the student a personal story about failure. Let the student know it is not necessary to be perfect—just to grow. *Never* embarrass the student or put him or her on the spot. When you are going to call on the student, let the student know several minutes ahead what you will ask so he or she has time to prepare an answer.

11. In every way show you are glad the student is in your class. Let the student help in ways that he or she can, such as watering plants or giving out papers. Make sure you positively recognize the child daily: "You have a wonderful smile." "That's a nice shirt." Get eye contact and say, "How are you today?"

12. If absenteeism is a problem, the student will continue to miss school until going to school becomes more pleasant than staying home. This may require that more than one person at school shows the student attention. One of my students had a history of missing over 40 days each year. The attendance office talked repeatedly with the parent who steadfastly maintained the student was "ill." Since the child returned without ever showing any residual symptoms, the teacher, counselor, librarian, and I decided we'd show the child more positive attention, including hugs. Bingo! Her attendance showed marked improvement. Several months later, we didn't give so much positive attention and the absences started again. Once the hugs and attention were reinstated, the student's attendance improved.

Student need for 1:1 help is another issue that regular teachers must deal with. Two issues must be considered: (1) Shall I help the student with this task or not? (2) Can I give the help that is needed or would it be more appropriate to ask the special education teacher to assist me?

In answer to the first question, regular teachers have consistently reported that identified children and "at risk" children require more 1:1 assistance. Teachers have expressed the need for class size to be reduced if they are to effectively help these children (perhaps the use of some sort of formula, such as counting each special child as being two).

When trying to decide whether to give 1:1 help, the crucial factor to consider is whether the student really requires that help to be successful with the task. Recently, I observed a fifth grade class where there were nine identified students who had just been fully included into the regular classroom. The teacher decided to do some phonics work because she felt all the students would benefit. She made a ditto which asked them to write five words that begin with gl, gr, br, and bl and then write a sentence using each word.

One student was not working. She went over to him and said, "Get to work." As it turned out, there were three very good reasons he was not working. First, he had not understood the directions because he had not listened. Second, he had a functional reading level of only 1.5 and could not look into his own head to find words that began with those letters. (Wisely, she

149

Figure 8-3 continued

gave him a dictionary.) Third, he was able to list five words with the given sounds by using the dictionary but it was only copy work since he could not read the words nor their definitions. This student needed her guidance to find words he could read, such as *glass* and *grow*. Once she helped him find five words he could read, he was able to successfully complete the assignment and gain some meaning from doing it.

If this student had been able to complete the assignment alone or with encouragement from a peer, it would not be necessary for the teacher to give help.

In answer to the second question regarding when to utilize special education help, there are two guidelines. Call for a consultation when:

1. A student needs help with every assignment.
2. You have tried everything you can think of and the student still doesn't get it.

Working with children from dysfunctional homes is an area needing more study. Clearly there are more dysfunctional homes now than formerly if you agree with my definition of "dysfunctionality." When using this definition, I am referring to homes where no one is functioning effectively and positively as a parent and role-model. This includes homes where the mother gives more time and concern to a boyfriend than to her children, as well as homes where the parents are simply not home during the hours the children are home (and do not take an active interest in rearing the children). It includes homes where drugs, alcohol abuse, or criminal behavior are a regular part of the picture. We occasionally see a home where the parents are taking an active part but their efforts are totally misguided (extremely poor parenting skills). When working with these children, engaging the parents in the process is usually more counter-productive than working directly with the child. For example, if homework is not done, you are more likely to get it by rewarding the child than by trying to get the parents to supervise the homework. You will get better results by trying to establish a relationship with the child where he or she wants to please you. Show the child you think he or she is a worthwhile person.

CLASSROOM MANAGEMENT 9

Teachers make hundreds of decisions every day—and with careful planning, the day can go more smoothly and productively. When a teacher does not exercise good planning skills, students tend to take advantage by misbehaving.

ENVIRONMENTAL DECISIONS

Creating a Utilitarian and Attractive Classroom

First, you want to create a safe, structured, and attractive environment. Although this means a lot of cleaning and organizing of materials, the effort pays off in time saved later when trying to find the things you need.

Next, decide how you want desks organized. There is no prescribed way, but you do need to give some thought to the kind of teaching you will be doing.

1. Rows of desks let students know you want them to face you and not talk to each other. Lecture will be the primary vehicle used in teaching.

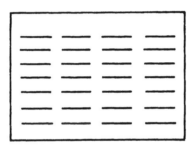

2. When desks are clustered in groups of four, this signals to students that there will be a lot of cooperative learning activity.

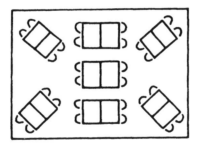

Sometimes a teacher will start the year with rows and then once rules have been taught, switch to a less formal arrangement.

3. When a teacher intends to have students role-play or perform, there are several possible arrangements, such as the two shown here.

153

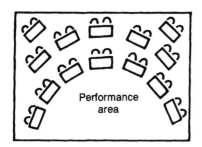

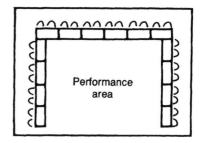

After arranging the furniture, decorate with plants, mobiles, student art work, a learning/listening center, computer center, a reader's corner (magazines, books, book shelves, chairs) and beanbag chairs. It is best to place items so you can supervise the behavior in the reading center.

Bulletin boards that can be used all year by merely changing the displayed items are time-savers. Sky blue makes a good background color.

Finally, you need to obtain essential equipment such as paper, pencils, scissors, glue, colored pencils and crayons, watercolors, chalk, chart paper, texts, and teacher's guides for curriculum.

BEHAVIORAL MANAGEMENT DECISIONS

Use a Classroom Aide Effectively

This was one of the subjects never discussed in my teacher training. Early on, I thought of myself as "the leader" or "the one in charge" and drove myself nutty trying to make detailed lists each night telling the aide what to do, hour by hour.

What I learned was I didn't have time to do this, my aide either complained of too much or too little work, and, further, she felt I didn't value her abilities; so I stopped making lists, told her to do what she saw needed to be done and to organize her own time just as I did. I did ask her to make time for each child to read aloud to her for 15 minutes a day, to record what they read and write some notes about their performance. When the class was doing an activity where more help was needed, she sprang to my side. The more I allowed her to do, the more responsibility she willingly took on.

Plan the First-Week Activities

Plan your first day and first week carefully. It is better to have more activities than the class can do than too few. Best choices are activities that:

1. are relatively short
2. require few directions (little or no new teaching should be involved so you can move around and get to know students or solve problems)
3. allow students to be successful and allow you to give positive feedback
4. build a feeling of belonging to the group

Your theme for the first month might be "Soaring to New Heights." One bulletin board with blue background might contain paper balloons of various colors in clusters of four (use real yarn to tie balloons into clusters). On the first day take each child's picture and put a number on the back of each photo. (If there are 12 students, you will put *1* on the back of three pictures; 12 divided by 4 is 3. If there are *32* students, 32 divided by 4 is 8 so you will write *1* on eight pictures.) The students with the *1*s are the first month's group leaders. Staple the photos with the *1*s to the bulletin board. Persons with the number *2* can then add their photo to any group; *3*s will then put their picture in a group; then the *4*s.

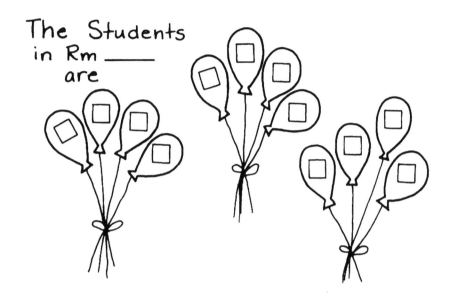

The Students in Rm ____ are

One of your early cooperative learning projects in *language arts* might be to have each group write a thank-you letter to the community for the school and its equipment, inviting the person who finds the letter to visit your classroom. Letters are then rolled up, placed in balloons filled with helium, and launched.

"Soaring to New Heights" is a theme easily expanded upon. In *health*, you might have students measure and record each other's height in inches at the beginning of the year and then at the end of the year, subtracting to see their growth. In *math*, you may review the skills they know now and talk about the ones they will learn this year (second graders learn subtraction, third graders learn multiplication, fourth graders learn division, fifth graders learn fractions, sixth graders work with decimals, etc.). You may want to introduce students to the idea of portfolio assessment, collecting samples of their work at different stages so they can show their parents they are growing/soaring to new heights.

If you teach at the secondary school level, you can also use the same theme. Display pictures of famous people on the bulletin board and ask the group to write a paper explaining how a particular person overcame hardships in order to soar.

Establish Rules

Post class rules in two locations. Some teachers like to have students participate in making rules; I never found this worked very well for me, so I would simply post rules as shown in Figure 9-1.

Figure 9-1

---

1. Complete your assigned task.
2. Let others work. Let your teacher work.
3. Be kind.
4. Respect the feelings and property of others.

During the first week, teach students:

1. what the rules mean

2. how to act in acceptable ways; role play

3. what the consequences will be when a rule is broken

4. how to become quiet as soon as a signal is given

For that first week, plan your lessons so you can watch for and handle violations of rules as they occur. This is one time when an extra pair of eyes (an aide or volunteer) can really help. When a student violates a rule, take him or her to the posted rules, point to the rule violated, and suggest another way he or she could have handled the situation. In handling first-week violations, be kind but firm about what you expect. For example, if the student was out of her seat at an inappropriate time, say "Jennifer, I'm sorry. You may not leave your desk now. It is disturbing me (point to rule #2). Why were you up?" If Jennifer has a legitimate need, such as "My pencil lead broke," you may want to stop the class and have other students suggest ways Jennifer might solve this problem.

Limiting movement in the room definitely increases the amount of on-task behavior. A class monitor might be a solution. This one person can sharpen a pencil or get a needed item for a student. (Monitor responsibility can be rotated daily so all students get a chance to do it.)

During the first week when students raise their hands, recognize them quickly.

After the first week, you must begin to assign logical consequences for rules violations. Any activity that results in students' failure to complete their work (such as talking or looking around) is logically followed by assigning them to come in on their own time to complete it (time after school, during lunch or recess the next day, homework plan if parent can be reached, loss of a privilege).

It is extremely important that students be held responsible for work production. Not all students must do the same assignment or the same length of assignment, but after you have modified an assignment, insist it be done. To fail to do so results in all kinds of difficulties for all involved (parent complaints, lack of student progress, poor student behavior). If a student does not complete an assignment, try to determine why by talking with the student in private. Write notes of the conference. Make reasonable adjustments, but let the student know you are required to keep the parents apprised if the student does not do the work. Older students today realize that teachers and parents are busy, so have learned to goof-off for long periods of time. They know that near reporting periods, they will need to produce more work. Teachers see this sudden increase in effort and want to encourage it to continue, so they raise the grade and tell the parent how much better the student is doing; then student effort declines after the report card has been issued. *Remember, frequent parent contact = higher student production.*

Create a Positive Feeling

You want a classroom where both you and your students feel comfortable. A four-to-one ratio of positive-to-corrective responses usually makes for a positive feeling tone. You may want to keep a tally in order to see how you are doing. Students report they like teachers who are "fair," "don't yell," "listen to us and care how we feel," "reward us for good work," "have a sense of humor," and "act as if they like us."

Shift from "Teacher" to Learning Facilitator

As children grow older (grades 3 and 4 are ideal times) it is helpful to introduce the idea that they are responsible for their own learning and that the teacher is just there to act as a learning facilitator. This shift makes the acquisition of both academic and personal skills the *focus* of the class. The teacher's role is to provide materials and directions, and manage the class in such a way that each child can maximize his or her learning.

To introduce the concept, ask the students, "Why do you come to school?" The first time I asked this question, I was shocked that today's students do not have a clear picture of why they are there. Responses ranged from blank stares to "My parents make me" to "So I can learn." When pressed with "Why do you need to learn?" it was an uncomfortably long time before someone said, "So we can get a job." For some youngsters, there is no concept that someday they will leave home to work.

Probably the best way to get this idea across is to make a homework assignment where they interview one of their parents by asking the following questions:

1. How old were you when you left home?
2. What was your first job?
3. What did you learn in school that helped you do that job?
4. At what age do you think children today should leave home?
5. What kind of job do you think I'd be good at?
6. What subjects do I need to take to do that?
7. What should I do at school to help myself learn?

Tell the students you will compile all the information given by the class members so they can bring it home to share with their parents.

Putting the focus on learning allows you to intercede for the "good of the group" whenever someone is doing something that is disruptive. After a while, surprisingly, students will begin to ask disrupters to think of the group and behave.

Placing the focus on learning also makes it possible to vary the assignments and the amount to be done. It helps a child understand that what he or she needs to work on may not be the same as someone else. Allowing students a choice of subjects to write about provides them an opportunity to pursue their individual interests. Giving them time to discuss their interests in their group may kindle someone else's interest.

Begin to encourage students to look at each new experience (movie, field trip, assembly program) and analyze it. "What did you get out of doing this?" At the end of the day ask five or six people to name something new they learned today. After awhile students will begin to do activities with the idea they should expect to be getting something out of it (that they are not doing it for the teacher but for themselves).

Equally important is for students to develop good "people skills." The most frequent reason for dismissal from a job is that the employee does not work well with co-workers. When a student has trouble working cooperatively in a group, it is definitely worth your time to help the student find ways to resolve the issue.

Introduce the concept that children need to analyze their own work for its merit and how they can improve the product. By working in pairs, students can edit each other's work before submitting it to the teacher. Model how to give constructive criticism mediated by compliments for parts that are well done, and have students practice criticism and compliments.

Set up dialogues between students that permit exploration of how answers were arrived at. Whether the assignment was how to solve a math problem or write a creative story, there is value in having students listen to how their peers got an answer. We all agree our nation needs a work force that can think creatively and cooperatively. (There is some exciting new computer software to help you do this. See Chapter 17 on technology.)

You will find these activities will help you feel more productive and prevent burnout because each period becomes an adventure in learning, with students actively participating rather than you having to drag results out of them.

Preventing Misbehavior

Find Better Ways to Talk to Students

It is not difficult to know how to talk to students—you simply speak to them with the same courtesy you expect them to use with you. If a student is rude to you, take them aside and say, "I will not call you names. I will not yell at you and I expect you not to do those things to me." Use the words "please" and "thank you" in your vocabulary. If there is a challenge to your authority, in private and in a tone that projects caring, say, "I am the person who has been appointed to be in charge here. How might we work this out so we are not working at cross-purposes? I am hoping you will let me know so we do not have to involve your parents." You may want to arrange for the student to go to some other supervised place while he or she gives some thought to your question. Students who are verbally aggressive often mellow after being given a timeout.

One thing a teacher must realize is that *all authority is granted, not seized.* The students in a class either decide to work with the teacher or they gang up, organizing an all-out assault that eventually results in the teacher leaving that situation. I have seen a few teachers who act like military drill sergeants who are able to survive but are not liked; they do not convey the image to students that they are people who want to be helpful.

Do not use embarrassment as a control technique. I can remember that only a few years ago if you got caught passing a note, the teacher read it to the class. For chewing gum you had to stand in the corner and moo loudly. Yelling at students, snapping your fingers at them, and saying things about flunking or low scores in front of others should never be done. When there is a problem, try to talk with the student in private. Sometimes an aide can do this.

Make your expectations clear. Instead of saying, "When you guys shut up, I'll begin," students are more likely to respond to "I want you to get out your math book and turn to page 56." Then on the board, write "Math Book, page 56." Allow enough time for 80 percent to comply and then begin your lesson. The stragglers usually will get their act together as soon as you start.

Each time you begin an activity, state the behavioral parameters for the activity. (Can they talk, work together?)

Provide Alternatives for More Able Students

Students work at different speeds, so you need to plan something to do for those who finish rapidly. Some possible suggestions are:

1. Allow them to act as coaches for those students who are less able.
2. Allow them to check practice papers and help students correct errors if it is not a test.
3. Set up a listening center and have interesting tapes (library books) there.
4. Allow them extra time to use the computer.
5. Allow them to begin their homework.
6. Agree to offer extra credit for extra work.
7. Allow them to read recreationally (age-appropriate student magazines and *National Geographic* are popular).
8. Have an art center with colored pencils and chalk and clay available.
9. If previously arranged, allow some to tutor in other classes.
10. Let them help you. If your boxes of mosaic pieces are running low, these students can replenish them; or they can collate/staple.

Provide Alternatives for Less Able Students

As you plan your lessons, decide ahead which students will need some modification of the assignment and what modification is most likely to be beneficial. Several kinds of alternatives are available.

1. Give less able students a different assignment at a lower level.
2. Shorten the assignment by choosing only the most important parts.
3. Allow the students additional time to complete the assignment. (It is not a good idea to send all unfinished work home to be completed. Many teachers do this; however, it can infuriate parents because they feel you are overloading the students and then *they* have to spend the entire evening supervising homework. The student feels overwhelmed and begins to hate school.)
4. Allow students to use "crutches" (calculators, a times table) for part of the assignment.
5. Allow students to do part of the assignment orally.

6. If reading is a problem, allow a more able student to read some of it to the less able students.

7. Help the students get organized.

8. Use school-based resources to meet students' needs, which requires parent consent. (We had a child whose IQ was 83 and, although she was a sixth grader, her math skills were at beginning fourth grade which was consistent with her ability. With the parents' permission, she attended a fourth-grade math class each morning. She was able to say, "Math is really hard for me. That's why I'm here." The younger children accepted her very well and the teacher took a real interest in helping her. This solution allowed her to learn those things she was ready to learn—division and fractions—and prevented the frustration that would have been caused had she been forced to be in a sixth-grade class where she lacked the prerequisites for what was being taught.)

Keep Environment Consistent and Structured

LD students have an incredible need for consistency and structure. Post a daily schedule for students to see. When you must alter the schedule, explain why and carefully outline what will happen, when, and what behavior you expect from them. Misbehavior can be prevented when these students clearly know what is coming and what they must do. When offered, free time must have structure, too. The students must be told what the parameters are for activity, noise, and movement. Classroom rules must be consistently enforced, which will require you to periodically review them.

Use Contracts to Prevent Misbehavior/Assure Work Production

When a student is having difficulty complying with classroom standards for behavior or work production, one of the tools teachers may try is the *contingency contract*. This written contract specifies what the student must do to get a given reward. The contract is made in private, with the teacher and student agreeing to its terms. Figure 9-2 shows a sample.

Figure 9-2

CONTINGENCY CONTRACT

I agree to complete my entire math assignment today. If I achieve an accuracy of 70% and complete it in 50 minutes, I will be allowed to have 15 extra minutes of computer time today.

_____   _____
Teacher signature   Student signature

I know one teacher who enters into such contracts with each of his students on Monday. The target behavior varies from student to student. If the student complies, the teacher allows the student to eat lunch with him on Friday, with the teacher supplying treats such as grapes or chips to supplement their brown bag lunches.

Use Lotteries to Prevent Misbehavior/Assure Work Production

Another effective technique is the lottery, whereby students are given tickets for good behavior or work production. Students deposit these tickets in a container and, on Friday, the teacher draws names for one or more prizes.

Use Token Economies to Prevent Misbehavior/Assure Work Production

In token economies, students earn points that are traded for prizes or privileges. (Figure 9-3 shows a sample points card.)

Figure 9-3. Sample points card.

week of _____	Name _____					
	Period 1	Period 2	Period 3	Period 4	Period 5	Period 6
Monday						
Tuesday						
Wednesday						
Thursday						
Friday						
Comments:					Total	

ACADEMIC ENHANCERS

Build Class Spirit/Increase Feelings of Belonging

It is essential that students feel accepted and good about themselves; however, this does not always happen naturally. My son's sixth-grade teacher understood this well. He had a golden retriever and each year his class called themselves the Golden Retrievers; the dog was their mascot. Each child received a yellow T-shirt with the logo. For the first four weeks of school, the students were invited to participate in Saturday-morning activities. They built a huge papier-mâché whale to go with the science unit; they had an overnight campout at school; they were invited to the airport to see the teacher's plane; and they could look at the stars through the teacher's telescope. The kids got to know each other in various social settings.

Today, with busing, this may not always work. Start the year by having the class give a play. (*Hansel and Gretel* is an easy one.) So that each student is involved, you may want to have two or three casts. Let each cast have a turn at performing, and ask students to make scenery and sew costumes. Your less gregarious students could be trees (brown clothes with green paper over their arms, which wave in the breeze).

Whenever a new child enters the room, be alert to make the child the center of attention for a few days. Involve the others in thinking of ways to welcome the child.

Offer Rewards

Rewards make learning more fun; the tricky part is that what is a positive reinforcer for one child may *not* be for another. If you want to find out what children at the age level you teach like, ask them. (Figures 9-4 and 9-5 offer sample reinforcers.) Another problem with rewards is that sometimes a child will get tired of a reward, so you have to find a new reward.

There is a hierarchy of rewards. (See Figure 9-6.) The most potent reward and one of the easiest to handle is edibles; they rarely lose their value and can be relatively inexpensive. Kids love cookies, small candies, popcorn, cheese crackers, and chips. When reward is tied to work production, you can gradually increase the amount while keeping the reward small. If reward is tied to behavior, the evaluation of behavior is subjective so you sometimes end up in arguments over whether the standard was met. Of course, it is extremely rewarding when a child no longer requires a reward to produce.

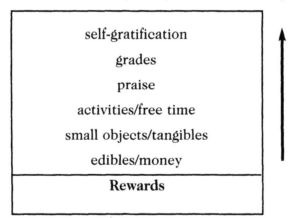

Figure 9-6

One activity you can use that is a high-level motivator as well as one that builds feelings of belonging is the "give ourselves a party" reward. To use this reward, give a pretest (this works well in math), average the students' scores, and share the results with the class. Next, say, "Let's give ourselves a party if we can raise that average score over the next few weeks to ___" (set a figure around 75% to 80%). Explain to them that

EVERYONE IS GOING TO HAVE TO HELP TO MAKE THE GOAL. Remind students daily of the goal and ask more able students to work with less able ones to help them learn the skill. When a goal is achieved (and it has been my experience that students will pull together to achieve it), set aside time for a party. You don't even have to furnish the goodies because of the phrase "give ourselves a party." Each person brings something!

Figure 9-4

REINFORCERS FOR ELEMENTARY-AGED STUDENTS

— Listen to radio/tapes/watch a TV program

— Talk to best friend

— Look at books, magazines

— Edible rewards (candy, cookies, ice cream, sodas, popcorn)

— Extra time for art, to play with clay, use colored markers

— Extra computer time

— Help out in a lower-grade classroom

— Help the teacher (carry out trash, pass out papers)

— Stickers

— Rewards such as pencils, notebooks, erasers, rulers

— Write on the chalkboard

— See a movie

— Extra recess

— Extra time with the teacher (small group goes with the teacher to fast-food restaurant, on a field trip, have a picnic, pizza party)

— Work on puzzles/play checkers

— Visit the principal

— Receive an award in assembly

— Money reward given by the parent

— Note/phone call to parents

"Earn a Grade"

One of the most effective techniques you can use is what I call *Earn a Grade*. At the beginning of each assignment, share with students exactly what they must do to get a given grade.

Let's say the assignment is to write sentences using the spelling words. You might say that to get an A, students must write 20 sentences and have corrected all errors in spelling, syntax, and mechanics. Each sentence must have a subject, verb, and at least one phrase. For a B, students must write 15 sentences with all corrections mentioned above. For a C, they must write and correct 10. You know which students (usually five or six) will need pushing and one-to-one help to reach a C. Your job is to arrange for that help.

Figure 9-5

REINFORCERS FOR SECONDARY-AGED STUDENTS

1. Free Time
   —watch TV/VCR
   —read books/magazines
   —typing/time on computer
   —peer tutoring
   —listen to records
   —play a game
   —earn a model/make it in class
   —draw, paint

2. Special Privileges
   —help as a teacher assistant
   —help the principal
   —do clerical work in the building (answer the phone, run the copy machine)
   —help the coach
   —be a library assistant
   —work with the custodian
   —run errands
   —extra time in shop, art, P.E.
   —food coupons/movie ticket/ticket to a game

3. Special Time with the Teacher (small groups)
   —field trips
   —go to a movie
   —picnic in the park
   —have a soda/go to a restaurant with teacher
   —note/phone call to parent

Involve the Principal

When students show improvement, arrange for them to "go to the principal." Tell the principal whom you will send (two to five students). Write at the top of each student's paper why it shows improvement; for example, "improved handwriting," "better score," "produced more," "nice ideas." The principal then reinforces your praise. This technique has several positive aspects:

1. Principals love it. They get tired of only seeing the kids who are in trouble. And the principals think you are a terrific teacher!

2. Since being sent is based on *improvement*, all students have a chance to be chosen. The students at the bottom of the class "need" this experience more than top students.

3. Doing this once a week or so inspires students to improve.

HANDLING MISBEHAVIOR

Preventing misbehavior is definitely preferable to handling it, but, alas, there are times when we must do so. When an offense is deliberate and recurring, it is a matter of weighing the total situation—were the directions clearly given and understood? Did the behavior cause harm? What would be the *logical consequence* for this behavior? How much punishment is required? What kind? Should parents and principal be involved?

Let's look at some more examples:

- Kanisha is continually one or two minutes late to class. The logical consequence is that Kanisha be given a short detention each time she is late. It is a good idea to inform parents of the problem and ask if your plan meets their approval. If they say *no*, then ask them how they want the matter handled. If they say they will take care of it, let them know that if the lateness continues, you will have to try the detention.

- Carl likes to play tetherball, but does not play by the rules. This results in pushing and shoving. The logical consequence is that each time this happens, Carl is removed from the tetherball court or the playground for that day.

- Mike trips others, says mean things, and hits. The logical consequence is referral to the office with a parent conference to follow. Students must be made aware that they may not assault other students at school.

The office may then give timeout, a suspension, or whatever else it deems appropriate.

"Ball in Your Court" Technique

When you have a student who is misbehaving, you have to confront that student. There is an easy and effective technique you can use. Let's say you ask Jaime to move and he complies, but shows his disgust by slamming his book down on the desk. Ask him, "Why did you slam your book down like that?" Use an inquisitive tone rather than a confrontational one. Jaime will either say "Sorry" or "I was mad." If Jaime says he is sorry, say "OK" and go on as though the incident did not occur. If Jaime says he was mad, say "I didn't mean to make you angry. We need to talk about this." Set up a nonclass time to do that. When you meet, ask Jaime to explain what made him angry. Listen attentively and then ask, "How can we resolve this so next time I ask you to move, you do not get angry at me?"

The "ball in your court" technique also works with irate parents. Say, "I can see you are upset. What is it you want to happen here? How can we work this out?" Listen attentively and try to honor as much of their wishes as you can. If you cannot, say, "I wish we could do that but we can't. What else could we do?"

Timeout

Timeout means a student is removed from whatever activity he or she was doing for a period of time. For less serious offenses, you may say, "Roberta, take a timeout in the library corner. You may return to the group when you are ready to do what we are doing without being disruptive." If a serious situation exists where Roberta continues to be belligerent or noncooperative, you may want her to serve the timeout somewhere else (another classroom) and you may want to set a time frame (such as, "for the rest of this period"). If the problem continues, then you may have to involve the office. In general, an office referral should *not* be your first line of defense.

Level Systems

Some teachers find it helpful to have a level system; usually there are three to five levels within the class. When a new student comes or at the beginning of the year when students are new to you, everyone is on level two. Students are proving themselves at this level. The only privileges enjoyed are recess and lunch. If a student proves him- or herself worthy, the student is moved to level three and has full privileges (to be a monitor, to have some free time). If a student messes up, he or she may fall to level one, which means losing recess and eating lunch in the room under supervision. Special day teachers are more likely to need level systems than regular classroom teachers.

INVOLVING PARENTS IN POSITIVE WAYS

Involve Parents in the Classroom

Try to have a conference with each parent during the first month of school so that you can prevent misunderstandings later. An easy way to do this is to invite about ten parents to a coffee klatch (have some lemonade, cookies, fruit, and cheese available). Offer door prizes (if you are a diligent garage-sale attendee, you can pick up some little vases or ring holders from $.50 to $1.00). When you invite ten parents, about half that number will come with the door prize incentive.

Sit informally around a table. Tell the parents a bit about yourself, such as where you were born and grew up, where you went to school, how long you have been teaching, if you are married and have children of your own, what your hobbies are, etc., and ask parents to share a bit about themselves. Let them know your homework policy (see Figure 9-7) and how they can get in touch with you; try to get them to tell you the best way you can contact them (times, place). To make it all sound friendly, say, "I'll make a deal with you. I won't believe half the things the kids say about you if you won't believe half of what they say about me!" Let parents know you would never intentionally hurt a child's feelings and, if the child ever indicates you have, parents should call you immediately. If some parents do not come, invite them to the next klatch.

Figure 9-7

SUGGESTIONS REGARDING HOMEWORK

Teacher's name:_____

Hours and # where you can reach me:

_____

1. Ask your child to tell you what the homework is.

2. If the child says there is no homework, have him/her get a book and read aloud to you for 15 minutes; then ask him/her to write a page about what he/she read. Contact me as soon as you can. (If you require the child work for the usual # of minutes, he/she will be less likely to try to get out of homework.)

3. Ask the child to begin the homework. After a few minutes, look at it to see if he/she understands what he/she is doing. If he/she does not, go to an alternative assignment. Send me what he/she did not understand.

4. The homework session should not exceed 1 hour for elementary grades; two hours for secondary grades. If a child is taking longer, please contact me.

5. Do not be afraid to teach your child or to help him/her make corrections. I always appreciate notes from you about how the homework sessions are going.

6. If you can come to school, please feel free to visit with us any day—even without prior notice. I may put you to work! I can always use an extra pair of eyes.

If you need help, call a parent and ask that he or she come on a particular day, at a particular time, and state what it is you want the parent to do. Parents are sometimes afraid of helping, particularly if their skills are not so good: but even these parents can watch while you teach and then if a student is off-task, they can gently remind the child to get back to work. It is wonderful to have this extra pair of eyes.

Having parents come to school serves two other purposes: (1) When parents see how busy teachers are and how much help children need, they are far more understanding and (2) children take more interest in school when parents participate. Be sure to let parents know their help is appreciated.

Money Therapy

Earlier in this chapter we spoke about rewards. Edibles do not seem to lose their potency, but there is always another reward that can be used continuously *if parents are trained in how to make it work.* That reward is money.

Our society revolves around money. I do not wish to debate whether this is good or bad, but this fact can be used to teach children from grade 1 and up.

First, a parent must require that a youngster perform a given amount of work for each monetary reward. The child soon learns that if he or she is to have what he or she wants, he or she must work for it. When a child says, "Can I have that?" the parent responds, "Do you have the money to buy it?"

In grade 1, a child needs about $1.50 a week. If he or she wants a book for $3, for example, it will take two weeks to get it. The parent then makes an arrangement. For each paper the child does satisfactorily at home or school, give a nickel. Cleaning their room may be worth 25 cents or 50 cents. The money reward is given immediately following the presentation of the papers or completion of the work. At first, the parent helps the child count the money every day so the child knows how much there is at all times (this prevents siblings from tricking the child). If you see the child's papers every night, you can see what he or she is being taught and how he or she is doing. *No money is just given, and buying goodies is limited to the child's savings.* If a child wants an expensive item, this is reserved for special occasions such as birthdays.

By grade 6, the child's needs increase to include movies or fast food, so the amount given for each job or paper is renegotiated.

Record Keeping

Profiles

Some districts require teachers to keep a profile on each student's progress. As a skill is mastered, allow the student to see you check it off the profile record. This gives a child a sense of worth.

Portfolios

Many school districts are instituting portfolio assessment because it is a direct reflection of the curriculum being taught. Portfolios allow for comparison of the student's work over a period of the year, are student-centered, and provide a way to get students more actively involved in their own learning. Students actively participate in selecting the contents and in judging the merit of their production against a set of criteria they helped to develop.

Portfolios are a great help in talking with parents at parent-teacher conference time. They make it easier to show the student's growth. Previously, we used test scores, which are often difficult for parents to understand.

Portfolios can contain papers across a wide range of subjects (tests, journal entries, notetaking samples, written projects from rough draft to published work) as well as anything else that both student and teacher feel will reflect growth (awards, student reflections on their work, peer reactions to a piece of writing, tapes of student's oral reading in September, January, and May). The major purpose of portfolio assessment is to engage students in their own learning.

Report Cards

Report cards need to reflect current performance levels as well as progress in each subject. They should contain as many positive comments as possible while still reflecting accurately how the student is doing when measured against the curriculum. Report cards also need to suggest ways parents can help at home.

Teacher-Parent-Pupil Conference

A good parent conference has several purposes: (1) it will let parents know what the student is doing, (2) it will allow the parent to share useful information about his or her situation and child with you, and (3) by the end of the first conference, you and the parent should part feeling you both have a clearer picture of what the child needs to do in school.

At the first conference, you may want to let the parents do most of the talking. What are their expectations for their child? What can they tell you about the child that will make it easier to teach him or her? What have other teachers said and do the parents agree with those teachers? Then you can share with the parents what you think is necessary to help the child. Start by telling them the positive things they should know, and then make a few suggestions of things you feel need to be worked on. Get the parents' input on how they think you might work together to get the job done.

Invite parents to participate in the classroom. Let them know they can come in *any time* to observe what is happening. If there is a concern or problem, tell the parents not to hesitate to call you. Inquire about homework and how it is handled at home. Does the child do it willingly or reluctantly? Offer suggestions or accommodations to make it easier on parents.

When the child reaches fourth grade, have the child attend the conference. Ask the child about his or her goals and previous school experiences. Ask how you can be more helpful to him or her.

Update I.E.P.s

When a student has an I.E.P., you want to be sure to keep it up to date. When you realize a student has mastered an I.E.P. objective, mark the objective achieved and file the proof of the accomplishment *that day.* If you do this, your I.E.P. record will always reflect exactly what the child needs to work on. You want to let the student know he or she has accomplished a goal; you may also want to notify the parent.

Hold Special Reviews to Rewrite I.E.P.s

If a student completes all I.E.P. goals earlier than expected, schedule a special review with the parent and write additional goals. Persons required to be present are the parent, teacher, Rsp, and principal.

If a student is not achieving the objectives in the I.E.P., you will need to apprise the parent. If you decide the original objectives are not appropriate, delete them after obtaining written parent permission and write new ones. Persons required for this type of meeting are the parent, teacher, Rsp, and administrator.

If a student is not adjusting well in the present setting, you will need to recall the entire I.E.P. team. The team may decide that a more restrictive setting is needed or may make further accommodations in order to maintain the student in the present setting. It is wise at this type of meeting to review the objectives to see if they are appropriate. If not, rewrite them with parent permission.

If a child is in a special day class and shows readiness to be returned to regular class with support, you will need to call the entire team back in order to change the student's placement and write goals that reflect regular class curriculum.

Although it is rare, occasionally you will have a student who is able to catch up and no longer qualifies for special education assistance. Call the entire team and formally dismiss the student with much praise. Do be sure to provide for continued monitoring of the student's progress as is required by Section 504 of the Rehabilitation Act of 1973.

21 TIPS FOR CLASSROOM MANAGEMENT

1. Make no more than five rules and consistently enforce them.

2. Be sure students understand they are in school to *learn.* Insist on work production, as working students are less likely to misbehave. As students begin to feel successful, they make gains in self-esteem.

3. Watch for and intervene to prevent frustration and stress.

4. Before beginning an activity, set parameters for behavior. "You may . . .," "You may not . . .," "When you finish your work you may . . .," "You may not . . ."

5. Reduce clatter and noise during working sessions. Have students practice whispering. Use white music/earphones to cover noise, and restrict movement.

6. Use signals instead of yelling. Sometimes you can reduce noise by *lowering* rather than raising your voice. If you yell, students may interpret it as a signal you do not have things under control.

7. Move parts of the group instead of the entire group. "Table 4 may line up" (orderly) instead of "Everybody line up" (chaos).

8. Plan for transitions. When students enter the room, give a short 5- to 10-minute activity or review worksheet so students are occupied while you do those things that must be done.

9. Keep directions short, clear, and supported by notes on the board.

10. Bring students to the immediate area or move closer to them when you are providing input or directions.

11. When walking down a hallway with a group of students, put three trustworthy students in front to lead. Walk at the back of the line so that from there you can see what the students in front of you are doing. If a student is not doing what is expected, call that student to the end of the line to be near you.

12. When you are going to do a class activity, be sure you either have enough materials for everyone or explain how they are to share.

13. Vary the activities: rest/activity; individualized/group; inside/outside.

14. Offer students some choice in the activities: where to work, with whom to work, what to do.

15. When you ask a question, tell students who put their hands up immediately that you are going to wait a minute so everybody has time to "think" of an answer.

16. Be sure you call on *all* students. Students need equal opportunities to answer questions. Research has shown that LD students are called on less frequently. Sometimes it is necessary to keep a chart to ensure you are not overlooking anyone.

17. Classrooms need to be colorful, inviting, and reflect what is going on. Display lots of student work.

18. Team teach with another teacher at your grade level and share ideas. Work together on academic preparations and disciplinary problems. Two heads *are* better than one!

19. Try not to yell. If a student needs a reprimand, go to him or her, get eye contact, and quietly deliver your message. One extremely effective message is to say: "Your behavior is inappropriate. Can *you* fix it?" (Wait for an answer.) My experience has been that students always say they can, and almost always do. Then, I am able to return to that student in awhile and thank him or her.

20. Do not allow grading and record-keeping chores to pile up. It is far better to occasionally risk that students may not grade their own paper accurately than to hold onto papers until the weekend or several days. By that time the assignment is no longer meaningful to the student. If you can do some of this at the end of each day, you will not be overwhelmed and your records will be up to date.

21. When students feel successful, they are less likely to misbehave. If a student is having problems or failing to complete the work, reexamine the amount of work assigned (too little/too much?); the level of the assignment (too easy/too difficult?); and the amount or quality of feedback you are giving to the student (too little/too negative?).

ACADEMIC MANAGEMENT CONSIDERATIONS

10

Schedule for the day:

9:00-10:30 Reading
10:30-10:45 Recess
10:45-12:00 Math
12:00-1:00 Lunch/Recess
1:00-1:20 Silent Reading
1:20-2:15 Science
2:15-2:30 Recess
2:30-3:30 Social Studies

Assignments:

Due today:
Math, p 113,
prob. 4-13.

English, p.17
paragraph on
"My Hobby"

Homework for tonight:
Book report
Write 10 sentences using
words from spelling list.

CURRICULUM FOR THE LEARNING DISABLED

When an LD child is being served in regular class under the collaborative-consultative Rsp model or the Inclusion model, the student is going to be "exposed" to the regular class curriculum tempered by accommodations and modifications. Therefore, the objectives written ought to reflect what is actually being taught in the regular class. Thinking educators will immediately ask, "How can a child who is almost a nonreader be expected to access the third-grade reader?" The critical word here is "exposed."

One of the compliance review issues is to assure that LD students are allowed equal educational opportunity to be *exposed* to the core curriculum. The degree to which each child is able to utilize that curriculum will vary. It is not expected every child will perform at the same level of proficiency. The task of the teachers in these settings is to try to help the children access the curriculum as much as they are able and to develop strategies that will allow them to become active learners.

The aim of these models is to de-stigmatize and re-integrate these children with their nonhandicapped peers; thereby, improving their self-esteem and socialization skills. We want them to develop adequate social skills.

Teachers of inclusion classes report the handicapped students are often able to perform as well as some of the nonhandicapped and demonstrate satisfactory progress in acquiring academic skills. They also report that behavior improves.

HOW CAN A TEACHER INCREASE STUDENT LEARNING?

The Importance of Task Analysis and Setting Goals

The purpose of curriculum guides and educational frameworks is to provide for systematic acquisition of skills across the curriculum. For example, by the end of the fourth grade, students are supposed to understand sentence structure, including nouns, verbs, adjectives, adverbs, capitalization, and punctuation.

These elements were introduced in third grade, so the fourth-grade teacher needs to determine early in the year what the students know. Can they write a complete sentence that makes sense and is mechanically correct? Can they look at a group of words and tell whether it is a sentence or a sentence fragment? The teacher usually gives some sort of informal assessment (see Figure 10-1 for a sample pretest). After giving the pretest and checking the papers, the teacher will need to carefully examine each youngster's paper to analyze the degree of understanding the child has and plan instruction groups that will zero in on those portions the child does not understand. This analysis is called *task analysis*.

Here are the answers to the sample pretest in Figure 10-1:

1. sentence
2. fragment
3. fragment
4. sentence
5. fragment
6. sentence

7. cookies, Bill, mother, store, house, one, dress

8. wants, was fishing, can come, fits

9. large, green

10. loosely

11. I, you, we

12. Answers will vary. Be sure students write complete sentences for numbers 2, 3 and 5 that make sense.

Then the teacher can set definite goals he or she wants to achieve. The pretest can become part of the portfolio; at the end of the year, after instruction, give the same test again. If you have taught effectively, there should be a marked increase in the child's score. *During the year do not teach to the test.* In daily practice it is acceptable to use materials that have similar format, but do not go over the exact sentences students will see again on the post-test.

Read the pretest directions to the students, and have them follow along by moving their finger. Then read the directions a second time. The purpose of this test is to determine whether the students know about sentence structure, *not* whether they can read. If a student needs to have the sentence read, that person will raise his or her hand and you will test the student later. When you do, you will read the words to the child. The sentences used in this test reflect a reading level of about 2.5. If a student claims not to be able to read these sentences, you will want to further check his or her reading ability.

Here are some of the possible goals you could work on:

- By the end of fourth grade _____ will be able to take 20 words he or she can read and classify them accurately either as a noun or verb. (You may have to teach a non-reader to recognize the 20 words first. I suggest: girl, boy, cat, dog, mother, daddy, baby, sister, brother, eat, sleep, want, come, run, get, go, can, come, did, stop.)

- By the end of fourth grade _____ will be able to take 10 groups of words he or she can read and classify them as a sentence or a sentence fragment.

- By the end of fourth grade _____ will be able to take a sentence fragment and rewrite it as a complete sentence.

- By the end of fourth grade _____ will be able to take 50 words he or she can read and classify them as nouns, pronouns, verbs, or adverbs achieving 70% or better on the activity.

- By the end of fourth grade _____ will be able to name at least 15 helping verbs from memory (am, are, be, been, can, could, did, do, does, has, had, have, is, may, might, must, should, will, would).

The importance of the pretest, post-test, task analysis, and goal setting is that when we set specific goals and work toward their achievement, learning is more likely to occur.

Name _____

Figure 10-1

Read the words below. Decide whether each group of words is a complete sentence. If you think it is, write "sentence" on the line next to the entry. If it is a sentence fragment, write "fragment." If you do not understand the directions, raise your hand.

1. Bill wants one of those cookies.   _____

2. I was fishing over by the   _____

3. My mother at a large store   _____

4. Can you come over to my house?   _____

5. After we eat before it gets dark   _____

6. Her green dress fits loosely.   _____

7. Using the entries above, list at least six words that are nouns.

   _____

   _____

   _____

8. Draw a circle around four verbs in the entries above.

9. Find and list two adjectives in the entries above.

   _____

10. Find and list one adverb in the entries above.

   _____

11. Find and list three pronouns in the entries above.

   _____

12. Read each entry again. Three of these are not sentences. On the back of this sheet, turn the three sentence fragments into complete sentences by correcting the errors.

Direct Instruction and Effective Lesson Design

Direct instruction has been shown to be highly effective in teaching language arts and reading skills for all children—including those with learning disabilities. Learning sessions are teacher-led and may even be scripted. The Open Court® reading series or Distar® are highly effective direct instruction reading programs.

You can develop your own direct instruction lessons if you learn the elements involved. First, you must be able to analyze a task for its steps. Let's say you want to teach 5-year-old May Li to make a puzzle of approximately 25 pieces and that child has had little or no experience with the task. What would be the first thing you would do? The steps as I see them are:

1. Have her *examine* the picture found on the front of the puzzle box so she knows how the finished product will look. Ask a few questions about the picture. Let's say the picture is of the Three Little Kittens. You say: "What are these?" The child answers, "Kittens." You say, "How many kittens are there?" The child counts and says, "Three." You ask, "What colors are the kittens?" The child says, "This one is yellow. This one is white and this one is black." You ask, "What are the kittens standing on?" The child answers "Grass." You say, "What color is the grass?" The child notes it is "green." You ask the child, "What is at the top of the picture?" The child says, "Blue sky." Place the picture where the child can see and refer back to it.

2. Next, have the child find all the pieces that are part of the frame. Start by showing her a piece that has a straight side. Say, "See how this piece has a straight side?" Put it against the table and show how the straight side lies flat. "I want you to find all the pieces that have a straight side." You watch. If she picks a piece that is curved, give immediate feedback. "That is not straight. See? It does not lie flat when you put the edge on the table. Here is a piece that has a straight side." Have the child put all the pieces to the frame on the table face up and put all the curved pieces into the bottom of the box.

3. Next, you want to have the child find the four corners that are pieces that have "two straight sides." Looking at the picture, see if she can place the corners in the correct position. Give help as needed, showing her how you knew (color or shape). Get her to locate all the pieces that appear to be blue sky. Give help at getting them assembled across the top of the puzzle as the picture shows.

4. Have the child find all the pieces that are green like grass and assemble the bottom portion of the frame.

5. Using the picture as a guide, get the sides done.

6. Finally, using the pieces that are left (those with curves), work on the interior part noting matching colors and odd shapes.

7. After admiring her handiwork, ask her to tell you the steps. The child will continue to make this puzzle daily using the exact same procedure while you give feedback (guided practice) until she can tell you the steps without prompting. Then she can show you if she can generalize what you have taught her by doing a new 25-piece puzzle without your prompting. If she needs to be reminded, do so. If not, she has mastered the art of puzzle-making.

The steps of lesson design are:

1. Get the student's attention.
2. State a goal. "Let's make this puzzle."
3. Give instruction in small increments, model.
4. Check for understanding at each step.
5. Practice is guided, with immediate feedback given if an error is made. Guided practice continues daily until the child demonstrates "readiness" to do the activity alone.
6. Provide for independent practice.
7. Reinforce the lesson at regular intervals to maintain the skill.

Direct instruction can be used in many subjects. To demonstrate, how would you teach a child to do long division? Using task analysis, you will come up with something like "divide, multiply, subtract, bring down." If you want to teach a child to use a microscope, what must he or she know and what is the sequence you will use to teach the child?

Peer Teaching

Peer teaching has also proven to be a valuable technique. Students are divided in groups of four to six. One student is appointed the leader, who takes charge of the group and acts as teacher to the group. This student may read materials to the group. The leader also appoints someone to take notes. Then the "teacher/leader" asks questions and directs the discussion so all members of the group participate. Through this interactive dialogue, inactive learners are drawn into listening and learning.

You may have a situation where two persons are paired and one teaches the other a skill. Once mastered, the one who was being taught then teaches someone else the same skill.

When using these methods, the classroom teacher circulates to monitor groups or pairs for on-task behavior and gives pointers as needed.

"Did you know that we learn 10% of what we read; 20% of what we hear; 30% of what we see; 50% of what we see and hear; 70% of what we discuss personally; 85% of what is personally experienced and 90% of what we teach someone else."

(Quote from handout given at the Regional Educator's Symposium, Palm Springs, CA, 1991.)

Cooperative Learning

Cooperative learning is another trend currently being widely used. When it was developed in the late 1980s, its primary purpose was to help integrate special education students into the mainstream. Now we find it to be helpful in teaching students to work cooperatively while developing a tolerance for individual differences and cultural diversity. In cooperative learning, every member of the group participates in activities that can only be completed through interdependent and cooperative effort. There may be a competition between teams, but the goal is cooperation *within* a given team. Teachers report the ideal number for a grouping is 4—one high achiever, two average achievers, and one low achiever. Groups remain together for a period of several weeks because it takes time to get them to learn to work cooperatively. A social goal is stated at the beginning of each lesson, such as learning to share one set of materials without squabbling. The class discusses how that should look and sound. Then a project is given with only one set of materials; students practice what they talked about, with the teacher circulating and giving accolades for groups who are able to do well at sharing and giving pointers or directions to those groups needing assistance. Other social goals might be learning to work using quiet voices, learning to engage everyone in participation, and giving and receiving criticism.

Usually grades are not assigned, but point systems are used to determine the winning group and a reward is given. Group work may be followed by a general class discussion about what they learned from the experience. Teachers often have students keep a diary of these experiences. If the project worked on is one that results in grades, the nondisabled students need to be assured their grade will not be negatively effected by the score of the disabled child. (Failure to do so can result in the disabled child being resented by the group instead of integrated.)

If you have not yet been trained in cooperative learning, you probably will be soon or you may want to request that kind of training when you have an opportunity to express your needs. To do a really good job of training takes many hours and is best done when teachers have a chance to use the techniques themselves before trying to involve students.

Metacognition

Metacognition simply means "understanding how you learn." When most of us approach a new task or something we must learn, we try to relate it to the knowledge we already have; we apply strategies that have worked well for us before as well as engage in "trial and error" behavior. Very few LD children or adults do that. In the face of an unknown task, they tend to give up without making an attempt.

Advance Organizers and Story Mapping

Advance organizers and story mapping are other techniques for increasing students' learning. A sheet of paper that must be completed is given to the student. The wording on the sheet forces the student to organize his or her approach to the material in some way. Figures 10-2, 10-3, and 10-4 are commonly used examples of such organizers. They are easy to do and markedly increase the amount of information a student gains from an assignment. They also can be used by the student to prepare for testing (a form of notes).

Figure 10-2

What do I already know about the subject?	What do I want to learn?	What did I learn from doing this lesson?

Figure 10-3. Story mapping.

Name of story _____

Author _____

Setting (time, place) _____

Main characters:

_____

_____

_____

_____

The plot/the problem:

_____

_____

_____

_____

The outcome:

_____

_____

_____

What value did I gain from reading this story?

_____

_____

Figure 10-4
ORGANIZER FOR A SOCIAL STUDY UNIT ON THE TRANSCONTINENTAL RAILROAD

1. **Meaning of Terms**

   transportation _____

   _____

   communication _____

   _____

   survey _____

   _____

   construction _____

   _____

2. Discuss the role played by Chinese workers in building the first transcontinental railroad, including the hardships involved.

   _____

   _____

   _____

3. Give the year and place where the Union Pacific and Central Pacific railroads were joined by a golden spike.

   _____

   _____

   _____

4. How did the transcontinental railroad affect:

   the Pony Express_____

   _____

   the stagecoach companies_____

   _____

STRATEGIES FOR LEARNING

At the *elementary level* we want to teach children appropriate school behaviors and organizational skills; strategies they can use to improve their daily performance; strategies for studying for and taking tests; reference skills; and how to read and interpret graphs and tables.

There is a very fine program for grades 3-6 available through Curriculum Associates, Inc. (1-800-225-0248). Written by Anita Archer and Mary Gleason, *Skills for School Success* provides scripted lessons so even the beginning teacher feels secure. It also provides student books so teacher time is not required to make materials. A skill is introduced at one level and reviewed at the next. Lessons are snappy because they are designed to be completed in one period of 20 minutes.

At the *secondary level* wonderful programs are available that will help students with word identification, paraphrasing, self-questioning, visual imagery, study skills in subjects such as science and social studies, improvement of memory, test taking, and writing skills (sentence building, paragraph building, and theme writing). Developed by the University of Kansas Institute for Research in Learning Disabilities, they are referred to as *The Learning Strategies Curriculum*. You can find more information on these strategies in Chapter 15.

The programs listed above have been tested and proven to be effective in helping LD students as well as regular class students. Unfortunately, you will need some training in order to learn to use them.

Higher Level Questioning

The use of higher level questioning is another trend that is prevalent in education today. In some places it is referred to as teaching critical thinking.

As we devise lessons, we can use low-level activities such as:

1. matching
2. filling in blanks
3. multiple-choice questions
4. defining
5. listing
6. paraphrasing

Or we can move into activities requiring multiple intelligences to demonstrate the application of facts, analysis of situations, and creating. These include:

1. make a diorama illustrating some portion of the story
2. use the events of the story to rewrite it in play form
3. compose a song or poem
4. hold a mock trial
5. compare and contrast two events
6. write an ad or draw a cartoon

7. debate a question

8. interview someone else about his or her viewpoint on an issue

9. make a list of questions that would be a good test

10. develop a project of your own to show you understood the unit

Item 10 is dynamite for the LD student whose IQ is above average but who has trouble with written expression. These students come up with elaborate and very creative projects.

The Importance of Feedback

Children vary greatly in their ability to absorb and integrate information. In order to ascertain exactly what a child has learned requires that you get either oral or written feedback. In classes where the teacher lectures and students listen, the opportunity for mislearning occurs. Several years ago, someone posted an amusing example of the kind of thing that can happen. The fifth grader involved had erroneously integrated information from several sources. The student reported:

"The human body is composed of three parts: the Brainium, the Borax and the Abominable Cavity. The Brainium contains the brain. The Borax contains the lungs, the liver and the living things. The Abominable Cavity contains the bowels, of which there are five: a, e, i, o, and u." (Associated Press—Seattle)

Every important discussion and lecture needs to be followed by feedback. Written feedback is appropriate for the majority of students; for those students not able to express themselves in writing, teachers need to provide them an opportunity to report what they learned in other ways.

6 TIPS FOR ACADEMIC MANAGEMENT

1. Place a copy of each student's I.E.P. in his or her portfolio so it is there to review regularly. As the student completes each objective, you can check it off in front of the student to give the student a sense of accomplishment. Be sure to keep the sample or test that supports the objective has been achieved. Date it and put the student's full name on it. If you also write the objective at the top, it is easy to tell which goal is satisfied by that particular paper.

2. Novelty, newness, props, and activities that are full of action enhance motivation and attention.

3. Within a given lesson, include as many learning channels (auditory, visual, tactile/kinesthetic input) as you can. Visual aids, tape recorders, overhead projectors, and movies stimulate and support lecture.

4. If you are delivering a lesson and you can see the lesson is not working, stop and have students do something else. Rework the lesson and try again another day.

5. Use a green pencil rather than a red one to grade. Make suggestions instead of criticisms. For example, instead of "This doesn't make sense," try "Tell me this in another way."

6. This next tip is specifically directed to new teachers. Before you begin *every* lesson, take a brief moment to reflect on your goals for that lesson. Settle on teaching a few concepts well and building on them daily rather than going over a lot of material poorly. All too often, a lesson consists of reading a chapter of material. When finished, the students have gone over the material but they have limited or no understanding of it.

It helped me to say to myself "When this child's parent asks him/her what was learned at school today, what do I want that child to say?" It really disturbs me to hear children say "Nothing."

Decide exactly what you want the child to take away from the lesson. It even helps to let children know specifically what you want them to remember. At the end of the lesson, you may want to have them read a summary of the main points; you may want them to take home a handout of notes on the major points that they can share with their parent; you will want to ask them questions to check their understanding and correct any erroneous ideas.

You will find that this simple exercise of deciding on a few goals at the beginning of *each* lesson will markedly increase the amount of learning gained by your students and help them improve their achievement scores.

11

TEACHING READING

Reading is considered to be the most important skill taught in school. Being able to read and understand what you read are skills critical to the acquisition of other knowledge. It is difficult to get by in our society if you do not read well; for example, in most states you must be able to read at a fourth-grade level to get a driver's license. When a child is referred to the SST in the early grades, it is generally because of a reading deficit. Many special education students are not able to read at the functional level of approximately grade 4 by the end of high school.

METHODS AND TECHNIQUES FOR TEACHING READING

Whole Language Approach

At the present time, the most prevalent method for teaching reading is the *whole language* method. The premise behind whole language is that if children read and listen to good literature read often, they will gradually build the skills necessary to become avid readers. The emphasis of whole language is on language development, semantic and syntax development within the natural flow of reading interesting stories. Words are recognized as wholes by sight. If you are in a whole language class, you will see the teacher reading the story to the children, the children listening to the story again on tape, the children rereading the story with the teacher chorally, or reading in pairs while the teacher circulates. In daily writing assignments, the child may use inventive spelling (for example, phone might be "fon"), but this is okay because the child will gradually pick up the correct spelling through repeated exposure to words. The components of whole language are reading, writing, and speaking. *How effective is the whole language approach?* It appears to work fairly well for roughly four out of five children.

The Basic Skills/Phonics Approaches

Reading programs using these approaches use readers that have controlled vocabulary. The stories in the readers are often deadly dull. If you have ever seen a basal reader, you will know what I mean: "This is Jane. Jane can run. Run, Jane. See Jane run. This is Dick. Dick can run. Spot can run."

When phonics is the approach, first grade begins with students learning the sounds of each alphabet letter and being taught how to blend letters together to get words. Various rules are taught as students progress in their understanding.

If you watch a class working with basic skills or phonics, you might see children using a skill-building notebook, with the teacher and other helpers listening to individual students read. You may see the teacher dictating isolated words (three-letter words) while the children try to listen for and write the letter sounds they can hear within the word.

How effective are basic skills/phonics programs? They appear to work with most students. Critical to their success is the degree to which each student is taught to blend sounds together to make words. This requires much one-to-one attention in the early years.

Combining Whole Language and Phonics

In response to criticisms leveled at the programs just described, some whole language texts have begun to include some phonics—primarily in grades 1 and 2. More and more teachers of whole language are trying to integrate some phonics knowledge into their classes by showing students how they can work out ("sound out") words.

Some newer phonics programs have begun to use more interesting books; those that have predictable endings are particularly popular. They have also eliminated the dull skill-pack work. By connecting a letter with a single referent and picture, these programs have been shown to be much more effective. When the students are confronted with the letters as well as a pictograph to support the letters, the phonics approach has worked well with mentally retarded students and LD students. If you are working with a student whose memory scores fall below the 10th percentile, that student probably will not learn to read without heavy emphasis on phonics. Having such poor memory, these students cannot grasp words in the time allowed by the whole language approach.

What method should you use to teach children to read? That's easy. *Use whatever works.* Research shows learning disabled children taught by phonics make a slow beginning, but after grade 3 they tend to do somewhat better than those taught by sight-word techniques (Bender, 1994).

Language Experience Approach

Some special class teachers use a *language experience approach.* In this approach students dictate their own stories to the teacher or other adult who writes them. Then the students read them back, looking carefully at each word.

Neurological Impress Method

In the *neurological impress method*, student and teacher simultaneously read a short selection several times. The child points to each word as he or she reads. With each subsequent reading, the teacher lowers his or her voice, eventually fading out almost entirely. The teacher may, at the end of each reading, elect to point out one or two words to the student for greater scrutiny.

Programmed Reading Instruction Method

You may encounter *programmed reading instruction methods*, with some being interactive with the computer. New information is presented in small increments, followed by requiring the student to use what was just taught.

Daily Word Lists

You occasionally will find a teacher who has students read *daily word lists*, periodically altering the order in which words are presented. The lists usually run about 50 words. When a student can identify all the words, a new list may be employed.

Cloze Method

Occasionally you may see a teacher use what is referred to as the *cloze method.* Using passages of approximately 250 words at the student's functional level, words are replaced with a blank. As the student reads, he or she must use the context of the story and his or her knowledge of linguistics to figure out the missing word. To give you an idea of how this works, consider the following excerpt from one such story:

Once upon a time, _____ were three little pigs. _____ day, their mother said, " _____ is time for you _____ leave home and build _____ own houses." The three little pigs had only gone a short way when _____ met a man carrying sticks. One little pig _____ , "Kind sir, will you give _____ some sticks so I can _____ a house?"

The student either writes or orally fills in the missing words. *Answers:* there, One, It, to, your, they, asked (said), me, build.

TECHNIQUES FOR IMPROVING COMPREHENSION

Marginalia

There are several excellent techniques available for improving comprehension. As previously mentioned, story mapping is one; but from third grade through sixth grade, you can't beat *marginalia*. Make a copy of the story to be read for each student. As students read, they interact with the text by writing comments in the margin, paraphrasing parts of the story in the margin or drawing a picture that illustrates their understanding.

Papers are scored as follows: A designation of "1" means the student made some attempt to interact with the text—even if it is only one word. A "2" indicates the student made multiple entries on each page. A "3" means the student related in depth to the story, relating it to his or her personal experience.

Figure 11-1 shows how two different students related to the same passage.

You will note that Student A did a more thorough job. He used a dictionary to look up the word "shocks" (the dictionary gave a picture). He relates to the words out of his own experience and makes predictions about what is happening from the clues. Student B, who is learning disabled, relates literally. Since beginning to use the marginalia strategy, this student's performance has markedly improved. He is more able to stay on-task and gets more out of the assignment. By examining his pictures, you can tell that you need to explain "shocks" to him and that it was a "full moon."

Self-Questioning

Another strategy is one that involves *self-questioning*. After reading a section of text, the student must attempt to answer the following questions:

Who is the story about?

What is the problem?

Where did the story take place?

When does the story take place?

Why does the main character do what he or she does?

How is the problem solved?

Predicting/Inferential Thinking

There is one skill particularly difficult for LD students: using clues to predict what will happen next. It is important to give students as many experiences with this skill as

Figure 11-1

Student A

I love Halloween. It is my favorite holiday. I like it better than Christmas

It was late in the evening—a cool evening

at the end of October. In the field beside the

house, the (corn stood in shocks) and a variety

of (pumpkins sat in a pile). You could tell

they were pumpkins because there was a full

moon that night. On the (fence) a big black cat

lazily washed her paws after having just

devoured a mouse who hadn't seen her in time.

Suddenly out of the corner of her eye, she saw

a (witch), a (ghost) and a (pirate) coming toward her.

I think these are children who are playing trick or treat. They will get some candy at the house.

moon

mouse in tummy

Student B

10 P.M It was (late) in the evening—a cool evening

at the end of October. In the field beside the

(house), the (corn) stood in shocks and a variety

of pumpkins sat in a pile. You could tell

they were (pumpkins) because there was a full

(moon) that night. On the fence a big black (cat)

lazily washed her (paws) after having just

devoured a mouse who hadn't seen her in time.

Suddenly, out of the corner of her (eye) she saw

a witch, a ghost and a pirate coming toward her.

meow

paw

you can because with practice, their ability to "think" improves. (See Volume II for student practice materials.)

TEACHING SAFETY WORDS

If a student learns nothing else in school, it is essential to his or her health and well-being that safety words are taught. The following words and phrases are important for survival. An attempt has been made to list them by importance.

1. Poison	18. Do Not Use Near Open Flame
2. No trespassing	19. Fire Escape
3. Exit	20. First Aid
4. Stop	21. No Left Turn
5. Keep Out	22. Proceed at Your Own Risk
6. Do Not Touch	23. No Swimming
7. No Admittance	24. Railroad Crossing
8. High Voltage	25. No Parking
9. For External Use Only	26. Yield
10. Do Not Enter	27. Slow
11. Restrooms	28. Watch Your Step
12. Beware of the Dog	29. Hospital
13. Slippery When Wet	30. Watch for Children
14. Wet Paint	31. School Zone
15. Out of Order	32. Wrong Way
16. Help Wanted	33. One Way
17. Don't Walk	34. No Smoking

TEACHING READING DURING SCIENCE AND SOCIAL STUDIES

Multi-Scan

One of the problems that LD students encounter is an inability to read many pages and complete a written assignment within the time limits set. You can help all your students by teaching them a study technique called *Multi-Scan*. Before beginning a new unit, have the students turn to the questions they will need to answer and read the questions aloud three times. Next, you want them to scan the question for the *key words*. Tell them that, in general, key words will be nouns. Have them make a list of those nouns. (See Volume II for lessons on teaching students to identify nouns.)

Now have the students go back to the first page of the unit. Instead of reading every word on each page, instruct them to read all captions, all words that explain a picture or chart, all bold print words. Through modeling and guided practice, have the students practice doing this. When they locate one of those nouns they listed from the questions, they need to read the information in that section of the text to look for the answer to the question.

When teachers give an assignment that involves lots of reading, followed by answering questions, LD students are at an immediate disadvantage. If they read the assignment word for word, or if they are not able to read the material, they can not complete the questions in the time required. The result is they get an F and experience all the bad feelings that are associated with failure. This failure increases the probability that the student will not attempt the next assignment. With Multi-Scan, the student reads the most critical parts, finds the answers to most questions, and probably obtains a passing score. The passing score makes these students feel they can do the assignment and increases the probability that they will attempt the next assignment.

HELP! JOHNNY STILL CAN'T READ AND I MUST HELP HIM: A TEACHER'S GUIDE FOR HELPING THE CHILD WHO FINDS READING EXTREMELY DIFFICULT

The purpose of this section is to give you a guide for working with students who are diagnosed as being dyslexic, students who have severe memory deficits, or students who have few, if any, reading skills. Since these students are primarily boys, the word "he" is used in this section.

- *First*, you will need to set aside at least 30 minutes a day everyday to work one-to-one with the student.

- *Second*, you must convince the student you can teach him to read even though other teachers haven't.

- *Third*, you need to explain that it won't be easy, but if he tries, he will learn. Let him know you will not be mad if he makes mistakes.

- *Fourth*, you will need to determine what he already knows. Use the following activities to help you assess the student. Ask the student to give you a sound for each alphabet letter, and record his responses (+ if correct and 0 if wrong) on the sheet shown in Figure 11-2.

Typically, what you will find is that most students can give you the correct sound for all consonants except *c* and *g*, which you will note are the only ones with two sounds. Likewise, they are confused by all the vowels. Why? Because they also have more than one sound.

Some students have problems with d/t, b/p, and v/f. Why? Because students do not know how much air to put out to make the sounds. You can show them by having them put their hand in front of your mouth to feel the air that is released for *t*, *p*, and *f*. T involves more air than *d*; *p* more than *b*; and *f* more than *v*.

You will usually find that no one has taught students to blend the sounds of the letters together to get words. They cannot "sound out." Children without LD pick up this skill almost incidentally, but LD kids do not. They can learn to do it but it takes lots of one-to-one practice to teach them. *If you take the time, they learn to read. If you don't, they'll remain illiterate.*

You will need to teach the student any sound he does not know. Be careful the student does not say *a* is *apple*. He needs only to make the *a* sound, as it sounds at the start of *apple*.

When you begin to teach him to blend sounds together, use two-letter words with short vowels. You can also take words he already knows by sight and unblend them so

Figure 11-2

_____ **A** sounds like the beginning of *apple*. If the student gives you the long sound (*a* as in *ape*), say "Yes, it does sound like that sometimes. Do you know any other sound for *a*?"

_____ **B** is a little poof of air that you hear at the beginning of words such as *ball*. If the student says "buh," you will need to reteach the sound until the student no longer adds the short *u* to the *b*.

_____ **C** is the sound you hear at the beginning of *car*. If the student gives you the soft *c* as in *city*, tell him that "It is true that *c* always makes an *s* sound when it is followed by an *e, i,* or *y,* but *c* has another sound. Do you know what it is?" Hopefully, he will come up with the *k* sound.

_____ **D** sounds like it does in the word *door*. Again we want to be sure the student makes a pure *d*, not "duh."

_____ **E** sounds like it does in the word *edge*. Remember that *e* can have the long sound as it does in *eel*.

_____ **F** sounds like it does in the word *fish*.

_____ **G** sounds like it does in the word *go*. If the student gives you the soft *g* sound as in *gym*, acknowledge that it does sound like a *j* when the *g* is followed by *e, i, y,* and ask if he knows another sound.

_____ **H** sounds like it does in the word *house*.

_____ **I** sounds like it does in the word *itch*. Remember that *i* can have the long sound also as it does in the word *ice*.

_____ **J** sounds like it does in the word *jar*.

_____ **K** sounds like it does in the word *kite*.

_____ **L** sounds like it does in the word *light* or *lamp*.

_____ **M** sounds like it does in *moon*.

_____ **N** sounds like it does in *nose*.

_____ **O** sounds like it does in the word *octopus*. As with the other vowels, it has a long sound also, like in *Ohio*.

_____ **P** sounds like it does in the word *pan*.

_____ **Q** sounds like it does in *queen* (*kw*).

_____ **R** sounds like it does in the word *red* or *her*. Be sure the student is not saying "ruh."

_____ **S** sounds like it does in *sun* or *snake* (a hissing sound).

_____ **T** sounds like it does in *tack*.

_____ **U** sounds like it does in *up*. It can sound like a long *u* as it does in *use*.

_____ **V** sounds like it does in *vase*.

_____ **W** sounds like it does in *water*.

_____ **X** says *x*.

_____ **Y** has three sounds. It can sound like it does in *you* or *yes*. It can sound like an *e* as it does in *happy* or *baby*. Finally, in some words such as *my*, it sounds like the long *i*.

_____ **Z** sounds like it does in the word *zoo*.

he can hear the three distinct sounds that make the word. Present the words with the pictographs below the letters so the student is not frustrated because of an inability to retrieve the sound from memory. Continue to present the pictograph until you note the student no longer needs it.

Do not despair if a student has trouble with blending. Continue to model how the sounds go together to make a word. Point to each letter as you slide through the sounds. The student will catch on.

Here is a list of one-vowel words you may draw from:

hug	cut	jug	pal	tax	in	set	rib	let
fed	up	mob	pat	on	left	am	bud	log
is	sit	on	fat	men	hit	dip	pat	off
us	pup	cup	pet	rid	if	get	not	hog
nap	dot	ham	mat	red	did	pig	web	neck
box	fan	dog	sad	pot	cat	lip	dad	ten
bed	at	bag	rub	lot	bug	hot	gum	hid
big	cot	rob	top	bus	had	ask	map	rug
gun	rat	jam	run	mud	yes	tip	fix	hen
lip	egg	nut	man	put	wet	but	sun	vet
pen	leg	and	ran	wag	has	fox	grin	hat
tuck	cast	brag	plan	fast	sell	miss	help	lost
lamp	back	best	sled	jump	plot	pull	slam	crab
raft	hand	soft	fact	trap	drum	gift	left	next
stop	bulb	flat	fond	doll	camp	mess	belt	lick
snap	spot	lack	scan	task	felt	hill	slid	
slap	bank	cost	flag	lamp	full	will	clip	
plug	cram	lift	send	milk	list	tell	spin	

Once the student clearly knows the short vowel sounds and can demonstrate he can blend most two- and three-letter words, he is ready to begin a reading series. The one I particularly like is *The Multiple Skills* series published by Barnell-Loft (958 Church Street, Baldwin, NY 11510). It is a carefully developed series that begins with materials at the primer level and gradually moves the student along. Even the primer level material is not offensive to most students—even older ones. The selections are short, which is helpful because it allows the teacher or student the flexibility to stop and start as the situation warrants (interruptions, student becomes tired). Once students reach Level C, they usually ask if the stories are true and are pleased to learn many of them are. This is not a programmed instruction series; the teacher needs to listen to the student read aloud daily, giving immediate feedback if errors are made.

At the point you note the books begin to use words requiring the long sound of the vowel, you will need to teach three rules.

Rule 1: If a word has only one vowel, it normally will carry the short vowel sound.

Begin to train students to analyze words to see how many vowels are in them. You will want to put up a bulletin board like the one shown here or furnish the student with the information.

Rule 2: If a word (or a syllable) has more than one vowel, the first vowel will usually carry the long sound.

To illustrate, take the word *hope*.

cvcv pattern

The *e* tells the *o* to say its alphabet name, not *o* as in *octopus*. I tell young children that the *e* is a "bully." It reaches over and threatens to hit the *o* on the head unless the *o* says its name. We look at many words where this happens.

Similarly, when you encounter a word such as *read*, the *a* tells the *e* it has to say its name.

cvvc pattern

Rule 3: If the word contains more than one vowel, see if the word follows the vowel consonant/consonant vowel pattern.

To illustrate, take the word *ham/mer.*

   vc/cv pattern

This word and many others will syllabicate between the consonants. Each syllable is then treated as a small word and the vowel assumes the short sound outlined in Rule 1.

As the text introduces special combinations such as *sh, ch, ou, ing*, you want to review them every day for at least a week. See the "Students' Reminder for Decoding" and the "Teacher's Resource List of Special Combinations" in Volume II.

Also begin working on spelling lists taken from *The First 100 Most Common Words.* (See the list in Volume II.) A good beginning list includes *can, eat, for, get, go, has, is, like, look, make, not, play, read, ride, stop, to, the, will, want, you.*

You will also want to introduce a dictation lesson three times weekly, as described in Volume II.

15 Tips for Teaching Beginning Readers

1. Start low; go slow.

2. When you introduce a new sound, work on it everyday until it is mastered.

3. While you may be "exposing" the student to the grade level text during the regular reading period, when you ask the student to read to you, if possible, choose materials at the student's functional level.

4. Empathize that you know it is hard, but praise the student's willingness to try.

5. Rewards promised for the completion of a given amount of reading will often keep a reluctant student reading.

6. When a student makes an error, be sure to give immediate feedback. If the word said is spelled almost like the word in print, show the student the words side-by-side (house, horse). Help the student see the difference.

7. If a student tends to "guess" a word after looking at only the first letter or two, encourage the student not to guess until after he has sounded out at least three letters.

8. Teach students to demand *sense* from what they read. For instance, if the student reads "The farmer's house was lazy," the LD student often does not self-correct. The teacher has the option of telling him the missed word or saying, "Tim, you said 'The farmer's house was lazy.' I don't understand." By far it is better to do the latter and wait for him to self-correct than to tell him; this forces the child to hunt for his own error and to learn to expect sense.

9. Reading and writing go hand-in-hand. Have students orally retell and then write summaries of what they read. For short selections, this may be only one sentence.

10. Markers are very helpful to students. They help students stay focused and eliminate the distracting influence of the rest of the print.

11. Have younger children make books to take home. ("Sixty percent of American homes failed to purchase even a single book last year." *Marilu* TV show, December 14, 1994.)

12. When parents ask to have a child celebrate a birthday at school, ask the parent to bring a gift-wrapped book for the class library instead of sweets.

13. Research shows that most beginning readers respond well to word/picture fading flash cards. Put a picture of a dog at the top of a 3″ x 5″ card. Print the word **d o g** at the bottom of the card. Make about 10 cards and begin flashing them to the child each day. After a few days begin covering the picture with plastic each time the child does the activity. As more layers of plastic are added, the picture gradually fades out. (Knowlton, 1980.)

14. Teach students word analysis. As they begin to read at the second-grade level, they will encounter root words, prefixes, and suffixes (for example, *happy* becomes *unhappy*). Use directed teaching lessons to enhance their ability to comprehend word meaning by having them learn that the *un* means "not."

15. To become a good pianist, you must practice. To become a good baseball player, you must practice. To become a good reader, you must read. Daily reading practice of 30 minutes is recommended (15 minutes at school and 15 minutes at home).

TEACHING LANGUAGE ARTS

Reading instruction and language arts go hand-in-hand. Reading requires a *blending* of sounds while spelling requires an *unblending* of sounds. Writing is by far the most difficult thing we expect of children in school because a whole series of cognitive abilities are simultaneously being brought into focus. The writer must decide what will be recorded and in what order it should go; then the writer brings into play his or her knowledge of semantics and pragmatics, while spelling correctly, using correct mechanics, and using good penmanship. Is it any wonder that children often forget what they intended to say before they get it all on paper!

The Value of Keeping an Ongoing Language Arts Notebook

If a student has a notebook in which to file vocabulary lists and other language arts handouts, the student finds it helpful and will use it later to refer back to.

Vocabulary Development

Research has shown that a majority of LD students have deficits in semantics (word meaning) and pragmatics (using words in specific ways so they convey exactly the meaning intended by the user). Research has also shown that the average student needs 20 to 30 exposures to commit new information to memory. If we utilize these two pieces of information, it is easy to see why students do not get much benefit out of the way new vocabulary words have been traditionally taught, i.e., the teacher puts several words on the board that are to be looked up in a dictionary. The student is to copy the definition.

First, this is a dull way to present information. Add to this the fact that LD students are inactive learners. What you will soon discover is *if* they do the assignment at all, it is rarely finished because they lack the skills to efficiently use the dictionary or lack the motivation to commit to such a tedious assignment. In the rare cases where the children have done it, they cannot tell you anything about what they wrote—they were too engrossed in the copying aspect of the assignment. They were not seeking meaning. One exposure is not sufficient to learn a new word and how to use the word in a sentence. So let's look at a way that does work.

1. Put the first word on the board, dividing it into syllables. Pronounce the word, then have students repeat its pronunciation. Have them write the word in syllables in their notebook.
2. Write a sentence using the word in context on the board. Read the sentence to students and have them read the sentence to you. Have them write the sentence in their notebook.
3. Using the context clues to help, discuss what they think the word might mean. For example: per sist.

We hope the good weather <u>persists</u> over the weekend.

(I usually ask the students to write their guesses on scratch paper. They often guess correctly and this make the activity more exciting.)

4. Have the students look up the word and raise their hands when they find it. (Note which students consistently take more than three minutes to find the word. These students will need training in how to use the dictionary more efficiently.)

5. Read together the definition and read any sentences given to show its use.

6. Have the students copy the definition that best suits the sentence. For example:

We hope the good weather <u>continues</u> over the weekend.

7. See Volume II for playing a concentration game to learn vocabulary.

Vocabulary Development and Its Relationship to Paraphrasing

Not all words have synonyms. (Sometimes it is necessary to define a word with a whole sentence.) Wherever possible, however, teach synonyms because when a student is asked to "put something in his or her own words," the student will only be able to do so if he or she has a knowledge of synonyms. Synonym knowledge is a prerequisite skill to comprehension.

Words That Describe Feelings

Another common deficit among LD students is having adequate vocabulary to describe feelings. You have probably found that when you ask a student how the character in a story was feeling, the student will almost invariably use the words "good" or "bad," or they may use the words "glad" or "sad." You may have just read a passage where the words *terrified, scared, frightened, horrified, afraid, panicked* should come to mind, but the student says "He was feeling bad" because the student does not have these other words firmly set in his or her vocabulary. The English language is particularly rich in providing additional words that describe the degree of the feeling. If the child says someone was "feeling good" or "feeling glad," have the student refer to the list of other words. Was the character *joyous, elated, gleeful, ecstatic*?

In Volume II you will find a list of Feeling Words as well as activities to help students improve their ability to use them effectively. Give students a copy of this list for their notebook.

Words That Drive Kids Crazy

This is another list of words kids need to have repeated practice using. (See Figure 12-1.) I used to use this list (students had a copy in their notebooks) whenever we ended up with 10 minutes before the bell. We would periodically look at the list, pronouncing the words and discussing the subtle differences between confusing things like *though, through,* and *thought*. It gave us a chance to reinforce things like the crazy *ei* that can sound like a long *a* and the silent *h* that occurs at the start of words such as *hour* and *honor*. As kids encounter other "crazy" words, have the students add them to their list.

Figure 12-1

LIST OF WORDS THAT DRIVE KIDS CRAZY

bear	laugh
	learn
begin	listen
being	
bring	neighbor
build	
busy	once
	one
could	
country	piece
county	
cousin	quiet
	quite
does	
	ready
edge	
eight	science
enough	sign
	since
find	sure
gnaw	there
great	they
guess	though
	thought
head	three
heavy	through
high	
hour	wear
how	we're
	where
island	who
	whole
knew	
knot	young
know	

TEACHING SPELLING

LD students can normally read or recognize words before they can spell them. The average nonhandicapped child at elementary level can spell 70 to 80 percent of the words he or she can read. The percentage for the LD child is 30 to 40 percent (Smith, 1990). If a student is attentionally deficit, his or her ability to spell will be adversely affected because the student doesn't see spelling relationships, such as the *the* in mo*the*r.

The whole language approach encourages that spelling be taught within the context of writing and the words chosen should be those needed by the student in order to communicate, especially those words used on a daily basis. Yet in most classrooms you will still find students receiving a weekly spelling list (usually one containing the vocabulary from the story being read) and taking a test on Friday. This is not a very effective way to teach spelling to anyone.

Which Words?

The question arises: *Which words should we be teaching?* In reviewing various lists widely used in the field, there is remarkable agreement on the 500 most often used words; so it seems we should begin with teaching those. If we could teach youngsters to spell these words and recognize them, we will have brought LD children to a minimum literacy level. After this goal is accomplished, we could move on to lists that go along with the students' reading series.

The next question that arises is: *How can we effectively teach spelling?* Spelling needs to be approached both phonetically and visually. To illustrate, when you see the word *quick*, you can phonetically hear the *ik* but you must also take in the visual details, i.e., the *qu* that sounds like "kw" and the *c* that cannot be heard at all.

Fifty percent of words in English are totally phonetically spelled. Most of the others you can come close enough with phonics that the reader can "ges" what you're trying to spell. Fortunately, there are very few words that are so perverse that a knowledge of phonics doesn't help. If the student can come close, in our days of technology, the actual spelling can be determined through the use of the "spell-check" on the computer or with an electronic dictionary.

Effective Ways to Teach Spelling

1. Have the student mark each letter he or she can hear in a word. If the word contains a special combination sound, circle it.

2. Have the student mark the configuration of the word.

3. Have the student color-code the words: vowels are written in red, consonants are in green. Using crayons, write the word *read* and then try *have*. Note how color makes you more aware of the letters within the word.

4. Ask the student to write the spelling words in dot-to-dot fashion. The main feature of this technique is that it will force inattentive students to think about what they are doing. I have never found a student who could not write words dot-to-dot, although several had to be encouraged to do it.

5. Teach the student to use *verbal rehearsal* to learn spelling words. Have the student look at the word and say each letter, for example, "l–e–a–r–n spells *learn*." Do this twice. Then teach the student to write the word without looking. The student checks the word for correctness, changing any part he or she missed.

6. Pair two students. Have the weaker speller call the words out to the stronger speller; they jointly check the paper. They then switch and the weaker speller writes the words, having first had the advantage of looking at them while dictating and checking his or her partner's paper.

7. For longer words, have the student write them by syllable, then color-code each syllable.

8. Use at least three *dictation* lessons a week. When developing your sentences, use words from the previous week's as well as this week's words. Caution students to listen carefully. Read the sentence three times. In the beginning, keep your sentences short (five to seven words). Have students repeat the sentence at least three times (this verbal rehearsal trains memory); then they write the sentence. If the student forgets, have the student read the part he or she has written to help him or her recall the entire sentence.

Allow the students to check each other's papers in four-person groups to help locate the mistakes. The students are then allowed to make corrections and get the better grade.

9. Give the students a *500 Most Used Words List* for their notebook and encourage them to use it for their work in all subjects. In the beginning if they ask you how to spell a word that is on the list, you will have to remind them to check their list. After a while, they will internalize the habit of checking the list.

TEACHING WRITING

At least half of students with learning disabilities have problems with penmanship or written expression. We need to examine some problem areas for LD students and talk about the accommodations and expectations that apply to them.

Penmanship

Many LD students are deficit in penmanship. Their errors fall in several areas: spacing, errors of letter height or formation, and letters that are not on lines. *Why is this so?*

First, we must look at children coming into kindergarten. Some have never had a pencil or crayon in their hand. When presented with these implements, they have no idea how to hold the pencil properly and they do not have the fine motor control to make the pencil go where they want it to go. For these children proper instruction in kindergarten would necessitate that someone diligently work with them to remediate the problem. These children are not ready to learn to make letters—they need to learn color. They are still in the 2- to 3-year-old stage of fine motor development (scribbling). Someone needs to teach them to "stay within the lines," how to make little strokes/big strokes, color in circles. Only months later will they be ready to learn to write legibly. These are often the same students who have poorly developed vocabularies, low general information funds, and language deficits. They will benefit from an extra year of kindergarten provided *specific efforts are made to help them develop these skills.* This does not mean one-to-one, but it does require small-group instruction of no more than one-to-three so the child is provided adequate feedback, attention, and assistance.

If a student has reached grade 2 and is holding the pencil wrong, it is extremely difficult to change this habit. If a student holds the pencil incorrectly, it will cause his or her hand to tire easily; thus, in later grades, the completion of writing assignments involving much writing is impossible.

If a student is right-handed, the proper way to hold the pencil and tilt the paper is shown in this illustration.

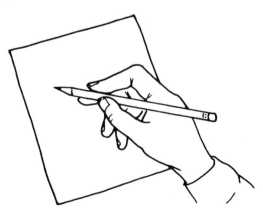

Left-handed students living in a right-handed world often write by "hooking," shown in the drawing on the left. This is tiring and easily corrected. Have the left-handed student tilt the paper as shown in the drawing on the right.

 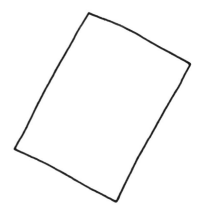

The primary goal of handwriting is communication. If it is legible, we can tolerate individual differences.

Written Expression Deficits of LD Students

Let's review some of the deficits common to LD students:

1. linguistic deficits (semantics, syntax, and pragmatics)
2. organizational deficits
3. fine motor deficits/visual perceptual deficits
4. poor vocabularies
5. poor memory
6. poor conceptual skills

If we propose to help students to improve their written expression, we must initiate remediation in all these areas. Speech therapists should work in the lower grades on syntax. Teachers at all grades and in all subjects should consistently teach new vocabulary words with great amounts of student feedback so that vocabulary is mastered and becomes a regular part of the student's writing and speaking.

In analyzing LD student's sentences, they usually do not exceed seven simple words. Here is a rather typical example. The adolescent student was asked to write about what he did on summer vacation; it is clear that his written expression is shockingly deficit.

It was hot.
I went swiming
Do you lik to swim?

When asking students to write stories, teachers need to use advance organizers such as outlines/paragraph clusters showing the correct sequence of events to help students who are about to write. Most LD students are not able to develop their own plots. For this reason, they cannot write even "primitive stories" with a beginning, middle, and end. Essential elements of plot, such as feelings and motives, are missing. Research suggests they rarely overcome this disability (Barenbaum, 1987).

12 Tips for Teaching Language Arts

1. LD students are more likely to expand the length of their sentences and the complexity of sentences when they are required to do argumentative writing, such as:

   - What is your favorite animal? Explain why.
   - How was the Boston Tea Party similar to and different from the political riots of today?
   - React to the statement "Young people should not be allowed to drive until they are 18."

2. Better writing occurs when it follows in-depth discussions of a subject with key words written on the board, movies that give a lot of information on a topic, or first-hand experiences such as field trips. Many LD students have low general knowledge, so teachers must give the necessary input.

3. When students sit down to write, encourage them to concentrate on what they want to say. Tell them not to worry about spelling, format, and mechanics. Although these things are important, they can be taken care of later in the self-editing (proofreading), editing, and rewriting stages.

4. Students who have extreme problems writing will benefit by using clusters or outlines or by following a pattern. For example, give students samples of great literature, such as a description of a character or place. Using that as a pattern or guide, the student writes about someone else or another place.

5. Students who have linguistic deficits are often panicked by writing assignments because they know this is an area of difficulty. If you start by being too picky, requiring too much, or failing to give encouraging words, they will hate writing. At first, you may have to accept some pretty bad stuff without having students change it; just compliment them for having done the assignment and for getting their ideas on paper. Later, when they consider you to be a friend, you can gently begin to teach them what they need to learn. Your expectation for each student's progress must fit his or her ability and willingness to produce. If students are happy to write, they will show progress.

6. Allow students to use the computer to edit and rewrite their stories. This often overcomes their resistance to the prospect of rewriting.

7. If a student cannot remember what he or she was going to say halfway through, show the student he or she can generally retrieve the idea by reading back the portion he or she has already written.

8. For students who are horribly deficit, teach them the skills they must know first; for example, writing notes to mom, to each other.

9. Daily journals can be great. Everybody keeps a journal, even the teacher! For 10 to 15 minutes each day, it is totally quiet and everyone writes. The easiest way to give students something to write about is to ask them to share something they learned in class today. In your journal, document the good things that occurred today and anything you need to remember. On Thursday and Friday, have the students pick one journal entry they want to read to the class. Likewise, you may want to share something good about the class or someone you wrote about in your journal.

10. Have younger students take stories they are very familiar with (such as *Cinderella*) and write them in their words.

11. Teach students to recognize and spell the 500 most commonly used words. It will make the student literate.

12. Teach students the patterns for spelling (rhyming families); for example, *light, might, night, fight, tight*.

Volume II offers detailed suggestions for teaching writing.

TEACHING MATHEMATICS 13

When children are identified as having learning disabilities, they often need help with reading, language arts, and math. Occasionally, you will locate a youngster who is only "dyscalculic" (math) such as the college student whose vignette was highlighted at the beginning of this book. When a youngster has trouble only in math, he or she is rarely referred for assessment. As was the case of Sarah, the student may not be identified until he or she reaches college and only then if someone recognizes the problem. The usual pattern is that the student flunks out, or becomes discouraged and drops out. This is too bad, for provision can be made so the student may receive extra help without cost to the student in order to pass the subject; or, if the deficit is too severe, the student may receive a waiver that allows him or her to graduate without completing math.

About one out of seven students will experience difficulty understanding math.

In the early grades, LD students' progress is most likely to be hampered by visuospatial deficits—beginning computation of adding/subtracting; while later they are hampered by verbal deficits—not able to figure out which process is needed to do a word problem or not able to use the internal self-talk that is so essential to math. For example, the student can not read $452 \div 132$:

$$132\overline{)452} \quad \text{or} \quad 452\overline{)132} \quad ?$$

Typically, the child who is going to have difficulty with math shows the problem right away. By the third or fourth week of school, the first-grade teacher can see that the student is not catching on. The child has trouble with one-to-one correspondence (miscounting sets); later he or she has trouble learning to recognize coins and learning each's value; and telling time is a disaster. If specialized remedial help would be brought in early and each time a student shows difficulty with a new concept, we probably could prevent half of these students from failing and could render them math literate. Unfortunately, we don't do that and the students go on failing. They then learn to hate, fear, and avoid math.

MANIPULATIVES VS. REPRESENTATIONAL INSTRUCTION

Young children need concrete ways to look at things. Typically, they count on their fingers. In kindergarten we sometimes give them counters or objects they can manipulate in order to do problems. Many children by ages 6 to 7 have a pretty good grip on counting and do not need manipulative objects to reckon with sums under 10; but this is not true of LD children. They may continue to need to count objects or their fingers even up to the age of 12 (Speece, McKinney and Applebaum, 1986). To tell such a child that her or she cannot do so dooms the child to failure.

Nonhandicapped children can look at pictures of halves, thirds, and quarters in grade 1 and understand what they mean. The LD child must have time to manipulate fractional pieces and requires one-to-one attention to develop the vocabulary that goes with that primary understanding of fractional parts.

Very young children and LD children have difficulty with a concept called *conserving*. Here are several examples of what is meant by the term. You ask a child to tell you what number you would get by putting 7 and 5 together. Most children of age seven will say "7-8-9-10-11-12." Children with maturational delays and/or learning disabilities cannot begin at 7 and count up. They will say "1–2–3–4–5–6–7 then 8–9–10–11–12." Another example of the inability to conserve occurs when you put out two piles of cubes (groups under 6). In one pile the six objects are laid end to end and in the other they are stacked. You ask the child if the number is the same in each pile. Nonhandicapped children usually can say yes without any evidence of counting, but LD children are not sure and have to lay the cubes end to end to compare.

The usual curriculum is shown in Figure 13-1. A child who has not mastered what should be assimilated in the primary grades cannot possibly do the math required at the intermediate grades. A student cannot learn long division, for example, without having mastered multiplication and subtraction; a child cannot add and subtract simple fractions, expressing them in lowest terms, without understanding how many pieces it takes to make a whole; a child cannot learn to understand numbers in the millions until he or she understands one thousands, ten thousands, hundred thousands. It is absolutely ridiculous, therefore, to have an LD youngster sitting in regular class being "exposed" to the core curriculum for an intermediate- or upper-grade math class if that student has not mastered the primary prerequisite skills. The point is this: *Someone will have to teach that child what he or she needs to learn.* Will it be the aide, the teacher, a parent volunteer, a classmate, or a special education person? Assignments will have to be modified to reflect lower level skills; otherwise, the child will make no further progress. Objectives on the I.E.P. must reflect skills at a lower level.

Figure 13-1

Primary (K-3)	Intermediate (4-6)
1:1 correspondence	division
numerals	fractions
sets	decimals
ordinal numbers	beginning algebra
calculations +, -, ×	harder calculations
shape recognition	beginning geometry
simple word problems	harder word problems
place value	harder place value
counting money	making change
time	harder measurement
simple measurement	

MAKING MATH ACTIVITIES RELATE TO REAL-LIFE SITUATIONS

This is a trend currently being seen in public schools across the nation. One such program seeks to engage the parents in teaching math through the homework process. Problems relate to doubling baking recipes, measuring and deciding how much material will be needed to make a cage, etc. Teachers who are involved in this family math program report only a small portion of parents who have LD children have been able to help the student (reasons include not being home evenings or not having the skills to help).

Using Math to Develop Critical-Thinking Skills

The movement to develop critical thinking has led to greater use of story problems whereby students are divided into teams of four and are given a word problem. The problems chosen frequently can be solved in a variety of ways. The students in each group set out to discover as many ways as possible to solve the problem, discussing their reasoning and demonstrating their solutions to others in the group. At the end of a certain time frame, the teacher facilitates a whole-class discussion of the ways to solve the problem. Students then write a solution in their math journal utilizing math terminology. The math journal may become part of the portfolio assessment.

Colleagues using this system report that while most students improve substantially in their ability to solve and explain solutions, LD students may learn to spell a few extra math words but often remain clueless as to solutions—even after having repeated experiences with similar types of problems.

LD students seem to be able to learn rote kinds of calculations (how to subtract with and without regrouping, how to count money, etc.), but they make very slow progress in the applications area. By beginning grade 4, the average child learns simple addition facts and subtraction facts by just having multiple exposures to them. This is not true of the LD student. They will not memorize facts unless someone makes a concerted effort to teach them.

20 Tips for Teaching Math

1. *Counting and 1:1 Correspondence:* Most nonhandicapped children can count to 10 before they come to school and—when shown one, two, or three objects—can tell you how many are there. LD children often cannot do that, so you will want to teach them. Begin orally. The song "Ten Little Indian Boys" and the game "Mother, May I?" are fun ways to teach these ideas. As soon as the child counts to 10, begin to work with objects, such as counting blocks or beans or Pogs™. "Show me six beans." LD students catch on to 1:1 correspondence quicker if you have them physically move the object as they say each number.

2. *Recognizing and Writing Numerals:* Put the numerals (1, 2, 3, 4, 5) on index cards. Make a number strip that contains the same numerals arranged in sequence. The child then matches the numeral on the strip with one of the cards. You both name the numeral and, when all five are in order, count 1, 2, 3, 4, 5.

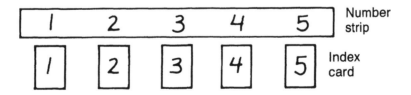

Next, have the child practice tracing a numeral on the chalkboard. Make the 1 and the 2 about a foot high. As the child traces the 1 (beginning at the top), have the student say "one." Likewise, follow the same procedure with 2. The next day do 1, 2, 3. The next day 1, 2, 3, 4, etc.

Looking at the numbers on the board, have the child sequence the index cards in order from left to right daily until the skill is mastered.

Give the child practice writing the five numerals one inch high on paper. First they trace it, then they write it free-hand looking at the model. Watch to be sure they begin at the top.

When the child has mastered the numerals 1 to 5, add one number at a time until you reach 10.

3. *Sets:* When you teach the student to do 1:1 correspondence, you put out sets of objects for him or her to count. When we are going to switch from the concrete manipulative to the representational picture, ask the child to look at a picture of objects and count them. Have the student write a number on each object and write the total for the set.

Most math books have several pages of this kind of material. LD students may need more experiences, so you may end up having to make your own worksheets.

4. *Joining Sets or Simple Addition: It is absolutely essential to the child's further understanding of math that at this point you teach the students to use the following type of self-talk while doing their problems.*

$$
\begin{array}{r}
5 \\
+\ 2 \\
\hline
7
\end{array}
$$

"I have 5. I get 2 more.

How many will I have in all?"

Begin to interject words as a prelude to future word problems.

"I have 5 *books*. I get 2 more.

How many books do I have in all?"

Tell the student it might be cats or marbles and reread the problem substituting cats for books. You might ask students to think of another word to substitute.

Tell the child that the beauty of math is that 5 + 2 is always going to make 7. Have the child repeat: "Five plus two more is always seven." Have them close their eyes and repeat it twice. Have them repeat it with their eyes closed and their fingers in their ears. (You are removing distracting or interfering stimuli.) Have them write the fact in the air with their eyes closed. (This activity forces them to visual-ize numbers.) Try the technique yourself now and you will see how effective it is.

NOTE: These techniques can be used to help a child memorize spelling as well.

Nonhandicapped kids pick up these facts incidentally. With LD kids, you have to frequently and actively teach them.

5. *Simple Subtraction/Undoing Sets:* Again it is absolutely essential that students be taught to use self-talk.

"I have seven puppies. I take two away. How many puppies are left?"

$$7$$
$$-2$$
$$\overline{5}$$

Show them with manipulatives that 5 blocks + 2 blocks = 7 blocks (you can make the plus and equals signs out of red construction paper). You can shift the order of the blocks and show that 2 + 5 is still going to be 7 and you can say:

"I have seven blocks. I take away two.

How many blocks are left?"

Family of Facts

Then show 7 - 5 with blocks. Teach children there are families of facts: 5 + 2 = 7
2 + 5 = 7   7 - 2 = 5   7 - 5 = 2

Thus, 2, 5, and 7 belong to a family of facts that make 7.

Subtraction is the opposite of addition. We put the numbers together in addition. We take them apart in subtraction. You know that; I know that; but LD children don't know that unless you keep telling them that until they clearly understand it. Even though they see it illustrated in the book and may even do it on their paper, they do not understand it until they can explain it to you in the right words.

6. *Counting to 100:* After you accomplish the preceding you will want to teach stu-dents to count from 0 to 100 and to write the numbers. To do this, use the student worksheet found in Figure 13-2. (You will need to increase its size so the spaces will accommodate a coin.) You will also need ten pennies and nine dimes.

Figure 13-2

	0	1	2	3	4	5	6	7	8	9
10										
20										
30										

As the student counts, lay one penny on top of the number 1; as the child says "two," put a penny on top of the 2. Continue to put a penny on each number until you reach 10. Then you tell the child to "Scoop up the pennies." The child trades them to you for a dime or "ten cents." On the worksheet, have the student write 11. Now put one penny on the 11. Pick up the dime and say: "This stands for ten pennies." Pick up the penny and say: "This is one penny. Eleven is equal to 10 (point to the dime) plus one (point to the penny)."

As the child writes 12, show that the 1 means 10 (the dime) and the 2 refers to two pennies. "Twelve is 1 ten and 2 ones." Keep on adding a penny to each space as the child counts until you reach 20. At that time the child again trades you the ten pennies for one dime. As the child writes 20, explain that the 2 means 2 tens and the 0 means no pennies. Keep on putting out pennies and trading them for dimes at the end of each row.

After you have done this activity for several days, teach the child to go down the left margin of numbers, saying "10, 20, 30, 40, 50, 60, 70, 80, 90, 100." You will need to do this many times with the student repeating. Then place the dimes and pennies in front of the student and say, "Build me 37." Show the student that the 3 means to put out 3 tens and the 7 means to put out 7 pennies. For several days, practice asking the students to find a number and then to build it with the coins.

After the child counts to 100, you will want to generalize this information by using other manipulatives such as Cuisenaire® rods.

7. *More/Less:* Using the preceding activities, you can also teach the concept of *more* or *less*. Have students build two numbers:

65	32
6 dimes	3 dimes

Point out to the students that we can tell which number is more if we check the tens column.

Later when they get into the hundreds column, you will need to extend your teaching to show students how to check the hundreds column for the largest number. You will need to show them, for example, how 105 is more than 95 since 95 has no hundreds in it.

8. *Ordinal Numbers:* You will need to teach the words *first, second, third,* etc. If the child is looking at a picture and trying to answer questions regarding the order, it is important that the child understand the order is determined by the direction from which you must count.

9. *Rounding Numbers to the Nearest Ten:* This is an extremely hard concept for LD children and one that must first be taught visually using a long number strip on which you have recorded every number from 0 to 100. **10, 20, 30, 40, 50, 60, 70, 80, 90,** and **100** are written in red while the others are in black. Ask the child to consult the strip to find out whether a given number, such as 27, is closer to 20 or

to 30. The child can "see" it is nearer to 30. Of course, when you give the child a number exactly halfway, you must also tell the child about the rule to round up. After using the strip for awhile, you will note one day that the child will answer the question without using the strip. When this occurs and the child habitually gets the right answers, you will know the child has conceptualized 0 to 100.

The same strip system can be used for teaching students to round numbers to the nearest hundred. Write **100, 200, 300,** etc., in red and put the midpoint in black. Explain that if the number is over 50, the number is rounded up to the nearest hundred because it is past the mid-point. For example, 465 falls between 400 and 500, but it is rounded up to 500 because the 65 is over 50 (the mid-point).

10. *Place Value:* By middle grade 2, students are expected to understand and read numbers that have ones, tens, and hundreds place value. The easiest way to teach this is by obtaining craft sticks (from a crafts store). Using wide rubber bands that do not break quickly, package most of the sticks in groups of ten.

You can then show students how to build larger numbers, such as ten sets of ten make a hundred. Using the sticks, show students what a number such as 135 means.

1 set of 100   3 sets of 10   and 5 single sticks

Teach students through guided practice to read all numbers from 0 to 999. Also teach them to expand numbers; for example, 347 (300 + 40 + 7).

11. *Teaching Addition Regrouping:* Using the same craft sticks, demonstrate to students the process of regrouping manipulatively.

45 means	4 tens	and	5 ones
If we try to join it to 37	+ 3 tens	and	7 ones
			12
			(1 ten and 2 ones)

Another group of ten is created when we put the 5 and 7 together. As you make that group of ten, slip a rubber band around it, place it physically with the groups of ten on the table, and show the children how to carry the one:

1		
4 tens	and	5 ones
+3 tens	and	7 ones
8		2

Likewise, with subtraction regrouping, put out the sticks to illustrate:

52 means	5 tens	and	2 ones
If we try to take away 28	- 2 tens	and	8 ones

(Activate the earlier self-talk to say, "I have 2. Can I take away eight?" The answer is "no" unless I can get some more.)

Show students how they can remove a rubber band from a group of ten so that now they have 12 single sticks and can complete the problem.

$$\overset{4}{\cancel{5}}\ tens \quad 2\ ones = add\ 10\ more \quad \overset{12\ ones}{\underline{8\ ones}}$$
$$\underline{-2\ tens} \qquad\qquad\qquad\qquad\qquad\qquad 4$$
$$2 \qquad\qquad\qquad answer\ 24$$

12. *Counting Coins:* The first step in teaching money is to teach children to recognize the coins and know their value. This task is best taught using real money. Tell children they can have the privilege to use real money as long as they do not lose any (know exactly what you give them to use). At the end of the period, be sure the children return all the coins.

If the child can read, teaching coins is easier because each actual coin is identified as one cent, five cents, a dime, or a quarter. Other clues you can give are that pennies are made of copper (which is brown), nickels are made of a metal called nickel, while dimes and quarters contain silver. Sometimes I'll ask children to remember other clues such as "the nickel has a building on the back" while "the quarter has an eagle."

Once a child can identify the coins, put out two coins and have the child assign the correct number of marks to each. Then the child counts.

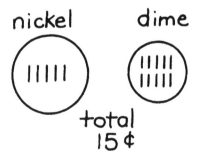

When the children become comfortable counting two coins, have them do three, and so on, until they are proficient.

When using coins you also want to teach counting nickels by 5's and dimes by 10's, and to teach: two quarters always make 50 cents, three quarters always will be 75 cents, and four quarters always will be $1.00.

13. *Teaching Time:* A child cannot learn to tell time until he or she can count by 5's to 60; so before beginning time, be sure this skill is known. Teach 5's as 0, 5, 10, 15, 20, etc. Have the student understand there are 60 minutes in an hour (not 100).

There are several other things children must know:

- They must clearly understand that both hands are moving in the same direction. Help students see that by moving the hands of a clock slowly while instructing them to watch carefully.

- They need to know the hour hand is the shorter one while the minute hand is longer.

- They must understand that it is two before it is three, and three comes before four. When the hour hand is between three and four, it is "after" three, but "is not" yet four so it is recorded as 3:__ __.

Have the students practice telling the hour only for several days. When students are proficient at finding the hour, have them begin counting the minutes and actually marking them on clocks.

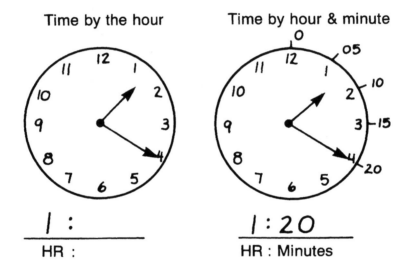

Teach them how to record time:

hour   minutes
3 :   15

For awhile do not confuse the child by doing times past 45 minutes after the hour. When you introduce this concept, show students with a real clock how close the hour hand is to the next number, but help them understand it really isn't yet the next hour.

We must be aware with the development of digital technology that LD students can bypass learning to tell time; but without understanding all the things just mentioned, they will not be able to do time-related problems, such as being able to tell how much time has elapsed between two given times. "I went to bed at 10:30. I got up at 7:00. How long did I sleep?"

14. *Reading Number Words:* It is important to teach students to recognize the following words:

one (1)	eleven (11)	thirty (30)
two (2)	twelve (12)	forty (40)
three (3)	thirteen (13)	fifty (50)
four (4)	fourteen (14)	sixty (60)
five (5)	fifteen (15)	seventy (70)
six (6)	sixteen (16)	eighty (80)
seven (7)	seventeen (17)	ninety (90)
eight (8)	eighteen (18)	hundred (100)
nine (9)	nineteen (19)	thousand (1,000)
ten (10)	twenty (20)	million(1,000,000)

Give students a variety of activities to do, such as "Write a number for seventy-one; for five hundred sixty-three."

15. *Doing Simple Word Problems:* Doing story problems is basically a reading comprehension activity. Teaching students to translate the words into pictures will help students solve them. Tell students to read each sentence (stopping at the period). Tell them to draw a picture of what the sentence said. For example:

You bought a dozen cookies.

You ate three and gave one to your mom. *How many are left?*

The solution to a word problem is frequently found in the question asked at the end of the problem. Certain words or phrases direct us to the solution process. Figure 13-3 gives a list of those *clue words* that can be a part of the student's notebook.

16. *Teaching Multiplication:* Again you will need to teach students to do some self-talk. When they see

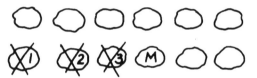

it means 3 groups of 4 items. It can be drawn as shown here. Teach students to draw pictures when they are first learning to multiply.

17. *Teaching Simple Division:* Again the self-talk must be taught. When students see 12 ÷ 3, they must be taught to say "12 divided by 3" and to understand they have 12 items they plan to group in threes.

In early division, it is wise to teach the students how to go a bit further—to obtain a remainder if there is one. (See example at top of page 226.)

$$\begin{array}{r} 3 \\ 4\overline{)15} \\ -12 \\ \hline 3 \end{array}$$

When students are taught to do this, it markedly facilitates moving on to more advanced problems later.

Be sure to also show students that division is the opposite of multiplication and that multiplication/division facts also can make families of facts.

$$3 \times 4 = 12$$
$$4 \times 3 = 12$$
$$12 \div 4 = 3$$
$$12 \div 3 = 4$$

Family
of
Facts

18. *Harder Calculations:* LD students often have trouble with multiplication when multiplying by more than one digit. Once they can multiply a problem such as the one on top of page 227:

Figure 13-3

CLUES FOR SOLVING MATH STORY PROBLEMS	

Addition {putting sets together}
• How many <u>in all</u>?
• How many <u>altogether</u>?
• Find the <u>sum</u>.
• What is the <u>total</u>?
	Subtraction {taking sets apart}
	• How many are <u>left</u>?
	• Find the <u>difference</u>.
	• How many <u>more/less</u>?
	• Comparing 2 numbers:
	  How much bigg(er)?
	        heavi(er)?
	         old(er)?

Multiplication {putting equal sets together} • How many <u>in all</u>? • How many <u>altogether</u>? • Find the <u>product</u>. Look for clues (last sentence)!	**Division** {taking equal sets from the whole} • Find the <u>quotient</u>. • What would <u>one unit</u> be? • If <u>shared equally</u>? • If <u>divided equally</u>?

$$
\begin{array}{r}
203 \\
\times\ 5 \\
\hline
1015
\end{array}
$$
show them that

$$
\begin{array}{r}
203 \\
\times\ 4\,⑤ \\
\hline
1015 \\
812\,■ \\
\hline
9135
\end{array}
$$

$$
\begin{array}{r}
203 \\
\times\ ⑤ \\
\hline
1015
\end{array}
\longleftarrow
$$

$$
\begin{array}{r}
203 \\
\times\ 4 \\
\hline
812
\end{array}
$$

For LD students, using a block for a space holder is less confusing than a zero. You will also want to show students how to use a hand calculator to do complex multiplication problems.

To teach long division to an LD student requires days and days of one-to-one guided practice, but they *can* learn to do it. If this objective is written, attention must be given to who will have the time and patience to do it everyday. It normally takes about 20 days for a student to habituate the four steps required to do problems such as:

$$
\begin{array}{r}
2\ 4\ 2 \\
3\,\overline{)\,7\ 2\ 6} \\
-6\downarrow \\
\hline
1\ 2 \\
-1\ 2\downarrow \\
\hline
0\ 6 \\
-\ 6
\end{array}
\qquad
\begin{array}{l}
\text{divide} \\
\text{multiply} \\
\text{subtract} \\
\text{bring down}
\end{array}
$$

It is important to teach older students to do long division using a hand calculator.

LD students who have difficulties in math always need to begin a concept as concretely as possible. If you decide to teach fractions, students will need weeks and weeks of experience using fractional parts. Milton Bradley makes fractional parts (manipulatives) called Fractions Are Easy as Pie™. You will need at least four sets in order to have enough.

Have the student sort parts and pile the halves in a stack, the thirds in another, and so on. Now go across the stacks and name them: "These are halves," "These are thirds," etc. Have the student repeat each stack's name. Next, ask the student, "Show me 3 fourths." You may have to demonstrate: "These are fourths and I asked you to show me 3 fourths. Pull them out and put them together, like this." Give the student several days' practice showing you different fractions combinations. Show the student how to write the numbers as shown in the illustration.

$$
\frac{1}{4} + \frac{1}{4} + \frac{1}{4} = \frac{3}{4}
$$

Later, you will say, "Show me 2 thirds. Now get out another 1 third. What will happen if I do this?" Lay a + between the parts and show the student how to move the pieces together so they make a whole. Help them understand that when the numerator and denominator match, you always will have a whole. Show them with pieces. With paper and pencil, write the problem and say, "This is how you write it."

$$\frac{2}{3} + \frac{1}{3} = \frac{3}{3} = 1$$

Show the students what happens if you have three entries.

$$\frac{2}{3} + \frac{2}{3} + \frac{2}{3} = \frac{6}{3} \text{ or } 2$$

When the student has spent several days doing practice with problems that end up making a whole, have them do some subtraction problems, such as:

"Show me 7 eighths."

"Now subtract 3 eighths."

"What do you have left?"

Then show them that 4 eighths is the same amount as 1 half by laying a half over the 4 eighths.

$$\begin{array}{r} \frac{7}{8} \\ - \frac{3}{8} \\ \hline \frac{4}{8} \text{ or } \frac{1}{2} \end{array}$$

LD students have trouble reducing fractions to lowest terms because they are not sure how to find the common denominator. You can get around this by telling them to use this *rule*:

Can you reduce both the numerator and denominator by dividing them by 2? 3? 5? or 7? If not, the fraction probably is already in its lowest terms.

$$2\overline{)\dfrac{2}{4}} = \dfrac{1}{2} \qquad 3\overline{)\dfrac{3}{6}} = \dfrac{1}{2} \qquad 5\overline{)\dfrac{5}{20}} = \dfrac{1}{4} \qquad 7\overline{)\dfrac{14}{35}} = \dfrac{2}{5}$$

Show students that sometimes you must divide the fraction more than once before the numerator reaches its lowest level.

$$2\overline{)\dfrac{6}{12}} = \dfrac{3}{6} = \dfrac{1}{2} \ \left(\text{lowest terms}\right)$$

Later allow the student to use manipulatives to do problems that result in improper fractions or mixed numbers.

More important than teaching LD students to do fractions, decimals, and other problems taught in upper grades is teaching them to make change, manage money, and avoid the misuse of credit (the skills we term "life skills"). These skills will be discussed in the next chapter.

19. *Spatial Deficits:* In your teaching you will encounter students who have difficulty spatially. They cannot line up columns of numbers, so graph paper that has large squares is often helpful to these students. They can write one number in each square.

There are also students who cannot copy a page of figures due to spatial deficits. There are several solutions to this:

- Allow someone else to copy the assignment for them.
- Give them an index card to place under the line of the first entry to be copied and move as they write the numbers.
- Insist that students finish each problem before going on to the next. This way they know they have allowed enough space to work the problem. I have seen LD students who will spend the entire period trying to copy an assignment and who never get even a single problem worked. They end up getting a grade of zero, which is totally defeating to them.

20. *Math Texts:* Watch out for math texts! Some will give only one lesson on each concept. I saw one recently that had one day's practice on how to teach students about equivalent fractions. The teacher giving the lesson was quite disheartened when she found that only a handful of students had understood the concept. She wisely did not go on to the next day's lesson; instead she spent two weeks working on equivalent fractions until every child could do them. She reviewed that one lesson everyday and then made her own worksheets for the kids to get practice.

In conclusion, LD students need to continually review and practice previously acquired skills so they will be maintained. The math books we typically use do not provide for this constant review practice. Teachers must give students at least twice-a-week review pages. These make excellent homework assignments because they involve skills previously taught and mastered. You can make these to provide the student with a smattering of each previously learned skill. See the sample sheet of review homework in Figure 13-4. It is appropriate for a student with skills approximating grade 4.

Figure 13-4

SAMPLE REVIEW FOR LATE GRADE 3 OR EARLY GRADE 4.

1. You have 2 quarters, 3 dimes, and a nickel. How much money do you have in all?

2. You buy a dozen cookies. You plan to share them equally with two friends. How many will each of you get?

3. There are 18 girls and 14 boys in your class. How many students are there all together?

4. Our school has 516 students. Forty-five are absent today. How many students are here?

5. 6,275 - 849 =

6. Put these numbers in sequential order (least to most): 1214, 2763, 596

7. There are four teams with seven kids on each team. How many kids are playing?

8. 36,714 + 24,008 =

9. You must catch a plane at 11 o'clock. You have to check in one hour ahead and it takes 30 minutes to get to the airport. What time will you need to leave home?

10. How long is this line?

11. What fractional part is shaded?

12. Candy is 45¢ a bar. You buy 6 bars. They cost:

230

TEACHING LIFE AND SOCIAL SKILLS

When you survey the curriculum of schools, you may not find life and social skills listed as such, but when you interview most teachers, they will tell you they teach them and feel these skills are very important, particularly today. They cite the decline of the family as the primary reason; many also mention the fact that interpersonal relationships are a weakness of LD kids.

Beginning in first grade, teachers feel it is important to teach students good manners, such as how to say "please" and "thank you." They also try to help youngsters assess their personal attributes, helping them to become aware of their uniqueness and fostering self-esteem. As students get older, they explore friendships and how to make friends. Using cooperative learning groups, students are encouraged to use the skills of listening and respecting the opinions of others. Telling time and counting money are covered within the math curriculum.

As students approach middle-school age, they participate in the DARE programs designed to help them say "No" to alcohol and drug use. They are exposed to their sexuality and attitudes toward that in classes entitled "Human Growth and Development."

As they move into high school, students take courses in "Family Life" and Vocational Education and, if they are lucky, have the opportunity to be employed part-time. Students are encouraged to set goals for their lives.

DO SCHOOLS NEED TO OFFER LIFE AND SOCIAL SKILLS COURSES?

If teachers are currently teaching these skills, do we need to offer full courses on them? The answer is *yes*. In one interesting study (Vaughn, 1985), strangers were taken into classes that contained LD and non-LD students. After only a short observation, they were able to identify the LD students. They described them as being different from non-LD students in several ways: were less likely to request additional information when they didn't understand, made more competitive/nasty statements, made inappropriate responses, were more egocentric and didn't put themselves in others' shoes, had more grooming problems, did not look or smile at conversation partner.

With the decline of the influence of the family, this is yet another area where the school needs to come to the rescue of the students. Deficits in social skills not only put children at risk of rejection by their peers, but will also hurt them later in life. Training in social skills needs to begin in kindergarten and continue right through high school. Many teachers do not feel competent to teach these skills, but would if they were trained and appropriate curriculum was provided.

HOW A LACK OF SOCIAL SKILLS AFFECTS SUCCESS IN LIFE

When teachers are asked to compare LD students with their nonhandicapped peers, they frequently describe the students as being less cooperative, less attentive and more distractible, less able to organize their work, less able to meet the demands of new situations, less socially acceptable, less responsible, less tactful, and less inclined to persevere until a task is finished (Perlmutter, Crocker, Cordray, and Garstecki, 1983).

Now let's try reading each of the above negative statements positively: is cooperative, is attentive, is able to organize, can cope with new situations, is socially acceptable, is tactful, and can persevere until the task is done.

Are these not the same attributes we would expect from a successful employee? Learning to get along with others certainly is important to success on the job, in marriage, and in all social relationships.

When you look at these facts, it is hard to minimize the importance of teaching social and life skills at every level. We need to do everything in our power to help students understand the importance of these behaviors and to practice these behaviors until they feel natural.

TECHNIQUES FOR TEACHING LIFE AND SOCIAL SKILLS

Sometimes it is hard to decide what is a social skill and what is a life skill because clearly there is a lot of overlapping; therefore, I have not separated them in this chapter. The techniques most used for teaching these skills are discussion and practice through role-playing. The teacher opens the discussion with a brief statement or problem to be solved and students talk about possible solutions.

An example of such a problem at the secondary level would be: What would you do if someone told you your best friend was saying unflattering things about you behind your back? First, a discussion occurs, during which someone may suggest that you must confront your friend. Students are then asked to role-play the confrontation. Role-playing allows students to learn how to tactfully approach others. If they are too confrontational, the players are able to say "erase" and try again, which they would not be able to do in an actual situation.

If students have difficulty figuring out what to say during role-playing, they have the option of asking the teacher for help, whereby the teacher models the solution. It is then important to have students practice the solution until it feels natural to them.

MAKING TIME TO TEACH LIFE AND SOCIAL SKILLS

Teachers say they often include these skills into other areas of the curriculum such as math, social studies, and language arts. It is a perfect way to foster *speaking* for students.

Use incidents that occur between students as a springboard to discussing and role-playing solutions. When applied to real situations, students get more benefit from the lesson.

CURRICULUM FOR TEACHING LIFE AND SOCIAL SKILLS

NOTE: Items with this designation * are suggested for the secondary level only.

Going to School

What Are the Rules?

Why Do We Have Rules?

Who Is in Charge Here? (identifying authority figures)

What Are Restrooms For?

What Is Recess For?

Being Safe on the Playground

What Is a Bully? (dealing with intimidation)

Dealing with Teasing/Name Calling

Showing Respect

Mine! Yours! Teacher's! (honesty)

What Do I Do When I Don't Know What to Do? (asking for help)

What Is Cheating?

When Should I Tattle?

*What Do I Do If I Am Failing?

Social Skills

Saying "Please" and "Thank You"

Starting a Conversation

Asking Questions That Stimulate Conversation

Listening

Giving and Accepting a Compliment

Apologizing

Introductions

Convincing Others

Giving Directions

Making Friends

Choosing Friends Wisely

How Do I Make a Friend?

Being a Friend

The Effect of Gossip

*The Circumstantial Nature of Friendship

*Handling Rejection (when friendships end)

*Dealing with Misunderstandings

*Joining Groups

*When a Friend Dies

Understanding the Feelings of Others

When Someone Else Is Angry

Asking Permission

Giving Help

When Someone Else Is Sad

Reading Facial Expressions and Body Language

Good Sportsmanship

*Negotiation

*Confrontation

*Providing Constructive Criticism to Others

Understanding Myself

Who Am I?

What Are My Strengths/Weaknesses?

What Is Lying?

What Is Stealing?

What Do I Do When I Feel Left Out?

What Do I Do When I Feel Lonely?

What Do I Do When I Feel Fearful?

What Do I Do When I Am Angry?

Standing Up for Myself

I'm Having a Problem—Whom Should I Talk With?

*Three Types of Decisions

Etiquette

Setting the Table

What Are Good Table Manners?

Talking with Older People

What Are Good Telephone Manners?

Writing a Thank-You Note

What Should I Know About Going to a Restaurant?

*What Should I Know About Attending a Wedding?

*What Do I Need to Know About Attending a Funeral?

Protecting Myself

Who Is a Stranger?

How Can I Be Safe When I Am Home Alone?

What Is Child Abuse?

What Are the Dangers of Drugs and Alcohol?

How Can I Avoid Fights?

*What Shall I Do When My Friend Wants Me to . . .?

Handling Emergencies

Calling 911

What Do I Do If My Clothes Are on Fire?

How to Put Out Various Kinds of Fires

What Should I Know About First Aid?

Taking Responsibility for My Own Behavior

What Do I Need to Know If We Have an (Earthquake, Flood, etc.)?

Working with Authority Figures/Obeying the Law

Speaking Respectfully with Parents

Cooperating with Teachers

*Speaking Respectfully with Police

*Working with Difficult Bosses

*What Is Vandalism?

*What Do I Need to Know About Going to Court?

*What Is a DUI?

Understanding My Handicap

*What Is a Learning Disability?

*Everyone Feels Dumb Sometimes

*Making a List of My Strengths and Weaknesses

*The Importance of Changing My Inner Language (daily activities for improving self-talk)

*Whom Should I Tell About My Learning Disability?

*Being My Own Advocate

Dealing with Stress

Relaxation Techniques

Leaving the Scene

Finding a Hobby

The Value of Exercise

*What Will I Do with My Leisure Time?

Family Living

Why Do We Have Families?

Getting Along with Others in the Home

What Does "Division of Labor" Mean in the Home?

When Parents Argue

Understanding Divorce

When a Relative Dies

Organizational Skills

Reading a Calendar
Keeping an Assignment Calendar
Ways to Help Myself Stay on-Task
The Price of Procrastination

Prevocational Skills

Telling Time
Counting Money
Making Change
Completing Simple Personal Information Forms
What Shall I Do with My Allowance?
Postponing Gratification
*Measuring
*Understanding Simple Fractions
*What Are My Interests? Can I Use Them to Make a Living?
*What Kinds of Jobs Are Out There?
*Reading a Bus Schedule/Road Map
*Setting an Alarm Clock

Work-Related Skills

*What Do I Need to Know About Grooming?
*Where Can I Get Job Training?
*What Do I Need to Know Before I Go on a Job Interview?
*How Do I Put Together a Résumé
*Avoiding the Five Deadly Work World Sins: Characteristics That Will Help Me Hold
 a Job
*What Is Sexual Harrassment?
*What Do I Need to Know About Taking Tests?
*Explaining a Problem to a Supervisor/Taking Responsibility for My Own Mistakes
*The Value of Having a Mentor/Choosing a Mentor

Dating

*Choosing a Special Friend
*Emotional Intimacy
*Protecting Myself Against AIDS
*To Have Sex or Not to Have Sex?
*Postponing Marriage

*Should We Live Together?

*Learning to Communicate Feelings

*When Conflict Occurs

*Is It Okay to Have a Baby Now?

Money Management

*What Do I Need to Know About Saving Money and Banking?

*How Do I Write a Check?

*What Kinds of Records Do I Need to Keep?

*What Do I Need to Know About Credit?/What Is the Cost of Interest? (an ideal time to teach students how to figure percentages)

*What Do I Need to Know About Budgeting?

*Writing a Business Letter

Consumer Skills

*Comparative Shopping

*Returning an Item

*Why Should I Get Insurance?

*What Do I Need to Know About Contracts?

*What Do I Need to Know Before Buying a Car?

*Finding a Place to Live

Community Services

*What Do I Do If I Need Legal Help?

*What Do I Do If I Need Medical Help?

*How Do I Get Food Stamps?

*How Do I Get Unemployment/Disability Benefits?

*Where Can I Get Job Training/What is Vocational Rehabilitation?

Some teachers like to develop their own lessons in these areas. Others prefer to seek out commercially prepared programs, such as Darlene Mannix's *Life Skills Activities for Special Children* (1991), *Social Skills Activities for Special Children* (1993), both for elementary-aged students, and *Life Skills Activities for Secondary Students with Special Needs* (1995), all published by The Center for Applied Research in Education. Or *The Social Skills Curriculum* developed by the University of Kansas Institute for Learning Disabilities, Lawrence, Kansas. This program includes an instructor's manual, workbooks, and activities for teaching social skills to adolescents.

Figures 14-1, 14-2, and 14-3 offer three sample lessons to help give you ideas for developing your own.

Figure 14-1

LIFE SKILL LESSON: HOW TO MAKE A FRIEND

Objective: The student will be able to name at least five techniques that can be used to make a friend.

Discussion: Today we are going to talk about making friends. I want you to think about the topic for three minutes. Be prepared to participate by answering these questions:

1. Why do we need friends?
2. What did your parents tell you about making friends? What pointers did they give you?
   After three minutes begin the discussion. List their answers to #2 on the board.

Possible answers include:

1. *Be friendly.* Look around you and find someone who is standing alone. With a *smile*, introduce yourself. "Hi! My name is Joan. What is yours?"
2. *Show interest in the other person.* "Have you gone to school here for a long time?" "Do you like parties?" "What do you like to do?" *Listen carefully.* Respond to what they say. Remember their name and use it when speaking to them. "Well, Jimmy, you look great! I really like that shirt!"
3. *Make others feel important.* Don't monopolize the conversation. Ask questions that will *get them to talk about themselves.* "What kind of music do you like?" "Do you play any sport?"
4. *Let others be themselves.* Do not tease others. Do not belittle their opinions. If you do not agree, you can say, "That's an interesting way to look at it. How did you come to that opinion?" Do not participate in name calling or shunning others.
5. *Be loyal.* Treat others as you want to be treated.

Set up scenarios. Let students role-play meeting a new person—at a friend's party, at work, at school—and having to begin a conversation.

Figure 14-2

LIFE SKILL LESSON:
FIVE DEADLY SINS THAT WILL CAUSE YOU TO LOSE A JOB

Read the following scenarios. Each person was fired or laid off. Write the reason on the line below each scenario. The first one is done for you.

1. Tom hated his job. On several occasions, he called in saying he was sick (when he really wasn't). Today his boss needed him to take inventory, but Tom really was too sick to go to work for several days. When Tom returned, his boss said, "Tom, I'm going to have to lay you off. Business is slow. Bill and I can handle it."

   <u>absenteeism</u>

2. Ann's job is to greet clients, answer the phone, and file folders. Her desk was stacked with folders. She broke a fingernail. Her boss came through looking for a folder, but she could not find it. Her boss asked her to work overtime that evening to get caught up on the filing. She said she couldn't because she planned to go to a movie with a friend. He fired her. Why?

3. Marshall works in a printing shop. He takes orders at the counter. Today he got fired. A man had come in and ordered some flyers. When he came back to pick them up, he would not pay for them because they were printed on white paper and he had clearly told Marshall to print them on pink paper.

4. Cindy works in an office. Her boss tells her they are going to computerize all their records and asks her to enroll in a computer training class. She begins to tell him all the reasons she cannot learn to use a computer. He tells her she is terminated.

Answers:
1. absenteeism
2. lack of interest in the job
3. not following directions/making costly mistakes
4. unwillingness to learn

Figure 14-3

LIFE SKILL LESSON: THREE TYPES OF DECISIONS

Objective: The student will be able to name the three kinds of decisions (awareness).

Discussion: Write these three headings on the board.

Type 1	Type 2	Type 3
Approach/Approach	Avoid/Avoid	Approach/Avoid

In the discussion, explain each type of decision.

1. *Approach/Approach decisions* involve making a choice between two pleasant or good alternatives. Examples include, "Do I want pie or cake?" or "Shall I watch this T.V. show or that one?"

2. *Avoid/Avoid decisions* involve situations where one has to choose between two unpleasant or bad situations. Examples might include, "Shall I go to the dentist (you hate shots/you find going to the dentist unpleasant) or shall I put up with this toothache?" or "Shall I write a term paper on this subject or that subject?" (You really don't want to write on either one.)

3. *Approach/Avoid decisions* are those decisions where you flip-flop your viewpoint depending on the distance you are from taking action on a decision. Examples might include: You decide to marry someone (approach) because you love him or her but as the wedding gets closer, you feel like backing out (avoidance) because you see some things about your future spouse that worry you. Another example is that you agree to take a job on May 1st because you need money but as May 1st draws closer you are more unsure about taking the job because you have legitimate concerns about it.

You can have students try to think of other examples of each type of decision or you can have them keep a diary/journal for a week and list any decisions they had to make. Then as a class you reopen the lesson and as a group they categorize the decisions under the appropriate type.

Note: The most difficult decisions to make are Type 3.

THE ROLE
OF THE SECONDARY SCHOOL

REGIONAL
OCCUPATIONAL
CENTER

—CDS

The Changing Needs of the Junior High School LD Student

The average 12- to 13-year-old has more to think about than whether the math grade is satisfactory. Around mid-sixth grade, there is an abrupt metamorphosis. The soon-to-be teenager is suddenly more aware there is a bigger world out there than was previously imagined. Perhaps this occurs because he or she is going to attend a new school soon.

The student discovers his or her body is also changing. Not only is growth occurring, but there are also emerging signs of sexuality. Hormones not previously there begin to influence thinking and interest in the opposite sex.

Almost overnight they become very concerned about what their peers think of them. They become almost obsessed with being popular and belonging to a group or at the very least blending in. Their mode of dress may give clues to their group affiliation.

The teenager is a sensation-oriented creature and often that desire for sensation or thrills leads young people into a collision course with danger. Lacking mature judgment, a youngster may be persuaded to cut school, joy ride, run away, shoplift, try a street drug, smoke, drink, or have sexual intercourse without thought to the possible consequences. It is extremely fortunate that we don't get negative consequences 100 percent of the time.

People expect more of teenagers. Parents may allow additional freedoms before the student is ready to handle them. Likewise, the school routine markedly changes. Instead of dealing with only one teacher a day, most intermediate-school students move from class to class. While elementary teachers focus on meeting the needs of the "whole child," intermediate and high school teachers tend to be more subject-oriented and expect the student to be responsible for his or her own education. Since they see about 150 kids a day (one subject per one period format), it is impossible for secondary teachers to get to know very many kids well. A certain amount of anonymity is experienced in the school setting.

Instruction at the intermediate level is primarily given through lecture supplemented by having the student read the text. Now here's the rub! The typical LD student enters the intermediate school with achievement scores around mid-third- to early fourth-grade level (see Figure 7-3 in Chapter 7) so he or she cannot get much from reading that textbook. Because of their continuing deficits in language (semantics, syntax, and pragmatics), secondary LD students are often unable to auditorally process information from the lecture. The teacher comes across as being aloof and uncaring. Research shows LD students are less socially acceptable to teachers and classmates than their nonhandicapped peers. It is not surprising, therefore, that:

- the LD students say "school is boring"
- the LD students either flunk or do very poorly
- many LD students develop an emotional overlay that further impedes their progress
- 50% of LD students do not complete high school

Efforts to Engage the Student in the Educational Process at the Junior High Level

Departmentalization/School Within a School

One plan that seeks to break down anonymity while allowing teachers to teach their "specialty" is the school-within-a-school approach. The faculty (a math teacher, a science teacher, a language arts/reading teacher, etc.) is assigned to a team. Each team serves around 150 students. The math teacher, for example, may teach two seventh-grade classes, two eighth-grade classes, and one ninth. Within a junior high school, it is common to find from three to six "teams" or "families" or "pods," depending on whatever the school chooses to call them. Each team, usually with its own counselor, is housed in an area of close proximity so students get to know other students in their pod and teachers can discuss with each other the needs of "their" 150 students. Students are then assigned to a team.

This approach has much to recommend it. In elementary school, the students had one teacher with 30 other kids; now their world grows to five or six teachers, changing classes and associating with a somewhat larger group, but they don't have to go all over the building, get lost, use lockers, and feel completely overwhelmed. There is more of a feeling of belonging because they have six or so teachers who share the responsibility to help them. Teachers meet as a team once a week to share information, but still have contact with other members of their department at departmental meetings once a month. Special education students may be assigned to only one, two, or three of the pods, making it easier for special education staff to give services to students.

Resource Rooms

Mild to moderately learning handicapped students are served in the regular classroom with the resource specialist either helping out in the room as a co-teacher/consultant or the student taking the regular class assignment to the *resource room* where he or she receives help completing it. In some cases, resource room efforts may be directed toward teaching students basic skills.

Self-Contained Special Day Classes

Severely handicapped students may be served in a *self-contained special day class* or may be served in an inclusion setting for a part of the day, with their teacher serving in the regular classroom as a co-teacher.

Curriculum for the Junior High School

The thrust at this time is to have all students access the regular class curriculum. For the LD student, this often means modifying the curriculum so the student can access it. In some cases, this merely means shortening assignments and providing tutorial help. For other students, it may mean either reading the text to them or assigning them a study buddy who will help them.

Strategies to Increase Metacognition and Learning

Some resource and special education teachers are teaching students who do not have the prerequisite skills to succeed in mainstream classes how to learn and how to perform in those classes through the use of strategic instruction. The Strategies Instructional Approach, developed and validated by researchers at the University of Kansas Center for Research on Learning (Deshler and Schumaker, 1988; Schumaker and Deshler, 1992), involves teaching students to acquire, transform, store, and express information by using strategic systems comprised of cognitive, metacognitive, and overt behaviors. Students are taught three strategy systems through explicit and intensive instruction in which mastery and generalization of the strategy system are emphasized. Student self-instruction in the performance of the strategy steps is facilitated through the use of an acronym. For example, the acronym for a reading comprehension strategy called the Paraphrasing Strategy (Schumaker, Denton, and Deshler, 1984) is "RAP," with the letters standing for:

R = Read a paragraph.

A = Ask yourself, "What were the main idea and the details?"

P = Put it in your own words.

For another example, the Error Monitoring Strategy (Schumaker, Nolan, and Deshler, 1985) enables students to identify and correct their own writing errors. The letters in the associated acronym "WRITER" stand for:

W = Write on every other line.

R = Read the paper for meaning.

I = Interrogate yourself using "COPS" questions:

   C = Have I capitalized the first word of each sentence and all proper names?

   O = How is the overall appearance?

   P = Have I used end punctuation, commas, and semicolons correctly?

   S = Do the words look like they are spelled correctly?

T = Take the paper to someone else to proofread.

E = Execute the final copy.

R = Reread your paper a final time.

Implementing the Strategies Instructional Approach requires training and practice. For information regarding the National Training Network associated with the University of Kansas Center for Research on Learning, call (913) 864-4780.

Reading in Junior High School

Most junior high schools have integrated reading and language arts into a 2-hour block. The trend is toward a heavier emphasis on writing skills than reading. Writing is almost always a deficit area for LD students, so teachers must plan ways to facilitate their writing. (See Volume II for suggestions.)

Mathematics for Living

The trend in math is toward problem-solving rather than calculations. Students usually work in pairs or groups, and solutions are written in a math journal. For LD students, this results in considerable frustration and anxiety. It is helpful, therefore, if the Rsp or the Rsp tutor is on hand to give help.

Teaching LD Students to Be Their Own Advocate

It is important to teach LD students to understand their handicap and to learn to ask for help.

Step 1 is to talk about "What is a learning disability?" During this first lesson, students are generally very quiet because they do not want to expose themselves. You will carry the ball by telling them the names of some very famous people who are or were learning disabled.

Start with the more recent ones, such as Tom Cruise who claims to have a reading disability. See if they know who Cher is; she is dyslexic. Henry Winkler (who was "The Fonz") has problems with math. Tell them how Thomas Edison's teacher told his mother that school was a waste of time for Tom because he was so "addled"; then explain that Thomas Edison invented the electric light bulb so people no longer have to use candles by which to read. Have students understand several geniuses, such as Albert Einstein, Winston Churchill, and Woodrow Wilson, have been learning disabled.

You may want to use the information from Chapter 2 to explain a bit about brain function: left/right brain functions, actions of chemicals such as neurotransmitters vs. neuroinhibitors, and the role of verbal rehearsal in helping you learn. End the lesson on two themes: (a) we do not all have to be carbon copies, we are unique and interesting creatures, and (b) everyone in the group has a learning problem. Ask them to try to figure out what they think it is and vocalize it, for example, "I have trouble remembering stuff."

Step 2 is to get LD students to feel they have worth in spite of their problems in school. Most LD students actually believe they are dumb. (Remember the note written by the student in Chapter 1?) It is important for them to realize there are jobs out there they can get and do well at, provided their attitude is acceptable and they try hard. There is a book called *The Success of Failures* by Brian Wilson (published by Mar*Co Products, 1443 Old York Road, Warminster Road, PA 18974) that was written by a young man who is severely dyslexic. Brian graduated from Humboldt State University in California at the age of 24. He could barely read, and writing was extremely tough, but he was personable, able to ask for help when he needed it, had parents who were very supportive, and made it with the help of the Disabled Students Services at the university. Though Brian had enormous strikes against him, he concentrated on what he did well—sports of all sorts. Today, he is employed at a resort as a host and ski instructor. Reading parts of his book may be helpful to your students because Brian offers good advice in a nice way. Part of your lesson in Step 2 is to get people to own up to feeling dumb in only one area. Begin the lesson by having two or three adults known to the group tell them what makes them feel dumb. Next, go around the circle and ask each person to confess to one area in which he or she feels dumb.

The next part of the lesson begins to teach students to mediate that feeling by saying something positive about themselves; for example, "I may not read very well but I can ride a skateboard far better than most people"; "I may not write very well but I can draw like crazy"; "I may not do math very well but I can outcook my mom." Begin to do daily exercises where students alter their self-talk. "I may not do math very well but I can listen and try." "I may not read very well but I can learn three new words today." It is also a good idea during this phase (which you may stay in for several days) to have kids express their feelings about their disability. They may be in denial, anger, guilt, or depression and *need to hear* "It's okay to feel angry"; "It's not your fault"; "You can succeed."

This is also a good time to talk about the fact that although we sometimes have no control over what happens to us, we *always* have control over our reaction to it. For example, two soldiers each lose a leg in wartime. One lies in bed saying, "Poor me" and refuses to accept what has happened. The other says, "Bad luck but it won't keep me down." He straps on a prosthesis and is walking in a few weeks. Ask, "What's the difference between these two soldiers?" Spend some time having students gather other stories and discuss what the influence of courage and persistence is on success.

Step 3 is to help students evaluate their strengths and weaknesses and to be able to verbalize them to other people; that is, to ask for help. For example:

- "I have a good personality and people like me. I'm pretty good at math but I need help with reading."
- "I can look at things and see how they work. I can fix things. But my memory stinks. I have trouble remembering things."

Step 4 requires students to practice asking for help, to teach them to be their own advocate. For example:

- "I'm learning disabled. I need . . . Could you help me . . . ?
- "I have a memory problem. I need to tape record your lecture."
- "I need to know exactly what material I need to study for the test."

One of my former students shared a story with me. One day when she was in seventh grade, her science teacher was angry because he had given a test and everyone in the class had failed it. As he passed back papers, he put each student on the hot seat with "And what's your excuse?" When he reached her, she looked up sweetly and calmly said, "I'm sorry I didn't do very well. I really wanted to, but I'm dyslexic and I can't read the book." The teacher thought she was pulling his leg, but checked her records and found out she was telling the truth. He called her in during conference time, apologized, and asked, "How can I help you?" Had she just suffered in silence, she would have continued to fail. She is now in her second year of college.

Step 5 is to teach students strategies for learning. This includes mnemonics training, note-taking strategies, and visualization training. (See Volume II.)

Step 6 is to teach students strategies for smart test-taking.

The Changing Needs of the High School LD Student

As LD students reach tenth grade, their basic skills seem to plateau. Average achievement hovers around the fifth- to sixth-grade level. At about age 16, students begin to turn their attention to preparing for employment, driving, marriage, and adult responsibilities. Students not doing well begin to drop out. We might be able to keep them in school if we could enhance two areas of the secondary school curriculum:

- work-study programs with on-the-job coaching
- development of a social and life skills curriculum to prepare students for independent living

Efforts to Engage Students in the Educational Process at the High School Level

Peer Counseling

Many high schools have embraced peer counseling programs. Recognizing that teenagers turn to persons of their own age for advice, many high schools offer training to students who wish to be peer counselors. These youngsters receive 80 or more hours of training and lectures covering a variety of subjects of concern to students this age. Students who want a peer counselor may request one. The peer counselor's job is to listen to the student and help the student explore options for solving problems. If the peer counselor is at a loss for solutions, he or she can go to an adult counselor for advice.

Family Involvement and Transition I.E.P.s

A second effort is family involvement and transition I.E.P.s. At the age of 14, districts begin to address "transition" on the I.E.P. At this age an effort is made to get students and their parents to begin thinking about what the student will do after high school.

Vocational Programs

A third effort is the vocational program offered by the school. Many high schools are cooperating with Regional Occupational Programs (ROP) to provide specialized job training. One of the problems that special education students face is they cannot read the texts required to take some of the courses offered: health occupations, microcomputer operator, drafting, etc. Therefore, they end up in lower-paid fields, such as food services and custodial services. Although the students can attend these ROPs at no cost and receive high school credit, we need to find ways to help them overcome the barriers to their success in completing such programs.

Independent Study Programs and Continuation High Schools

Independent study programs and continuation high schools can offer salvation for many LD students. These programs place students in noncompetitive classes with faculty dedicated to helping them stay in school and graduate. It often works!

CURRICULUM FOR THE SENIOR HIGH SCHOOL

If you look at course offerings at the senior high level, you will find that typically students are required to take 4 years of English, 3 years of math, 3 years of science, 4 years of social studies, 2 years of P.E., and 1 year of fine arts/foreign language. In addition, students have an option to choose between skills development classes or college prep classes.

Special educators need to actively help students take advantage of vocational educational offerings. LD students are under-represented in these programs. Ten percent of regular students are in these programs, while only two percent of LD students are.

Many districts have a transition office (whose staff's responsibility is to let students and parents know what is available) and Career Centers. The problem is that students and their parents do not take the initiative to contact the transition office staff or Career Centers, which means the students will not receive adequate transition services.

If a student elects to use the transition office's services, the staff can follow that student from high school through vocational rehab or college and onto the job.

In California, state funding for Project Workability seeks to encourage employers to hire handicapped students. The project pays the student's salary for 100 hours as he or she learns a job and provides staff to help iron out problems that develop on the job. Perhaps your state offers a similar program.

Finally, we need to look at the program for LD students in high school and try to determine why it is that our students in grades 10, 11, and 12 are showing little increase in achievement. See Figure 7-3 in Chapter 7 and note that students tend to "plateau" after ninth grade. Is this because we are not doing a good teaching job? Is it because the curriculum does not meet these students' needs? (Recognizing their skills levels are still at grades 4 and 5, perhaps the curriculum being offered is just so difficult that they are getting no benefit from it.) Is there something wrong within the students themselves that causes them not to be able to make progress at this time in their lives?

BEYOND HIGH SCHOOL

When I began teaching 30 years ago, we thought we could "fix" or help students overcome learning disabilities. Now we know this was a myth. Some individuals find ingenious ways to compensate for their disabilities and enter adult society without being recognized as "learning disabled." For instance, I remember one young lady who was extremely bright and had beautiful training in her social skills who became a receptionist and a secretary. She was very likable and her people skills were incredible. Clients coming into the office loved her! Her boss nearly lost his mind, however, because she could not remember what she did with things. Files were misplaced; important details forgotten. Her husband received a job transfer and they moved just short of the time when she would have been terminated.

How many learning disabled adults do you know by name? Probably not very many. What happens to LD kids after they get out of school? From the somewhat limited research that is available, we know that:

- LD students who drop out prior to graduation have the greatest difficulty finding and keeping jobs, and experience more periods of unemployment than students who graduated.

- LD students who "hang in" through graduation generally take jobs that require little reading and/or writing.

- Most LD workers are in minimum-wage or entry-level jobs.

- LD students who have above-average IQ seem to fare better; about 20% of LD students go onto college or trade schools. Of this number, the ones who are successful have coping strategies (assignment calendars to remember what is due and when, know how to highlight and take notes, ask friends to study with them).

- Sixty percent of learning disabled adults continue to live with their parents (Sitlington, Frank, and Carson, 1992).

SERVICES AVAILABLE TO LD STUDENTS GOING TO COLLEGE

Section 504 of the Rehabilitation Act of 1973 mandated that services be provided for all individuals with handicaps to assist them to become economically self-supporting. Today over 500 colleges and universities offer services to students with disabilities. LD students, for example, may apply to take entrance exams under modified circumstances (alone in a quiet room, extra time).

Once admitted, they benefit from the same kinds of program *accommodations* previously discussed:

- assistance with registration and strategic placement in classes with empathetic instructors
- extra tutorial assistance (without cost to student)
- tape-recorded lectures or textbooks and assistance with note taking
- provision of notes by instructor
- access to word-processing equipment, calculators, and computers
- access to the Learning Lab where they are taught specific strategies for study
- proofreading services/typists to help with papers
- waivers for some courses, such as math

255

- permission to reduce course load without loss of full-time student status
- highlighted texts
- alternative modes of testing and arrangements for testing
- assistance with time management and personal organization
- psychoeducational testing and therapy
- support groups
- social skills training

As is always the case, how good the student support services are is largely dependent on the individuals hired to provide such services. Thus, parents of youngsters going onto college need to seek out those institutions that demonstrate their commitment—those with sympathetic faculties. Visit the campuses. Talk to the personnel in the Office for Disabled Students Services.

Occasionally a person will reach college with a learning disability that has never been recognized. Sarah, in Chapter 1, was such a student. She squeaked by in high school but finally realized she had a terrible problem in math. At the age of 25, she requested assessment, but her request was met with resistance. Finally, after threatening to file an appeal with the Office of Civil Rights, she was assessed and identified. Students who are going onto college need to be helped to develop strong self-advocacy skills.

VOCATIONAL REHABILITATION SERVICES FOR THE LEARNING DISABLED

Some individuals with learning disabilities are accepted for training through the various vocational rehabilitation services, such as Goodwill or state departments of rehabilitation. Again, whether this avenue is worthwhile is dependent on the knowledge and dedication of the staff.

Vocational rehabilitation services may include a combination of services from the following list:

- books and tuition for trade school/college
- transportation
- job training
- reader/interpreter/note-taking services
- tools or other equipment needed for a job
- initial stock or supplies in a small business
- medical services if needed
- job-seeking skills training
- placement in a job
- a "job coach" on the work site to help the student learn the job
- follow-up on the job to make sure both employee and employer are satisfied

LEARNING DISABLED ADULTS

The employment rate of learning disabled students who completed high school is not significantly different from their nonhandicapped peers—about 75 percent. What *is* different is where they are after several years of working. They are still in entry-level jobs, usually earning minimum wages, may only be employed part time, and are often dissatisfied with the job they do have (Sitlington, Frank, and Carson, 1992).

Research (Okolo and Sitlington, 1986) suggests there are three reasons why the mildly LD are underemployed:

1. They lack interpersonal skills (work habits and social communication skills).
2. They lack job-related academic skills.
3. They lack specific vocational skills.

Many LD students are ashamed of their handicap and will try to deny it or hide it; they feel inferior, as if they don't belong; and they often feel helpless. Young people with LD will sometimes tell you they might not have dropped out had vocational education been arranged for them. If teachers have empathy for their plight and go out of their way to work with these students on a personal basis, they feel less ostracized.

If you are a high school teacher, talk to students one-to-one about their future. Go with them to the transition office and to see other people who can help them. By doing this, you can improve a youngster's entire life. It may be the difference in whether he or she becomes a productive adult or a burden to society.

The Role of Technology in Learning disabilities

COMPUTER-ASSISTED LEARNING

By the year 2010, the way we teach school today probably will seem as antiquated as the one-room schoolhouses of 100 years ago seem to us. Technology and the Information Superhighway are about to revolutionize how youngsters are taught.

In my crystal ball, I foresee that each student will have a personal computer workstation (or two students will share a workstation, each working there for several hours each day). Student programs will be highly individualized. Students will work at their functional level using materials that satisfy their interests and academic needs. There will be a large screen at the front of the room for whole-class viewing of lessons and discussions. Students will be able to answer questions about the lesson and the teacher will receive immediate feedback regarding which students need to have the lesson reshown or clarified. On-line services will allow students to talk with people all over the country and receive the latest information (including access to up-to-date references such as encyclopedias).

The teacher's role will be that of learning facilitator, progress monitor, and advisor. As the learning facilitator, the teacher will organize the classroom and help students maintain satisfactory behaviors. He or she will monitor what the student works on, what degree of proficiency the student attains, and keep appropriate records. As advisor, the teacher and student will jointly plan and select software that will be beneficial for the student's progress. Students may take a much more active part in selecting what they want to study.

A few years ago, I could not envision that a machine would ever be able to teach a child to read, but today's computers with voice synthesizers can. If you have not experienced the *Wiggleworks®* software available from Scholastic, Inc., I urge you to try to visit a school that has it. Using the whole language approach, the student listens to a story read as many times as he or she wants. The computer can highlight the text as it reads to the child. The child then reads to the computer. The computer keeps a record of the student's performance so the teacher knows what words were missed. The software then provides the student the opportunity to write about the story and to individualize the story. The child's writing of the original story can be printed so he or she can take it home. What a marvelous feature for those children who come from print-impoverished homes! *Wiggleworks®* begins with kindergarten and moves upward. The software program comes with books (72 titles) for grades K-2. The books are sequenced, so as the child moves through the series, they become more difficult but also reinforce words previously encountered.

Some people fear the shift to computer-assisted learning, worrying that children will become slaves to their machines; for example, the child who will play tennis on the computer instead of playing tennis outside. Parents and teachers will have to insist children turn the machine off periodically.

In the year 2010, teachers will still plan the student's day so there is a balance of activity—rest, play, computer learning, teacher-led lessons, cooperative learning, and opportunities to engage in dialogue.

Likewise, even though there are some tremendous word-processing programs that will help students learn a great deal about mechanics and pragmatics, they do not totally take the place of the teacher. Before printing, the teacher needs to sit with the student and review the proposed document for syntax and pragmatics. The teacher may still be needed to help the student make the corrections that will improve organization and meaning, even though the software has already made some suggestions along this line.

Unlike TV, many new computer programs are interactive. A child can sit like a blob watching TV in an almost "brain-dead" state; interactive computer programs, however, require thinking and a response on the student's part. Indeed, with some programs, such as *The Oregon Trail®* (by Mecc), a history simulation for grade 5 and up, the student is presented with a scenario and must complete the program by making decisions. There are some programs that have the student make a choice and then, based on the choice made, the computer shows the consequences of the choice. If the child does not like the consequences, he or she can replay the scenario and make a different choice. In the math line, there are many interactive programs such as *Millie's Math House®* (by Edmark) to help K-1 children—through music and animated characters—bring math concepts to life.

Students with artistic talent make good use of the mouse or crayon modem to produce outstanding graphics. Older students enjoy authoring their own quizzes and programs (Mather, 1988).

Word processors are a boon to the LD student. The processor's features help the student overcome such deficits as poor fine motor control, organizational problems, spelling errors, and mechanics errors. Many students are helped by being able to see and edit the paper prior to printing. Upon printing, the student is amazed at how good the paper looks, so they are willing to produce more written work.

WHAT DOES RESEARCH SAY ABOUT COMPUTER-ASSISTED LEARNING?

Early research suggests that computer-assisted learning is extremely effective with LD students. Why?

- It increases on-task behavior. Typical on-task behavior for LD students is 30 to 60 percent; but with the computer, it jumps to 80 to 90 percent (Cosden et al., 1987).

- Students are more likely to do the drill work necessary to the acquisition of math facts; drill practice that is hooked up with a game format motivates students to do the practice necessary to acquire the skill (Malouf, 1987-1988).

- Computers help students develop better decoding and vocabulary skills.

- Instruction can be individualized to the students' needs and functional level as well as their learning speed.

- Students receive immediate feedback of results.

- The multi-colored graphics and game formats with sound appeal to students more than traditional paper-and-pencil tasks.

- The ability to correct errors without messy erasures or redoing the task is a big help to LD students who are easily frustrated and defeated. It has been found that when students were allowed to use the computer, they produced more written work (MacArthur, 1988).

HARDWARE

Minimally, the modern classroom needs to have a TV, a VCR, one or more tape recorders, a movie projector, an overhead projector, and several computers (minimally six to eight with sound capability). Word processors are cheaper than computers, so you might be able to reduce the number of computers by having several word processors—perhaps six computers and two word processors. Choose word processors that have separate upright monitors, spell checks, and mechanics checks. Some are even compatible with the computer.

Franklin Learning Resources produces a line of hand-held dictionaries (some with a voice component) that are reasonably priced. As a word appears on the screen, it is highlighted and said aloud. These language masters also give the definition, divide the word into syllables, and tell the part of speech. Some provide a thesaurus feature and vocabulary enrichment games. A set of eight would be a real asset in a classroom, but—I warn you—you will need to be sure you retrieve and carefully store these because students like them so well they will take them!

SOFTWARE

The variety of software available is astounding. Software companies are entering into partnership contracts with school districts that allow each district to acquire multiple copies of popular software at substantially reduced prices. For example, what would normally cost a district $1,299 under regular purchasing can be purchased through one company's program for $500.

Software is being developed so rapidly now that programs that seem to be "on the cutting edge" of technology today may be upstaged by better ones within only a few months. Each school district needs to be constantly evaluating new releases.

For a catalog of offerings, you may wish to contact:

- Educational Resources at 1-800-624-2926
- Macmillan at 1-800-428-5331
- Franklin at 1-800-525-9673
- Microsoft at 1-800-426-9400
- Computer Plus at 1-800-446-3713
- National School Products at 1-800-627-9393
- Queue, Inc. at 1-800-232-2224
- The Learning Company at 1-800-852-2255
- Orange Cherry New Media Schoolhouse at 1-800-672-6002
- Steck-Vaughan Company at 1-800-531-5015
- Milliken Publishing at 1-800-325-4137
- CDL at 1-800-637-0047
- The Electronic Bookshelf at 1-800-327-7323
- Electronic Learning at 1-800-544-2917

A CALL TO ACTION

18

Joseph Kozol, author of *Illiterate America*, says:

- 60 million Americans are illiterate.
- 85% of juveniles coming before the courts are functionally illiterate.
- 50% of prisoners are illiterate.
- The cost to society of this illiteracy exceeds 200 billion dollars a year.

According to "Dateline," March 17, 1995:

- In 1990, the U.S. Census found that one out of every third baby born in the U.S. was born to an unwed mother.
- By 2000, this statistic is expected to be one out of every two babies will be born to an unwed mother.
- 50% of high school students are sexually active before they leave high school.
- The U.S. has the highest rate of teenage pregnancy among the industrialized nations.

The April 25, 1994 issue of *Newsweek* reports:

- One of every 5 children is living in poverty.
- Over one million referrals for child abuse and neglect are made each year in the U.S.

Clearly, all is not well.

HOW CAN WE PREVENT LEARNING DISABILITIES?

We know teenagers are sexually active. Many will become pregnant. For a substantial number of these young mothers, that results in going on welfare and raising their offspring in poverty. Learning disabilities occur more frequently in young mothers and in persons raised in poverty.

Discourage Teenage Pregnancy

We suggest that our young people say "no" to drugs. We need also to suggest that they say "no" to unprotected sex by either not engaging in it or by using a condom. We need to mount campaigns *discouraging teenage pregnancy* by encouraging youngsters to do "their best" and to stay in school. If a girl does become pregnant, we need to provide that teenager something other than a welfare check to squander on unwise purchases or boyfriends. We need to have centers where these young women can live to receive counseling and prenatal care while continuing their schooling. They need to be taught how to prepare nutritious meals on a budget (actually shopping for the center's groceries under supervision and working in the kitchen). They need vocational guidance and training. Once employed, they need to be taught how to manage their money and live within their means outside the center. We also need to provide these girls with birth-control information.

267

Initiate Early Infant Program

Embodied in this plan would be an *early infant program*. Each girl would be required to work in the infant care center of the center for a portion of the week. There they would learn about caring for children, what normal development looks like, disciplining without harming a child physically or emotionally, and stimulating cognitive and physical development.

EARLY SCREENING AND IDENTIFICATION

Another change we need is early screening and identification of children who will need some special services. This means doing more in our colleges and universities to prepare doctors, nurses, and teachers to ask the right questions and make referrals on children who seem to have problems.

We know that *Headstart* was a worthwhile program and it probably follows that we need to allow all students to attend one if their parents so desire.

At the age of five all children could be subjected to *screening* designed to locate those youngsters not ready for an academic kindergarten experience. No child would "flunk" or be retained. Upon *identification* these children would enter *junior kindergartens* where the emphasis is on developing those skills necessary for success in academic kindergarten. The curriculum would help these children learn how to play cooperatively, how to sit and listen for five minutes, how to color and write their name, develop the gross and fine motor skills, work on receptive and expressive language, develop pre-literacy skills, and provide compensatory experiences that develop the general knowledge fund. Schools also would provide *junior first programs* for students needing greater attention (low teacher:pupil ratio) who are not ready for grade one. All children would enter grade one by age 7. Dyslexic children would be identified and given appropriate services earlier.

ATTENDANCE

Another area needing to be fixed is *attendance*. It is not uncommon to find that children who are having problems with academics or behavior develop a pattern of poor attendance. Our current truancy laws are not dealing with this problem.

When have you heard of a parent being arrested for not sending his or her child to school? When a child consistently misses more than one day a month, or 10 to 12 days a year, we can predict that it will hamper the student's progress. I am estimating that under this definition at least 10 percent of our school population would be classified as having an attendance problem. In today's society, children are kept home to babysit, taken on vacations during the school term, and allowed to remain home when not truly ill. I personally have tried to talk with parents who have done these things and they feel entirely within their rights to do whatever they please with their child.

GETTING PARENTS INVOLVED WITH EDUCATION

Across the country there are districts experimenting with various *programs to get parents involved with education*. Probably most effective is a program whereby employers insist and pay the parents' wages while they help out for two hours per month at their child's school. Under this program parents seem to enjoy the experience and there is a strengthening of support by the parent for the teachers' efforts. One of the current problems is that many parents are suspicious of teachers and their motivations. The parents may align themselves with their child against the school. When parents do this, the child always loses because the child cannot relate to the teacher in a healthy way.

Somehow we need to convince parents to supervise their children's TV viewing. Left unsupervised, children will sit like zombies watching the tube. This keeps them from pursuing more worthwhile activities and frequently exposes them to a steady diet of violence. There is research support now that says children who *watch* violence *become* angry and violent. Communities need to develop after-school programs—on school sites—so we do not have so many latchkey kids. There needs to be dance classes, music, tutoring programs, as well as recreational programs. A well-supervised, busy child is less likely to become involved in drugs or trouble.

STRENGTHENING VOCATIONAL PROGRAMS

The ultimate goal of education is for the child to become a productive citizen; therefore, we need to strengthen our *vocational offerings*. LD children will benefit from participating in a *work-study program* during the last two years of high school. Even students planning to attend college often have to work part time. How helpful it would be if they had a marketable skill! When students have participated in work-study programs, it has been documented that they are suddenly more interested in learning their school subjects. High schools need to offer training in a wide variety of areas. Many high school districts are connected to Regional Occupational Programs (ROP).

In tenth grade, every student should be given an interest inventory, an aptitude test, and counseling by trained career counselors as to fields they might want to pursue and opportunities for training in those fields. It would be nice if parents were a part of these interviews as well. Following this, the school counselor would work with parent and student to *develop a meaningful high school program*, choosing courses that would best *complement the vocational area selected or the work-study program*. If continuing onto college is chosen, school counselors could actively assist students and parents in making that transition. For these students, there should be a minimum of at least two semesters of note-taking instruction and they absolutely must be able to use the computer proficiently. For special education students, the transition counselor will help the students choose an institution sympathetic to their needs or area of pursuit and do those things necessary to put the students in contact with the college's Office of Services for Disabled Students.

ADULT EDUCATION

We now have adult education centers that offer a *second chance program* for students who did not apply themselves well to regular school. We need to expand these programs and possibly pay students a small stipend to attend as incentive to better themselves.

When a student drops out of school, we need to go after him or her and try to get that person into an independent study program or into a continuation high school.

When a student is involved in a crime and comes under the jurisdiction of the juvenile court system, extraordinary efforts need to be made to turn that youngster around.

We need to enforce laws already on the books that prevent discrimination against the handicapped in hiring. Many employers will not hire LD persons if the person says he or she is LD (Minskoff et al., 1987).

PROFESSIONAL ISSUES

We need to look at how we are *staffing programs for learning disabled students*. It was the intent of the legislatures that specially trained teachers would direct programs for LD kids. Unfortunately, there are not enough of these trained persons around, so what is actually happening is not in keeping with the intent. Instead of the students having the best-trained teachers, due to the shortage they often end up with the least well-trained teachers (people on emergency credentials). Some incentive must be offered to entice good people to continue to get all the additional training required to become fully certified. This might come either in stipends to cover the cost of training or in salaries that inspire teachers to take the training.

Meanwhile, we need not "kill off" those trained people we already have on the job. One way to avoid this would be for districts to provide extra aides to help serve both identified and at-risk students. With direction from the teacher, aides are often able to do the instruction necessary to help the students; thereby, freeing the teacher to handle the assessment, volumes of paperwork, planning/initial teaching, consultation with other staff members, and training paraprofessional staff.

A final consideration needing attention is *dissemination of knowledge within the field*. It is so important that we help teachers stay current with the research and developments in the field so they achieve the best results possible. I would like to see a bi-yearly newsletter published by the federal government and sent to teachers free of charge. Currently, the National Information Center for Handicapped Children and Youth (NICHCY) does publish a newsletter and you can obtain a copy by writing NICHCY, P.O. 1492, Washington, D.C. 20013.

In conclusion, we teachers need to assume a leadership role in our communities. What's wrong with American education is that it simply reflects the general apathy in our society. As a nation (according to the 1983 report *A Nation at Risk*), we have become a nation that accepts mediocrity. In response to that report, school districts and teachers have redoubled their efforts, but we need to tell it like it is—instead of patting ourselves on the back for what we are doing, we need to reach out to parents and industry for support.

Some studies suggest the answer does not lie in extra money for schools. What seems to be needed is a revival of a spirit of personal responsibility. We all need to be talking to youngsters about how they can make things better. *We need to inspire them to develop their talents*. We need people around to answer each child's questions, reward effort, and—when a child is feeling inadequate—give the encouragement and attention necessary to give the task a try. Who can do that better than the child's own parent? A teacher is with the child for a year; the parent will be there for the whole school career.

I dreamed I stood in a studio
And watched two sculptors there,
The clay they used was a young child's mind
And fashioned it with care.
One was a teacher; the tools he used
Were books and music and art;
One was a parent with a guiding hand,
With a gentle, loving heart.
Day after day the teacher toiled,
With touch that was deft and sure,
While the parent labored by his side
And polished and smoothed it o'er.
And when at last their task was done,
They were proud of what they had wrought,
For the things they had molded into the child
Could neither be sold or bought.
And each agreed he would have failed
If he had worked alone,
For behind the parent stood the school,
And behind the teacher the home.

—Anonymous

APPENDIX

1

LIST OF ORGANIZATIONS AND SOURCES OF HELP

Organizations

Association for Children and Adults with
  Learning Disabilities
4156 Library Road
Pittsburgh, PA 15234
412-341-1515

Provides general information on LD; lists
  of special schools, colleges, and camps
  for LD.

Association for Persons with Severe
  Handicaps
7010 Roosevelt Way, N.E.
Seattle, WA 98115
206-523-8446

Offers support to parents. Publishes a
  journal and newsletter.

Children with Attention Deficit Disorders
1859 North Pine Island Road, Suite 185
Plantation, FL 33322
305-384-6869

Provides parental support, information.
  Publishes a newsletter.

Clearinghouse on the Handicapped
Office of Special Education
  and Rehabilitative Services
U.S. Department of Education
Switzer Building, Room 3132
Washington, D.C. 20202-2319
202-732-1214

Answers questions regarding programs,
  housing, transportation, legislation, etc.
  Provides referral services to parents.
  Publishes a newsletter.

Council for Exceptional Children
1920 Association Drive
Reston, VA 22091
703-620-3660

Provides information on laws, policies,
  and materials on special education.
  Advocates for legislation to benefit persons with special needs.

Council on Learning Disabilities
P.O. Box 40303
Overland Park, KS 66204
913-492-8755

Disseminates professional information via
  a journal.

Epilepsy Foundation of America
4341 Garden City Drive
Landover, MD 20758
1-800-332-1000

Provides information and brochures.

National Association for the
  Education of Young Children
1834 Connecticut Avenue, N.W.
Washington, D.C. 20009
202-323-8777

Provides information, kits, and brochures.

National Association for Hearing and
  Speech Action
10801 Rockville Pike
Rockville, MD 20855
1-800-638-TALK

Provides information on services for
  speech/hearing impaired and children
  with communication disorders.
  Publishes a newsletter.

National Information Center for Children
  and Youth with Handicaps
P.O. Box 1492
Washington, D.C. 20013
1-800-999-5599

Answers questions, and provides advice
  and lists of agencies and services for
  children with special needs.

National Legal Resource Center for Child
  Advocacy
1800 M Street, N.W.
Washington, D.C. 20036
202-331-2250

Provides information on educational services for children with special needs.

National Mental Health Association
1021 Prince Street
Alexandria, VA 22314

Provides information on services and legislation for people with mental or emotional disorders.

Orton Dyslexia Society
724 York Road
Baltimore, MD 21204
301-296-0232

Provides information and brochures.

President's Committee on Employment of the Handicapped
1111 20th Street, N.W. (6th floor)
Washington, D.C. 20210

Provides pamphlets.

Tourette Syndrome Association
42-40 Bell Boulevard
Bayside, NY 11361
718-224-2999

Provides programs, brochures, and newsletters for persons interested in Tourette Syndrome.

Sources of Help

Directory of Educational Facilities and Services for the Learning Handicapped, 12th ed. (1987)
Academic Therapy Publication

Lovejoy's College Guide for the Learning Disabled (1985) Simon & Schuster,
1230 Avenue of the Americas, New York City, NY 10020

Pro-Ed
8700 Shoal Creek Boulevard
Austin, TX 78758

APPENDIX

2

TEACHER'S GUIDE TO BEHAVIORAL PROBLEM SOLVING

"He's out of his seat. He touches other people's things. He talks all the time. He does very little work. He yells out for help. I know he needs help but I have 30 other youngsters to worry about. I can't sit with him all day."

STEPS TO PROBLEM SOLVING

1. *Write* down all the things the student does that annoy you.
2. *Analyze* which behavior bothers you the most.
3. *Choose* no more than two behaviors to work on.
4. *Discuss* the target behaviors with both student and parent.

In order to change behavior, a person first must become aware of the behavior and then want to change the behavior. It has been my experience that once parent support is enlisted, students are more likely to want to change their behavior.

In discussing the behaviors with parents, it is not the fact that the behavior annoys you that is important. It is that the behavior is interfering with the student's social life or academic achievement.

5. *Decide* on appropriate rewards and aversives and who will use them.
   - *Use* the least amount of reward necessary to get the appropriate behavior and the least amount of aversive necessary to illicit the desired behavior.
   - *Decide* how you will measure whether the student's behavior meets your expectations.
6. *Write* a contract and *model* the expected behaviors.
7. *Set up* a two-way daily communication system with the parents so they are kept informed of progress.
8. *Remind* the student at the beginning of each period of the behavior expected.
9. During the period, *use a pre-arranged signal* to let the student know when behavior is not satisfactory (a tap on the shoulder).
10. *Give* work that the student can be successful with.
11. *Be consistent.* Avoid unclear parameters for behavior.

APPENDIX 3

WHAT YOU NEED TO KNOW ABOUT ADD: A GUIDE FOR PARENTS AND TEACHERS

WHAT IS ATTENTION DEFICIT DISORDER?

Attention deficit disorder without hyperactivity (ADD) or attention deficit hyperactivity disorder (ADHD) are two forms of a condition that occur in about 5 to 10 percent of our children. Their primary characteristics include an inability to concentrate and complete school work, low tolerance of frustration, and impulsivity (does things before considering the consequences). The child with ADD may present as a tired child (head frequently on table or leaning against wall).

The child with ADHD has difficulty staying in his or her seat, fidgets constantly, and is very easily distracted. Incessant talking or mouth noises are also frequent complaints.

Children with both forms of the condition generally have either normal or superior intelligence, but are not able to truly benefit from instruction because they are off-task.

They may also have a learning disability.

It is not uncommon for the parents to report that other family members have had the problem.

As these children get older, they may cause a lot of trouble in the home because they do not get along with brothers and sisters. In turn, their behavior can cause parents to argue.

HOW IS ATTENTION DEFICIT DISORDER DIAGNOSED?

At this time there is no medical test for the condition; rather, it is diagnosed by its symptoms. If you went to a doctor and said, "I have a fever, I'm coughing, I have a headache, and I ache all over," the doctor would say, "I think you have the flu." Likewise, if you say, "My child is not able to complete school assignments in the allotted time, is distractible, forgets and loses things, and is impulsive," these are symptoms* the doctor should want to pursue because we know that children with these symptoms are going to be underachievers if they do not get help. Unfortunately, there are some doctors who know very little about ADD/ADHD and others who do not pursue the issue unless the child's behavior in the doctor's office is out of line. If this happens, parents need to seek a second opinion.

Doctors will want a referral letter from the school, may want to talk personally with the teacher, or ask you and the teacher to complete a behavior scale. Based on what they learn from you and the school, a trial period on medication may be recommended.

IS MEDICATION NECESSARY?

Many parents are concerned about giving children pills—especially central nervous system stimulants. Insulin is given when a person's body does not produce enough to cover the person's sugar intake. Likewise, if your child does not have enough natural chemicals to stay alert and vigilant, the child may need medication to provide the missing substance. Medication often reduces the stresses that have kept the family on edge. You need to make a list of questions to ask your physician so that, if medication is used, you understand what it should do to help, what side effects you should report, and what the long-term effects may be.

*There are other things that can cause children to show this kind of behavior, so you want to be totally open when talking with your physician. When asked, "How are things going at home?" don't say "Fine" unless things are really fine.

283

If medication is given, supervise its storage and use. Children should not be allowed to get their own pills and you need to be sure the child takes it (does not spit or throw it out).

Someone at school needs to monitor your child's behavior to see whether the use of medication is beneficial. It sometimes takes several weeks to get the dosage right, because the effect of the medication varies from child to child. There needs to be a lot of communication among teacher, parent, and doctor at the beginning.

You may have heard that a child's hyperactive behavior can be controlled with changes in the child's diet or by restricting sugar intake. It would be nice if this had worked. For most children, it does not.

Many doctors will suggest that in addition to medication, you will want to seek counseling. Family life will run more smoothly if you have help learning additional parenting skills because these children are more demanding. These children will require a lot of your time—they need to be taught social skills if they are to fit in and have friends.

Finally, you will want to become very knowledgeable about the condition. You will need to become your child's advocate at school. Unfortunately, just as some doctors are not totally familiar with the condition, you will find some teachers who do not know how to help. The following suggestions will help you and the teacher in working with your child.

SUGGESTIONS FOR CLASSROOM MODIFICATIONS

Here are classroom modifications that will assist the ADD/ADHD child.

- Shorten assignment and/or decrease the workload. A child may balk at a long assignment that he or she would willingly attempt presented in small increments. For example, give five problems, check and praise, then give five more, and so on. Some children seem to be overwhelmed when confronted with a long task such as a research paper; however, if they do one small part a day, eventually it will get done.

- Allow for oral answers if writing is a barrier to success. Also allow student to dictate to an adult or cross-aged tutor.

- Limit distractions. A carrel out of the traffic pattern or even the use of ear plugs may help.

- Arrange for a daily two-way communication system (notebook or phone call) between parent and teacher.

- Arrange for a reward system (parent gives rewards) for work completed. It is easier to measure a goal for work completion than a behavioral goal.

- Allow the child a choice of assignments when appropriate. Try different seating arrangements until you find the best. Arrange an escape valve! If the child needs a timeout, have a place arranged (another teacher's room, the office, the nurse's room); timeout, however, must not get the child out of working (an alternative assignment may have to be substituted for the original).

- For children who get in trouble at recess, make plans (time in library or time with an aide) to prevent this.

- If changes of scheduling are necessary, discuss this with the child and explain what to expect.
- Use a touch, whisper, a signal, or verbal reminder (firm but not ugly) when the student's behavior is inappropriate. For example, if the child is climbing over, under, around or through a chair, say, "Johnny, sit properly."
- Remove any objects that are distracting the student, saying "This is distracting you. I want you to listen and look at me." (Return objects at the end of the day.)
- Be specific in giving directions. "Jaime, look at the board."

SUGGESTIONS FOR HOME MANAGEMENT

Parents will find the following home-management suggestions helpful.

- Provide as much consistency as you can. Making and following a daily schedule helps immensely. For example, having bedtime occur at the same time nightly makes for fewer hassles. If the child is allowed to stay up even once by begging, you may be sure your life will become a nightly nightmare of begging and arguing.
- Excessive television watching is detrimental for children. Recent studies suggest that children who watch TV for long periods of time are likely to be more angry and aggressive, so limit TV viewing to less than two hours a day. Monitor the programs for wholesomeness. ADD/ADHD children should not watch action films or violence (even in cartoon form).
- The best bedtime activity is getting the child into bed, and either reading to the child or playing soothing music.
- ADD/ADHD children require adequate rest—ten hours a night on average. When they are having a bad day, being sent to bed is often the best solution.
- Since ADD/ADHD children may be impulsive, accident-prone, and have a tendency toward aggression, you will need to supervise their activities more closely. Non-competitive sports such as gymnastics and swimming, gardening, art lessons, and music lessons (drums) are good outlets. Martial arts, boxing, war games, and highly competitive sports are contraindicated for ADD/ADHD children.
- Prepare the child for experiences such as shopping trips, church, doctor's or dentist's office, a friend's house, or restaurant. Explain what to expect, the behavior expected, and offer a reward for proper behavior. Under no circumstances should the child be allowed to disturb other people or touch their things. If you cannot keep the child from doing this, remove the child from the situation or premises.
- All children need social skills training. They need to practice good manners ("please, thank-you, hello, good-bye, excuse me, may I . . ."). They need to be taken into a variety of settings and given immediate but quiet feedback on their behavior, including modeling for them any areas needing instruction.
- Keep the child's environment quiet, calm, and structured.
- Mark belongings with a label so—hopefully—they are recovered if lost.
- Train the child to listen for and follow oral directions. Start by giving *one* direction and waiting for and insisting on compliance. Later move to two directions.

- Children, especially attentionally deficit ones, need help to organize themselves. Insist on an organized bedroom, an organized desk, a place for everything and everything in its place.

- Encourage them to concentrate on one thing until it is done. These children tend to be fragmented and scattered, flitting from one thing to another and finishing nothing. You will hear them say they need to "hurry up and do" their work; but there is little concern whether the job is done well.

- Homework must be done in a place that has as few distractions as possible (*no* TV). For elementary children in grades 1-3, confine homework to 30 minutes a day. For grades 4-6, confine it to 1 hour. For secondary students, homework of less than 2 hours a day is suggested. If these suggested limits do not allow time for full completion, ask the teacher to prioritize assignments in the order of importance.

- Reward yourself with time away from your ADD/ADHD child if you can. You need to have a life beyond parenthood.

APPENDIX 4

WHAT YOU NEED TO KNOW ABOUT LD: A GUIDE FOR PARENTS AND TEACHERS

WHAT IS A LEARNING DISABILITY?

Learning disability (LD) has been called the "invisible" handicap. Its victims do not look different; they have near-average, average, or above-average intelligence; and their hearing and vision are normal. Yet they have troubles the rest of us do not experience. To understand this, you must know there are many learning disabilities and each person so diagnosed has a profile unique to him or to her. Among the multiple areas of disability are:

- *Visual perceptual deficits.* The child's visual acuity is normal, but the mind misinterprets what was seen. Some examples are letter reversals (b/d) or sequencing errors (*was* is called "saw" and vice versa). These children almost always have difficulty learning to read and may have trouble copying.

- *Visual motor deficits.* The child has trouble making the muscles do what he or she wants them to do. The child may be awkward, accident prone, and have illegible handwriting.

- *Auditory perceptual deficits.* The child may have difficulty understanding what is said and may not be able to distinguish between similar sounds. Children with this problem are really going to have trouble in school since so much of what we learn depends on listening.

- *Memory deficits.* The child has difficulty remembering what is seen or heard. This results in poor language development and low general information funds. Children with this problem do not learn information that is encountered incidentally. They require drill to retain facts. They also forget and lose things.

- *Spatial deficits.* The child lacks a sense of space and direction. He or she may get lost in familiar circumstances. This deficit may be reflected in the child's writing (cannot write on a line, letters collide with each other, or there is no space between words).

- *Conceptual deficits.* The child with this disability has trouble seeing relationships between objects and has difficulty reasoning.

NOTE: While attentional problems are not classified as a learning disability, we know that 20 to 33 percent of all children with learning disabilities also have trouble staying-on-task, which further hampers their ability to learn.

Immaturity is also often a component of learning disabilities.

While emotional problems are not necessarily part of the conditions, many LD children develop them. This may occur because of the increased frustration they experience.

Other terms associated with learning disabilities include:

— "dyslexia" which refers to dysfunctions in learning to read

— "dyscalculia" which refers to deficits in learning math

— "dysgraphia" which refers to difficulty in learning the multiple skills required to communicate in writing

When your child has been diagnosed as having learning disabilities, it is important for you to find out in detail what kind of situations are going to be difficult for him or her. You have a legal right to a copy of the psychological report, but you will want to talk in depth with the people who did that assessment in order to truly understand it. Make notes about your child's areas of strengths and weaknesses. Ask what you can do to help.

WHAT CAUSES LEARNING DISABILITIES?

Once in a while we can point to a specific episode that might be the cause—such as oxygen deprivation, multiple ear infections, or a family history of LD—but usually we do not know. Trying to find the cause, however, does *not* help the child.

WHAT IS THE INCIDENCE OF LEARNING DISABILITIES?

Five percent of the general school population has been diagnosed as LD so we know the incidence is at least that high. In any classroom there are usually two or three youngsters who seem to have the problem. Most learning disabled children are not diagnosed until they reach third or fourth grade; by that time, they are one to two years behind in their academic achievement. It is rare for a child to "catch up."

WHAT IS THE PROGNOSIS FOR THE LEARNING DISABLED CHILD?

In large measure this depends on how serious the disabilities are and how the situation is handled. Some well-known people have been learning disabled—Albert Einstein, Winston Churchill, Thomas Edison, Tom Cruise, and Cher, to name a few. It is particularly important that parents take an active role in helping their child. The job cannot be left to the school if a desirable outcome is to be achieved. Parents will have to maintain at least weekly contact with the teacher, will need to provide either outside tutoring or daily help with school work at home—particularly reading to the child and having the child read to them. Most LD children show deficits in reading and writing skills; some also have trouble with math.

WAYS YOU CAN HELP A LEARNING DISABLED CHILD

1. *Be understanding.* Many times LD children get in trouble for disobeying when in actuality he or she simply did not understand what you were saying or expecting. Since these children require more reprimands than other children, they often think of themselves as being "bad." Since they make poor grades or realize they can't do what other children can, they feel worthless and inadequate. Teachers and parents need to let them know they care about them/love them and give them some extra time. Parents need to listen and empathize with how hard school is for them, but encourage them to "do their best." Encourage them to express their feelings and opinions in socially acceptable ways.

2. *Look for and give positive feedback.* The child needs to know when he or she does the right thing. "Thank you for making your bed." "You sat very still in the restaurant." "You look nice today." Positive feedback needs to *exceed* negative feedback.

3. *Keep life predictable.* Have a daily routine as a family or a class. If the routine must be adjusted, explain to the child how it will be changed and how he or she should act. Each child needs to have a place where homework is done. Parents need to help a child get started, periodically check its progress, and give help to make corrections. If the child does not understand something, explain it and let the teacher know that the child needs extra help with it. You may need to help the child read the material.

4. *Be firm.* You don't have to yell or spank, but you do need to wait to see that the youngster follows through when you give directions. You will find these children are more likely to follow through if they "buy into" or understand why they are doing something. Rewards can encourage compliance.

5. *Arrange for outside activities.* Sports, gardening, scouts, music, arts, and gymnastics offer these children outlets where they may feel more successful.

6. *Teach social skills.* Teach these children to be socially appropriate. Good manners and a pleasant demeanor will help the child tremendously now and later. Learning to say "Could you show me how to do that?" and "I'm sorry I did that. How can I make amends?" are important skills.

7. *Help in your child's class on a regular basis.* If you do this, it will have several advantages. First, you will know what is being taught so you can help at home. Next, you can see what kinds of modifications and methods the teacher uses to help your child. Third, your child will see that you think school is important. Because you are there regularly, the child will usually try harder so the teacher gives a good report each time you come.

BIBLIOGRAPHY

Abel, Ernest L. *Fetal Alcohol Syndrome and Fetal Alcohol Effect.* New York: Plenum Press, 1984.

Abramson, M., Willson, V., Yoshida, R.K., and Hagerty, G. "Parents' Perceptions of Their Disabled Child's Educational Performance." *Learning Disability Quarterly*, 6, 184-194, 1983.

Ackerman, P.T., Dyksman, R.A., and Gardner, M.Y. "Counting Rate, Naming Rate, Phonological Sensitivity and Memory Span: Major Factors in Dyslexia." *Journal of Learning Disabilities*, 23, 319-327, 1990.

Alves, A. and Gottlieb, Jay. "Teacher Interaction with Mainstreamed Handicapped Students and Their Nonhandicapped Peers." *Learning Disability Quarterly*, 9, 77-83, 1986.

American Psychiatric Association, *Diagnostic and Statistical Manual of Mental Disorders*, 3rd edition. Washington, D.C., 1980.

Archer, Anita and Gleason, Mary. *Skills for School Success.* North Billerica, MA: Curriculum Associates, 1989.

Ariel, Abraham. *Education of Children and Adolescents with Learning Disabilities.* New York: Macmillan, 1992.

Barenbaum, E., Newcomer, P., and Nodine, B. "Children's Ability to Write Stories as a Function of Variation in Task, Age and Developmental Level." *Learning Disability Quarterly*, 10, 175-188, 1987.

Bateman, B. "Who, How, and Where: Special Education Issues in Perpetuity." *Journal of Special Education*, vol. 27 (4), 509-520.

Begley, Sharon. "Why Johnnie and Joanie Can't Read." *Newsweek* Magazine, August 29, 1994, 52.

Behrman, Richard E. and Vaughan, Victor C. "Attention Deficit Disorder." In *Nelson's Textbook of Pediatrics*, 12th edition. Philadelphia: W.B. Saunders, 1983.

Bender, W. N. *Learning Disabilities, Characteristics, Identification and Teaching Strategies.* Boston: Allyn & Bacon, 1992.

Bender, W.N., Bailey, D.B., Stuck, G.B., and Wyne, M.D. "Relative Peer Status of Learning Disabled, Educable Mentally Handicapped, Low Achieving and Normally Achieving Children." *Child Study Journal*, 13, 209-216, 1984.

Benson, S. "Biophysical Intervention Strategies." *The Pointer*, 31 (3), 14-18, 1987.

Benz, M.R. and Halpern, A.S. "Transition Services for Secondary Students with Mild Disabilities. A Statewide Perspective." *Exceptional Children*, 53 (6), 507-514, 1987.

Birely, M. and Manley, E. "The Learning Disabled Student in a College Environment. A Report of Wright State University's Program." *Journal of Learning Disabilities*, 13, 7-10, 1980.

Bryan, J.H. and Bryan, T.S. "The Social Life of the Learning Disabled Youngster." in James McKinney and Lynne Feagans (Eds.), *Current Topics in Learning Disabilities*, vol. 1. Norwood, NJ: Ablex Publishing, 1983.

Bryan, T.S. and Wheeler, R. "Perceptions of Learning Disabled Children: The Eye of the Observer." *Journal of Learning Disabilities*, 5, 485-488, 1972.

Budoff, Milton and Hutten, Leah R. "Microcomputers in Special Education: Promises and Pitfalls." *Exceptional Children*, 49 (2), 123-128, 1982.

Chapman, J.W. and Boersma, F.J. "Learning Disabilities, Locus of Control, and Mother Attitudes." *Journal of Educational Psychology*, 71, 250-258, 1979.

Cohen, S.E. "Coping Strategies of University Students with Learning Disabilities." *Journal of Learning Disabilities*, 21, 161-164, 1988.

Comings, David E. *Tourette Syndrome and Human Behavior.* Duarte, CA: Hope Press, 1989.

Cone, T.E., Wilson, L.R., Bradley, C.M., and Reese, J.H. "Characteristics of LD Students in Iowa: An Empirical Investigation." *Learning Disability Quarterly*, 8, 211-220 1985.

Cook, Ruth, Tessier, Annette, and Klein, Diane. *Adapting Early Childhood Curriculum for Children with Special Needs*, 3rd edition. New York: Macmillan, 1992.

Cosden, M.A., Gerber, M.M., Semmel, D.S., Goldman, S.R., and Semmel, M.I. "Microcomputer Use Within Microeducational Environments." *Exceptional Children*, 53, 399-409, 1987.

Cosden, Pearl R. "Sizing Up a Situation: LD Children's Understanding of Social Interactions." *Learning Disability Quarterly*, 5, 371-373, 1982.

Davis, W.E. "The Regular Education Initiative Debate: Its Promises and Problems." *Exceptional Children*, 55, (5), 440-446, 1989.

Deshler, D.D., Schumaker, J.B., and Lenz, B.K. "Academic and Cognitive Interventions for LD Adolescents: Part 1." *Journal of Learning Disabilities*, 17, 108-117, 1984.

Deshler, D.D. and Schumaker, J.B. "An Instructional Model for Teaching Students How to Learn." In J.L. Graden, J.E. Zins, and M.J. Curtis (Eds.), *Alternative Educational Delivery Systems: Enhancing Instructional Options for All Students.* Washington, D.C.: NASP, 391-411, 1988.

Diehl, W. and Mikulecky, L. "The Nature of Literacy at Work." *Journal of Reading*, 24, 221-227, 1980.

Edgars, E. "How Do Special Education Students Fare After They Leave School? A Response to Hasazi, Gordon, and Roe." *Exceptional Children*, 51, 470-473, 1985.

Epstein, Mark A., Shaywitz, Sally E., Shaywitz, Bennett, and Woolston, Joseph L. "The Boundaries of Attention Deficit Disorder." *Journal of Learning Disabilities*, 24 (2), 68-71, 1991.

Fofard, M.B. and Haubrich, P.A. "Vocational and Social Adjustment of Learning Disabled Young Adults: A Follow Up Study." *Learning Disabilities Quarterly*, 4, 123-130, 1981.

Gardner, Howard. *Frames of Mind: The Theory of Multiple Intelligences.* New York: Basic Books, 1983.

Goldman, Susan R. and Pelligrino, James W. "Information Processing and Microcomputer Technology: Where Do We Go from Here?" *Journal of Learning Disabilities*, 20 (3), 144-153, 1987.

Halpern, Andrew S. "Quality of Life as a Conceptual Framework for Evaluating Transition Outcomes." *Exceptional Children*, 59 (6), 486-498, 1993.

Hasazi, S.B., Gordon, L.R., and Roe, C.A. "Factors Associated with the Employment Status of Handicapped Youth Exiting from High School from 1979-1983." *Exceptional Children*, 51, 455-469, 1985.

Hoffman, F. James, Sheldon, Kenneth L., Minskoff, Esther H., Sautter, Scott W., Steidle, Ernest F., Baker, Deborah P., Bailey, Mary Beth, and Echols, Laura D. "Needs of Learning Disabled Adults." *Journal of Learning Disabilities*, 20 (1) 43-52, 1987.

Idol, L. "Group Story Mapping: A Comprehensive Strategy for Both Skilled and Unskilled Readers." *Journal of Learning Disabilities* 20, 196-205, 1987.

Idol, L. and Croll, S. "Story-Mapping Training as a Means of Improving Comprehension." *Learning Disability Quarterly*, 10, 214-229, 1987.

Ingrassia, Michele, and McCormick, John. "Why Leave Children with Bad Parents?" *Newsweek* magazine, April 25, 1994, p. 53.

Jenkins, J.R., Larson, K., and Fleisher, L. "Effects of Error Correction on Word Recognition and Reading Comprehension." *Learning Disability Quarterly*, 6 (2) 139-145, 1983.

Jones, Karen H. and Bender, W.N. "Utilization of Paraprofessionals in Special Education: A Review of the Literature." *Remedial and Special Education*, 14 (1), 7-14, 1993.

Keilitz, I. and Dunivant, N. "The Relationship Between Learning Disability and Juvenile Delinquency: Current State of Knowledge." *Remedial and Special Education*, 7 (3), 18-26, 1986.

Knowlton, H.E. "Effects of Picture-fading on Two Learning Disabled Students' Sight Word Acquisition." *Learning Disability Quarterly*, 3, 88-96, 1980.

Kolich, Eileen M. "Microcomputer Technology with the Learning Disabled: A Review of the Literature." *Journal of Learning Disabilities*, 18 (7), 428-431, 1985.

Lender, Toni W. *Play Based Assessment.* Baltimore: Paul K. Brookes Publishing, 1983.

Levin, E.K., Zigmond, N. and Birch, J.W. "A Follow Up Study of 52 Learning Disabled Adolescents." *Journal of Learning Disabilities*, 18, 2-7, 1985.

MacArthur, C.A. "The Impact of Computers on the Writing Process." *Exceptional Children*, 54, 536-542, 1988.

Malouf, J. "The Effect of Instructional Computer Games." *Journal of Special Education*, 21 (4) 27-38, 1987-1988.

Mastrapieri, Margo A., Scruggs, Thomas E., and Levin, Joel R. "Mnemonic Strategy Instruction with Learning Disabled Adolescents." *Journal of Learning Disabilities*, 18 (2), 94-99, 1985.

McKinney, J.D. and Feagans, L. (1983) "Adaptive Classroom Behavior of Learning Disabled Students." *Journal of Learning Disabilities*, 16, 360-367, 1983.

McKinney, James D. "Longitudinal Research on the Behavioral Characteristics of Children with Learning Disabilities." *Journal of Learning Disabilities*, 22 (3) 141-150, 1989.

McLoyd, V.C. "Socialization and Development in a Changing Economy: The Effects of Paternal Job and Income Loss on Children." *American Psychologist*, 44, 293-302, 1989.

Miller, Michael (Ed.) *Development of the Central Nervous System: Effects of Alcohol and Opiates.* New York: Wiley-Less, 1992.

Minskoff, E.H., Sautter, S.W., Hoffman, F.J., and Hawks, R. "Employer Attitudes Toward Hiring the Disabled." *Journal of Learning Disabilities*, 20, 53-57, 1987.

Moon, Charles, Marlowe, Mike, Stellern, Jon, and Errera, John. "Main and Interaction Effects of Metallic Pollutants on Cognitive Functioning." *Journal of Learning Disabilities*, 18 (4), 217-221, 1985.

Newcomer, P.L. "The New and Improved Holy Grail." *Learning Disability Quarterly*, 12, 154-155, 1989.

Okolo, C.M. and Sitlington, P. "The Role of Special Education in LD Adolescent's Transition from School to Work." *Learning Disability Quarterly*, 9, 141-155, 1986.

Outhred, Lynne. "Word Processing: Its Impact on Children's Writing." *Journal of Learning Disabilities*, 22 (4), 262-263, 1989.

Perlmutter, B.F., Crocker, J., Cordray, D. and Garstecki, D. "Sociometric Status and Related Personality Characteristics of Mainstreamed Learning Disabled Adolescents." *Learning Disabled Quarterly*, 6, 20-30, 1983.

Pierangelo, Roger. *A Survival Kit for the Special Education Teacher.* West Nyack, NY: The Center for Applied Research in Education, 1994.

Radius, M. and Lesniak, Pat. "Student Study Team Manual." California Department of Education, 1987.

Rief, Sandra F. *How to Reach and Teach ADD/ADHD Children.* West Nyack, NY: The Center for Applied Research in Education, 1993.

Ross, A.O. *Psychological Aspects of Learning Disabilities and Reading Disorders.* New York: McGraw-Hill, 1976.

Sabornie, E.J. and Kaufman, J.M. "Social Acceptance of LD Adolescent." *Learning Disability Quarterly*, 9, 55-61, 1986.

Salisbury, C., Evans, I., and Palombaro, M. "On the Nature and Change of an Inclusive Elementary School." *Journal of the Association for Persons with Severe Handicaps.* 18 (2), 75-85, 1993.

Salvia, J. and Ysseldyke, J.E. *Assessment in Special and Remedial Education*, 4th edition. Boston: Houghton Mifflin, 1988.

Saski, J., Swicegood, P., and Carter, J. "Note-taking for Learning Disabled Adolescents." *Learning Disability Quarterly*, 6 (3), 265-271, 1983.

Sattler, J.M. *Assessment of Children*, 3rd edition. San Diego: James Sattler, 1988.

Schumaker, J.B., Denton, P.H., and Deshler, D.D. *The Paraphrasing Strategy: Instructor's Manual.* Lawrence, KS: The University of Kansas Institute for Research in Learning Disabilities, 1984.

Schumaker, J.B, Nolan, S.M., and Deshler, D.D. *The Error Monitoring Strategy: Instructor's Manual.* Lawrence, KS: The University of Kansas Institute for Research in Learning Disabilities, 1985.

Schumaker, J.B. and Deshler, D.D. "Validation of Learning Strategy Interventions for Students with LD: Results of a Programmatic Research Effort." In Bernice Y.L. Wong

(Ed.),*Contemporary Intervention Research in Learning Disabilities: An International Perspective.* New York: Springer-Verlag, 1992.

Semmel, M.I., Abernathy, T.V., Butera, G. and Lesar, S. "Teacher Perceptions of the Regular Education Initiative." *Exceptional Children*, 58 (1), 9-21, 1991.

Shalock, R.L., Wolzen, B., Ross, I., Elliot, B., Werbel, G., and Peterson, K. "Post Secondary Community Placement of Handicapped Students: A Five-year Follow-up." *Learning Disability Quarterly*, 9, 295-303, 1986.

Sharpe, Rochelle. "To Boost IQs, Aid Is Needed in First 3 Years." *The Wall Street Journal*, April 12, 1994.

Shaywitz, Sally E. and Shaywitz, Bennett A. "Introduction to the Special Series on Attention Deficit Disorder." *Journal of Learning Disabilities*, 24 (2) 68-71, 1991.

Shin, M.R., Habedank, L., Rodden-Nord, K., and Knutsen, N. "Using Curriculum-Based Assessment to Identify Potential Candidates for Re-Integration into Regular Education." *Journal of Special Education*, 27 (2), 202-221, 1993.

Siperstein, Gary N. and Goding, Melinda. "Teacher's Behavior Toward LD and Non-LD Children: A Strategy for Change." *Journal of Learning Disabilities*, 18 (3), 139-143, 1985.

Sitlington, Patricia L., Frank, Alan R., and Carson, Rori. "Adult Adjustment Among High School Graduates with Mild Disabilities." *Exceptional Children*, 59 (3) 221-233, 1992.

Smith, Corinne Roth. *Learning Disabilities, The Interaction of Learner, Task and Setting.* Boston: Allyn and Bacon, 1991.

Snell, M.E. and Drake Jr., G.P. "Replacing Cascades with Supported Education." *Journal of Special Education*, 27 (4), 393-409, 1994.

Speece, D.L., McKinney, D.P., Applebaum, M.L. "Longitudinal Development of Conversational Skills in Learning Disabled Children." *Journal of Learning Disabilities*, 19. 302-317, 1986.

Tarnapol, L. and Tarnapol, M. *Brain Function and Reading Disabilities.* Baltimore: University Park Press, 1977.

Taylor, Ronald L. *Assessment of Exceptional Students, Educational and Psychological Procedures.* Englewood Cliffs, NJ: Prentice Hall, 1989.

Torgeson, J.K. and Licht, Barbara G. (1983). "The Learning Disabled Child as an Inactive Learner: Retrospect and Prospects." In James McKinney and Lynne Feagans (Eds.) *Current Topics in Learning Disabilities,* vol.1. Norwood, NJ: Ablex Publishing, 1983.

Vaughn, Sharon. "Why Teach Social Skills to Learning Disabled Students." *Journal of Learning Disabilities*, 18 (10), 588-591, 1985.

Vogler, George P., De Fries, J.C., Decker, Sadie N. "Family History as an Indicator of Risk for Reading Disability." *Journal of Learning Disabilities*, 18 (7), 419-421, 1985.

Wadsworth, Barry J. *Piaget's Theory of Cognitive Development*, 2nd edition New York: Longman, 1979.

Webb, G. "Left/Right Brains Teammates in Learning." *Exceptional Children*, 49, 508-515, 1983.

West, James, (Ed.) *Alcohol and Brain Development.* New York: Oxford University Press, 1986.

Wilson, Brian. *The Success of Failures, A True Story of a Learning Disabled Student.* Warminster Road, PA: Mar*Co Products, 1993.

Witt, J.C., Elliot, S.N., Kramer, J.J., and Gresham, F.M. *Assessment of Children: Fundamental Methods and Practices.* Madison, WI: W.C.B. Brown Benchmark Publishers, 1994.

————. *Handbook of Special Education.* San Bernardino, CA:San Bernardino City Unified School District, 1993.

————. "A Genetic Flaw: Closing in on the Cause of Dyslexia." *Newsweek* Magazine, October 24, 1994.

————. *Federal Register.* United States Office of Education, 1977.

Made in the USA
Columbia, SC
27 August 2023

22147944R00176